Redefining Theatre Communities

Redefining Theatre Communities

International Perspectives on Community-Conscious Theatre-Making

Edited by Marco Galea and Szabolcs Musca

intellect

Bristol, UK / Chicago, USA

First published in the UK in 2019 by
Intellect, The Mill, Parnall Road, Fishponds, Bristol, BS16 3JG, UK

First published in the USA in 2019 by
Intellect, The University of Chicago Press, 1427 E. 60th Street,
Chicago, IL 60637, USA

A catalogue record for this book is available from
the British Library.

Copy editor: MPS Technologies
Cover designer: Aleksandra Szumlas
Cover image: Photo by Irina Vosgerau/isuvo, Athens.
From the *Dourgouti Island Hotel* project/UrbanDig, 2015–16.
Production manager: Naomi Curston
Typesetting: Contentra Technologies

Hardback ISBN: 978-1-78938-076-7
Paperback ISBN: 978-1-78938-862-6
ePDF ISBN: 978-1-78938-078-1
ePUB ISBN: 978-1-78938-077-4

To find out about all our publications, please visit
www.intellectbooks.com.
There, you can subscribe to our e-newsletter,
browse or download our current catalogue, and
buy any titles that are in print.

This is a peer-reviewed publication.

Contents

Table of Figures

Acknowledgements

The editors are grateful to a large number of people without whose help and encouragement this book would never have been published. First of all we would like to thank all the practitioners and academics who participated in the conference entitled *Redefining Theatre Communities: Community Perspectives in Contemporary Theatre-Making*, which was held at the Gozo Campus of the University of Malta. For their assistance before and during this conference, we would like to thank Joseph Calleja and Marvin Grech. We are particularly grateful to Professor Joe Friggieri, then pro-rector responsible for the campus for his generosity and expert support and to the Conference and Events Unit, especially Lucienne Bugeja, for going out of their way to help us.

The University of Malta has supported this project from the beginning through an ongoing research grant that financed the organization of the conference and many of the expenses involved in producing this book. The Department of Theatre Studies at the University of Malta also provided financial support, but it is the constant moral and intellectual support from all colleagues in the department that is most appreciated.

We are also grateful to the Creative Literary Studio (UK) especially Manuela Perteghella and the University of Bristol's Theatre Department for being partners in our conference venture. Thanks also goes to Kate Nagy, whose help and insightful knowledge in publicizing this project was invaluable.

We are humbled by the faith shown in this book project by Intellect Books and are grateful to Naomi Curston and Tim Mitchell who guided the process with a lot of patience and even more knowledge towards the finishing line. For his technical assistance in preparing the manuscript, we would like to thank Reno Fenech.

Introduction

Marco Galea and Szabolcs Musca

In early 2015 we embarked on an exciting new project, an international collaboration between the University of Malta's Department of Theatre Studies and New Tides Platform, UK. Our aim was to facilitate a lively debate on the ever-changing relationship between theatre and communities as part of an international conference that eventually took place on the unique island of Gozo in Malta in mid-September 2015. The three-day conference entitled *Redefining Theatre Communities: Community Perspectives in Contemporary Theatre-Making* introduced and discussed a whole array of perspectives on the changing relationship between contemporary theatre and communities. Participants from around twenty countries were involved in this event, mapping new approaches and shifts in the theatrical environment on an international level. Aesthetic, social, cultural and political aspects of community-conscious theatre practices were discussed in a variety of formats. Academic papers, practical workshops and practice-led talks were equally present at the conference. The conscious decision to invite scholars and researchers as well as theatre directors, actors, dramaturgs and cultural managers proved to be a constructive one. Participants gained insight on emerging theatrical projects and transnational initiatives with strong social and community engagement, and also had the chance to experience new modes of community building and devising via practice-based workshops. Academic presentations addressed and contextualized topics such as temporary communities, spaces and politics of community engagement, translocal communities in theatre and performance, formation of new theatre communities and new forms of spectatorship. Established and early-career researchers from diverse cultural backgrounds shared their current projects and discussed ideas of mutual interest. Lively debates were an important part of the programme and it often continued beyond the formal settings of the conference. One of the main outcomes of this project was the establishment of an international network that brought together academics and theatre practitioners from around the world expanding our understanding on contemporary theatre-making and communities.

This edited collection was born from the stimulating discussions that took place in Gozo, bearing the intellectual imprints of both the 30 plus conference participants and the historically and socioculturally complex environment that this Mediterranean island represents between Europe and Africa. *Redefining Theatre Communities* is rooted in the collective effort of both academics and theatre-makers. The majority of the chapters in this volume directly relate to the conference, but given the distance in time since the event, connections to the topics deepened and more detailed reflections took shape, hence the collection itself became a platform for creatively *returning*, *rethinking* and *redefining* the multiple forms in which contemporary theatre connects with its various communities internationally. The multiplicity of contributions is core in this process. The collection presents different voices from various cultural backgrounds and embedded in various theatre traditions. We do not wish to create the illusion of a single-authored monograph. On the contrary, we believe that this diversity of voices is one of the assets of this volume.

Redefining linkages between theatre and communities is of course an ongoing critical process rather than a renewed attempt to establish rock-solid meanings. Our aim is to map new forms of communication, dialogue and engagement by which contemporary international theatre connects with its diverse communities. The volume explores the interplays between theatre practices and communities: the aesthetic, social and cultural aspects of community-conscious theatre-making. While doing so, the book reflects on recent transformations in structural, textual and theatrical conventions and traditions, and changes in the modes of production and spectatorship in relation to theatre communities. We hope to expand understanding on the changing notion of theatre communities by presenting a whole array of emerging perspectives on the politics, ethics and practices of community representation on the contemporary international theatre landscape. We acknowledge, however, that our collection draws mainly on perspectives from European theatre and performance, keeping Europe's diversity in mind. This book aims to challenge a long-standing continental European theatre tradition, whereas, historically, community issues were employed in mainstream theatre-making almost as a metatheatrical element, often kept on the side or diluted within the aesthetic modalities and subordinated to artistic philosophies of individual directors/ensembles. Due to social, demographic and cultural changes and shifts, such attitudes are fast transforming, together with changes not only in European societies, but also in national theatre ecologies. This collection aims to discuss and reflect on these shifts and how they can facilitate new links between theatre and communities.

By engaging with processes of redefinition, we aim to re-position theatre communities within the debates on contemporary theatre. Traditionally, community-conscious theatre-making is discussed and debated within the fields of 'applied theatre' and 'community theatre'. We believe such framing of the debate on theatre communities almost exclusively within these academic fields often removes theatre communities from professional theatre practices and positions it within a narrow view on amateur or semi-professional theatre-making. Diverse areas of theatre and performance scholarship started to engage more robustly with community issues in recent years. In fact, one of the key aims of this book is exactly to highlight and discuss how areas such as theatre and architecture, theatre historiography, theatre translation and adaptation, festival studies, theatre and health, political theatre and intermedial performance among others engage with issues and shape notions of community. Framing our area of investigation as/ within 'community-conscious theatre making', our intention is to present perspectives not readily available in applied/community-theatre scholarship, but ones that respond to artistic/sociocultural/institutional transformations of recent years.

We hope that the contributions in this volume will open up the discussion to wider considerations on this complex relationship. For this, our collection aims to facilitate a dialogue between different ways of working and forms of engagement and various historical, spatial, ideological, aesthetic and dramaturgical perspectives. The book presents a holistic understanding on the links (historical and contemporary) between theatre and communities in this respect, by placing theatre communities within recent theatre developments and shifts in the theatre environment internationally.

Community-conscious theatre initiatives are also making considerable efforts to re-evaluate traditional linkages between theatre-making and audiences; hence, in this volume, we also attempt to re-examine historical divisions between audiences and theatre productions within contemporary practices. All these important considerations are raised from the grounds of theatre-making, hoping to contribute to scholarship by channelling in and embedding practitioners' perspectives into the discourse. Ongoing debates during our conference and beyond convinced us that disseminating artistic viewpoints in academic discourses is not only necessary (given the growing importance of industry insights in academia), but a fruitful way to foster new perceptions and ultimately generate new communities of thinkers with a multitude of artistic and academic expertise.

Contextualizing Transformations

The issues discussed in this book acquire a sense of urgency because of the multitude of economic, social, political, demographic – and not least – cultural transformations that have altered the relationship between theatres and the communities surrounding them during the past two decades. Changes were manifested on core levels of theatrical creation: in new or (re)emerging theatrical forms and practices, modes of reception, and on levels of theatre structures as well. The public theatre structure faced profound challenges throughout Europe. Public theatres are expected to serve a wide range of audiences as well as to contribute to artistic innovation and community linkage. Around them the social patterns are continuously changing, as are demographics in the urban landscape of the European cities, created by increased mobility and migration. Addressing different communities with various cultural and social backgrounds is increasingly important and needs to be reflected on both creative and organizational levels. As a result, socially engaged theatre productions feature more prominently on the theatre programmes across Europe and beyond, verbatim or documentary theatre is also gaining ground, while community theatre initiatives are strongly emerging alongside (or even instead of) public theatres. Addressing, involving, representing and thematizing particular communities or community-specific issues have become a key element of the international theatrical landscape. New forms of contemporary theatre-making have also shifted the modes of reception towards a more comprehensive involvement in the performance event. Because of the nature of theatre, changes occurring on either of these levels quickly feed into the overall ecologies of theatrical systems and theatre-making. *Redefining Theatre Communities* examines these culturally and artistically important shifts and presents contemporary theatre communities within an ever-changing theatrical ecology.

Almost two decades ago, Hans Thies Lehmann reflected on core transformations in theatrical modes of expression in his *Postdramatic Theatre* (2006, originally published in German in 1999). He stressed the 'de-dramatization' of contemporary theatre, arguing that dramatic plots and/or narratives are increasingly becoming secondary in contemporary performance, and dramatic texts no longer have primacy over the theatrical performance (Lehmann 2006: 49). As Lehmann pointed out: 'It is no longer the stage but the theatre as a whole which functions as the "speaking space"' (2006: 31).

Meanings and narratives are often exclusively created by physicality/movement, the usage of spaces, visuals, music or the montage of all these. According to Lehmann, postdramatic theatre does not need to create fictional situations around itself:

> In postdramatic theatre, the theatre situation is not simply added to the autonomous reality of the dramatic fiction to animate it. Rather, the theatre situation as such becomes a matrix within whose energy lines the elements of the scenic fictions inscribe themselves. Theatre is emphasized as a situation, not as a fiction.
>
> (2006: 128)

Verbatim or documentary theatre productions are likewise positioned between reality and its aesthetic processing on stage. Here, the dramaturgy follows the logic of the pre-existing materials (various documents, interviews etc.), and meaning is conveyed through the presentation of these documents by actors, or the interviewees themselves. Events are not acted out but told by the performers. Lack of sets, costumes, music and other elements that create the fictional dimension of theatre productions, and an equal treatment of the sources (avoiding positioning the sources hierarchically) are other aspects of documentary theatre that prompt the audience to develop their own (political) point of view. Arguably, the emergence of such theatrical forms and practices involves different attitudes on the spectator's part. Hence, modes of reception are also shifted towards a more comprehensive involvement in the performance event. As Lehmann argues:

> The task of the spectators is no longer the neutral reconstruction, the re-creation and patient retracing of the fixed image but rather the mobilization of their own ability to react and experience in order to realize their participation in the process that is offered to them.
>
> (2006: 134–35)

Lehmann here outlines the forming of a new relationship between theatre and its audiences, a form of spectating where audiences are mobilized physically as well as psychologically. Thus, a more participatory stance is expected from the theatregoer (also see Burzynska 2016).

In the special issue on the spectator of *Critical Stages*, Peter Boenisch also talks about 'participatory theatre's [...] renewed manifest engagement with the audience' and the effects this creates on dramaturgical strategies (2012: n.pag.). He observes that a shift occurred in the 'central role of the relation between actor and spectator' and that is inevitably altering dramaturgical practices (Boenisch 2012: n.pag.). Boenisch's response informed by similar theatre practices is the proposal of a 'relational perspective on dramaturgy' or simply 'relational dramaturgy' (Boenisch 2012: n.pag.). This is necessary as contemporary dramaturgical solutions activate an interplay between performers/performance and audience/reception. Dramaturgy here is understood as a '[...] relational aesthetic practice [that] forges relations, changes relationships, and calibrates a dynamic interplay' (Boenisch 2012: n.pag.).

Arguably, the changes in the interplays between text and performance, actors and audience, spaces and meaning creation and 'the production's spectatorial relations', challenge the traditional functions of theatre-making especially in the context of audience relations (Boenisch 2012: n.pag.; see also Radosavljević 2013). Intermediality in theatre and performance further adds to the complexity of the relations between theatre and its communities. Digital technologies and the presence of diverse media within the theatrical space is actively creating new modes of engagements and links with theatre communities. This not only alters the perception of what theatre and/or performance means in the twenty-first century, but, arguably, produces new communities around intermedial productions (see Chapple and Kattenbelt 2006). Looking beyond the creative processes, it is also important to highlight here that theatre institutions are also increasingly turning to digital technologies to reach out to a potentially larger audience base and with this extending the contexts of reception and getting through to more diverse communities. Such institutional outreach is of course influenced by changes and challenges in the theatrical, social and cultural structures of contemporary societies (also see Van Campenhout and Mestre 2016).

Dragan Klaic gives an extensive analysis of the profound challenges the public theatre structure faces throughout Europe. In his posthumously published monograph, *Resetting the Stage: Public Theatre between the Market and Democracy* (2012), Klaic argues that public theatres are in transition as they are challenged by financial, social and demographic changes and these changes have a direct effect on their productions (Klaic 2007: 22–33). In defining the public theatre system that dominates the European theatre landscape, Klaic points out that today's public theatres are 'artistic in orientation and subsidized by public authorities', working in ensemble structures or otherwise, 'staging a diverse repertoire in a recognizable stylistic key' often led by directors (Klaic 2012: 5, 7). As publicly funded, they are expected to serve a wide range of audiences as well as to contribute to artistic innovation and community linkage. Pressured by commercial forces, public companies are increasingly adopting commercial strategies in order to respond to the market forces and not least to respond to expectations coming from their funders. What effects can we map on aesthetic, social and cultural levels as a result of these tendencies? Klaic points out one aspect concerning the audience:

> An audience in a subsidized theatre is a micro-community of citizens, engaged in deliberative democracy, whereas in commercial theatre it is a group of consumers paying to be amused.
>
> (2012: 15)

Drawing such a sharp division between audience groups is questionable, certainly considering that these audiences frequently overlap. Nevertheless, Klaic makes a point on one of public theatre's important aspects to enhance community cohesion, which is, of course, rather limited in a seller versus consumer type of relationship that commercial theatre venues often represent.

As stressed several times beforehand, the public theatre structure is shaped by three main factors: economic, social and demographic, arguably interconnected throughout. In terms of finances, a constant expectation to increase income and hence reduce dependence on public funding is often met by reducing costs (along with sponsorship and other campaigns). As Klaic observes, this practice has a direct effect on 'artistic choices and determine[s] the programming' (2012: 26).

In terms of programming, Klaic stresses that in many cases repertoire ensembles replaced the '*rotating repertory* [...] with a *sequential repertory*', meaning that productions would have a limited run (2012: 26, original emphasis). This also means that short-term commissions will be preferred as opposed to a long-term artistic employment. Again, this is a fundamental change in the mode of theatre-making in the case of ensemble theatres for instance.

Social changes represent yet another challenge for the public theatre sector, though often theatres are reluctant to address concerns coming from a social level. As social patterns changed over the past two decades, not least due to the rapid changes in affordable technology (digital goods of all varieties), theatre became a 'minority option' amid a broad variety of leisure options (Klaic 2012: 26). Theatres are already addressing these changes by introducing considerable changes in their artistic offerings, programming and their facilities (e.g. on-site restaurants and external caterers, children's playing areas etc.). Creating a balanced repertoire that combines artistic innovation with spectator satisfaction is a complex task. This often involves commissioning further training, in the case of adding musicals and other popular genres on their repertoire for instance. Companies with long-standing tradition in staging dramatic forms find it particularly hard to adjust their working style and the aptitudes of their artistic staff. Changes in repertoire structures can also result in reduced performance time – an effect that does not particularly favour classics or lengthy performances for instance. Programming/ scheduling also needs to fit in with working life patterns of the audience and with rival cultural events. Changes are implemented to reach out to more and diverse (in terms of cultural, social and age groups) audiences, and to 'increase seat-occupancy rate' (Klaic 2012: 23). With these alterations comes an even more complex transformation on a sociocultural level, as the traditionally middle-class audience base shifts towards a socially and culturally more diverse audience. Consequently, new viewpoints and expectations appear in spectatorship (also see Malzacher and Warsza 2017).

As Klaic observes, theatres often fail to recognize the demographic changes in the urban landscape of European cities, created by migration and increased mobility from inside and outside Europe (see Klaic 2012: 29–31). Arguably, migrant communities are still under-represented while theatres try to sustain inclusiveness. As he highlights:

7

> [...] public theatre suffers from the individualisation of taste and sensibilities, an emancipation process to which theatre has been catering since the Renaissance and that now works against it by making any envisaged audience opaque and diffused.
>
> (Klaic 2012: 31)

Klaic campaigns for an artistic and institutional engagement with cultural diversity arguing for a comprehensive approach: '[...] described as a "4P approach" covering programming, partnership, personnel and public outreach' (Klaic 2012: 30).

Addressing different communities with various cultural and social backgrounds is core and must involve thematization on both the creative (e.g. themed repertoire, casting and so forth) and organizational levels (personnel, educational and outreach programmes). Klaic concludes that:

> Both cultural uniformity and cultural diversity challenge the public theatre and force it to define its own specific cultural position more sharply than before, as well as delineating its field of action in terms of what other cultural producers and intermediaries cannot and will not do.
>
> (2012: 31)

What the above argument stresses is a new or reformed pathway public theatres should consider in order to legitimize their public character. Engagement with the reality of a demographically heterogeneous public would ensure relevancy and a contribution towards social cohesion (on theatre and migration also see Cox 2014).

A range of transformations have been presented so far, some artistically more favourable for theatres than others; nonetheless, all of the changes highlighted here shift organizational, textual/literary and theatrical/performative conventions and traditions towards a multilateral institutional and creative (co)existence. Both in artistic offerings, modes of production and spectatorship, new viewpoints appear as a result of financial, demographic and sociocultural changes. Today, intercultural encounters, exchanges and cultural diversity are more and more on the public theatre's agendas to various degrees. On an artistic level, this might be manifested in a new repertoire building strategy to include marginalized voices (through a series of thematic performances for instance), staging of a play from or about an under-represented cultural context or setting up workshops for cross-cultural exchange in actors' training. In the modes of production, cooperative creation is frequently used. This often combines exchange of ideas, approaches and theatrical practices with the opportunity to raise and discuss (social) issues present in several countries.

On the reception level, educational programmes, post-show discussions and other outreach programmes are also increasingly present in managerial objectives. Touring and performing at various venues is also a form of ensuring an extensive outreach, though this often goes hand in hand with national cultural promotion. The new ways of collaborations and exchange are encouraged by public authorities, though often for economic (shared production cost and financial benefits), political (nation and/or region branding) or societal (in integrating different communities) reasons. Nevertheless, cultural dialogues and dynamic relationships between creative and institutional systems are continuous. Theatres are frequently positioning themselves within international theatre platforms, either by organizing/establishing such events, festivals and projects etc. or by participating and presenting work. Analysing the main directions of these platforms of theatre creation and sharing/exchange is of key importance.

In this book, we survey these systemic changes and map emerging responses, positioning the interplays between theatre and communities at the forefront of our investigation. We are hoping that by looking at community-conscious theatre across a range of national and cultural contexts within and outside Europe, we will be able to outline an emerging theatre landscape that genuinely embraces community engagements on both artistic and institutional levels. As the contributions to this volume demonstrate, such close connections are a much-welcomed reality in today's theatre environment.

Structure

Connecting to the overarching principle of this book to present a wide variety of initiatives and approaches, the studies are edited into five sections, each covering community perspectives within historical, spatial and sociocultural settings (Part I), politics and ethics (Part II), global vs local initiatives (Part III), emerging practices (Parts IV and V) and new modes of audience involvement (Part V). An interview section (Part IV) is also developed, linking together theoretical perspectives (Parts I–III) with reflections on emerging community-conscious theatre practices (Part V). In the interviews with international theatre-makers and artistic directors, new insights emerge regarding actual artistic practices and institutional policies alike. As seen in the above description, the volume's intention is to draw a more holistic understanding on issues specific to theatre and communities. Each section of the volume is briefly introduced by the editors, reflecting on possible discursive connections between individual contributions in the respective sections. We also provide further readings at the end of each chapter in an editors' note in order to contextualize the essays within most recent scholarship, but also to point out further discourses and directions related to the subject matters discussed by the authors.

The opening section (Part I) of the book examines notions of theatre communities historically, within theatre spaces and through modalities of belonging. Through three distinct approaches (historical, spatial and sociocultural), the authors reflect on aesthetic, social and cultural aspects in the relationship between theatre and communities. In the opening chapter of the book, Stefan Aquilina gives an important historical reconstruction of amateur theatre in post-revolutionary Russia, drawing parallels between the worker-actors' *do-it-yourself* ethic in the early 1920s and contemporary theatre communities, arguing that communities are not only defined by the space they inhabit, but increasingly by shared values and aspirations. Aquilina's chapter is an important contribution to this volume also because he gives a historical insight into the process of constructing a theatre community, something that can be viewed as an early example of contemporary devised theatre.

Ruben Paul Borg and Vicki Ann Cremona draw on extensive research and documentation of performance spaces in Malta to argue in favour of a decentralized approach to the use of theatrical space that would lead to an increase in participation in theatre and an increased use of spaces that are already available and are often situated in a strategic position that can contribute to the sense of community if it is reactivated. Like in Aquilina, the focus is on amateur theatre as activity that is born in the community, reflects it and reinvigorates it.

Zoe Zontou deals with a specific form of theatre that is guided by professional theatre-makers but involves non-professional performers who are recovering drug abusers. The chapter discusses how the main tool for recovery in this practice is the process of substituting the existent belonging to a community of drug users with a new belonging to a community of performers, who not only use performance as therapy but also become contributors to the wider community.

The second part of the book (Part II) focuses on the politics and ethics of community-conscious theatre-making. It looks at the mechanisms of power and the politics surrounding community engagements, the problematic notion of 'national theatre' and social segregation in relation to building and addressing theatre communities in contemporary theatre. By doing so, the authors reflect on various theatrical forms such as adaptation and socially engaged theatre. Maria Elena Capitani looks at contemporary English and Scottish rewritings of ancient tragedies as spaces of ethical encounters and affection, actively forming a 'temporary and heterogeneous communal body' during the theatrical representation. As Capitani argues, the radical adaptations and appropriations of Sarah Kane, Martin Crimp, Liz Lochhead and David Greig, by enhancing spectatorial participation in the performance event, foster rethinking of personal and communal identities and facilitate ethical reflections.

Shifting geographically from Britain to India, the second chapter in this part of the volume discusses a living and working grass-root theatre group in rural Bengal. Pujya Ghosh's contribution goes beyond the parameters of a case study and critically revisits concepts of political theatre, with a focus on spatial, aesthetic and community intervention through the lenses of a somewhat radical, socially engaged theatre practice and community. Ghosh's chapter neatly connects to Capitani's arguments on building communities in reception via communal empathy and ethical reflections. Given its subject matter (communal living and working), Ghosh's study goes on demonstrating that by taking direct ownership over the aesthetics and economics of theatre-making, Tepantor's community has 'the power to create a rupture in the social structure' in and around them.

Marco Galea's chapter at the end of Part II opens up the discussion towards a much larger theatre community, that of the national. His very timely analysis on the strategies and (often failed) attempts of forming a national theatre in and for Malta shows just how complex and politically charged such a theatrical and cultural endeavour can be. Galea rightly points out that forming a national theatre – being that a commissioning centre or a national theatre ensemble – should build equally on a consensus on the multiplicity of (national) identities and the fostering role of an artistic community. In the lack of such rigorous debate and strategy, national theatre building almost certainly finishes as either a political assertion or a personal (vanity) project.

The third part of the collection (Part III) focuses on (inter)cultural and social perspectives of new modes of engagement between theatre and hybrid communities. It reflects on the tensions between local and global in the contemporary theatrical environment and the ways in which theatre productions and institutions create and negotiate 'glocal' values and communities.

Szabolcs Musca sees international theatre festivals as meaningful temporary communities that necessitate a specific theatrical practice, one that maintains a fine balance between portability of content and authenticity. This balance is maintained mainly through different strategies of translating and adapting performances for different audiences.

Closely linked to Musca's analysis of international theatre festivals as hybrid cultural spaces powered by translating communities, Evi Stamatiou takes a close look at the development and mechanisms of the economic communities within Edinburgh's August Festivals (EAFs). Informed by personal experience as a theatre-maker present at the EAFs, Stamatiou gives a highly relevant account of the power geometries that influence the artists' 'sense of space', multiple communal identities and ways of belonging to an imagined theatrical community. Stamatiou shows the importance of various economic interactions in creating a sense of 'local membership' within a 'universal [festival] community'.

Belonging is also an issue tackled in Hasibe Kalkan's discussion of postmigrant theatre in Berlin. Referring to the postcolonial term 'métissage', Kalkan explains how through theatre training and performance, second- and third-generation descendants of Turkish migrants move from being at odds with both their culture of origin and their adoptive culture to becoming agents of communication between the two, even though their access to formal training is limited.

Part IV of the volume is dedicated to practitioners' perspectives and contains three interviews with established and emerging international theatre-makers and artistic directors. The interviews touch on social and cultural projects and communal theatre practices.

Vicky Featherstone will probably be the most familiar of this group among English-language readers. Mark O'Thomas, who has worked as a dramaturg and translator for the Royal Court Theatre, interviews the current artistic director about the theatre's work in and with London communities. The Royal Court is a good example of an established metropolitan theatre that reaches out to the local community that is not traditionally part of its audience. In order for this to be successful, a different approach to theatre-making has to be adopted, one that sees the communities (especially its children and youth) as collaborators rather than consumers.

A comparable approach is used by UrbanDig Project in Athens, even though the context could hardly be more dissimilar. As George Sachinis explains in his conversation with Zoe Zontou, UrbanDig exists specifically to create performances in local neighbourhoods, where residents, usually of marginalized communities, become co-creators of communal activities that help them and the collaborators coming from outside the community to better understand their neighbourhood and thus acquire a sense of empowerment.

In their conversation with Romanian theatre director and activist David Schwartz, Marius Bogdan Tudor and Ionuţ Sociu bring yet another important perspective to this volume, that of the politics of memory. Besides reflecting on the social and political context that shaped contemporary community and political theatre in Romania, this interview draws a symptomatic map of the 'social and human impact of the post-socialist transition' in Central and Eastern Europe. As a well-known community theatre-maker in Eastern Europe with an increasing reputation in various parts of Western Europe as well, David Schwartz is interested in 'counter-hegemonic perspectives towards local and global history'. By discussing his work with various marginalized communities in Romania, the discussion unfolds the intimate connections between theatre-makers and communities, ultimately attempting a re-evaluation of complex personal and communal histories.

The closing part of the volume (Part V) analyses emerging theatre practices and methodologies, both textual and theatrical. The section focuses on new modes of theatrical communication, looking at communal dramaturgies and participatory aesthetics in the context of intermedial, 'cyberformance' and verbatim/documentary theatre. The authors in this section map new modes of spectatorship and the creation of unusual theatre communities.

Opening the section is Ágnes Bakk's intriguing chapter focusing on the different ways in which new technological tools and game design elements are transforming both processes of theatre-making and spectating. By analysing alternative forms of performative storytelling, she highlights emerging methodological considerations in audience engagement and argues for a more comprehensive development of new virtual theatre communities that also brings data protection to the fore in the context of cyber performances and generally amidst transmedia products.

Technology is also a major player in Rimini Protokoll's performances. Naďa Satková uses her experience as participant in *Remote Vilnius* (2015) to dissect the format created by Rimini Protokoll to form a temporary community that engages with the urban landscape and become aware of issues they might never have noticed, even if they live locally. At the same time Satková problematizes the particular relationship created between the participants, who are led to almost be remote controlled and have limited possibilities of communicating with each other.

By discussing Moisés Kaufman's *The Laramie Project* (2000), Bettina Auerswald explores the potential of verbatim theatre to engage with a community and create a discussion about a local tragedy that had been made impossible by the invasive intervention of national media. In this example, verbatim theatre helps the community come to terms with the tragedy and shoulder responsibility. However, Auerswald is also interested in establishing the limitations or systematic failures of verbatim.

As seen in the above content outline, the chapters of this volume deal with a wide variety of issues surrounding contemporary theatre's complex relationship with communities. Alongside a multitude of artistic and scholarly perspectives, this collection also presents divergences and convergences between national, sociocultural contexts and different theatre traditions. Ultimately, understanding community-conscious theatre-making in the twenty-first century involves a continuous re-examination of theatrescapes and sociocultural ecologies both nationally and internationally. We hope that our venture will contribute to further discussions and genuine debates on the shifts and systemic changes in the relationship between theatre and communities.

REFERENCES

Boenisch, Peter (2012), 'Acts of spectating: The dramaturgy of the audience's experience in contemporary theatre', *Critical Stages*, 7, December, http://www.critical-stages.org/7/acts-of-spectating-the-dramaturgy-of-the-audiences-experience-in-contemporary-theatre/. Accessed 4 March 2019.

Burzynska, Anna R. (ed.) (2016), *Joined Forces: Audience Participation in Theatre*, Berlin: Alexander Verlag.

Chapple, Freda and Kattenbelt, Chiel (2006), *Intermediality in Theatre and Performance*, Amsterdam and New York: Rodopi.

Cox, Emma (2014), *Theatre and Migration*, Basingstoke: Palgrave Macmillan.

Klaic, Dragan (2012), *Resetting the Stage: Public Theatre between the Market and Democracy*, Bristol and Chicago: Intellect.

Lehmann, Hans Thies (2006), *Postdramatic Theatre*, London and New York: Routledge.

Malzacher, Florian and Warsza, Joanna (eds) (2017), *Empty Stages, Crowded Flats: Performativity as Curatorial Strategy*, Berlin: Alexander Verlag.

Radosavljević, Duška (2013), *Theatre-Making: Interplay Between Text and Performance in the 21st Century*, Basingstoke: Palgrave Macmillan.

Van Campenhout, Elke and Mestre, Lilia (eds) (2016), *Turn Turtle! Reenacting the Institute*, Berlin: Alexander Verlag.

PART I

Theatre Communities:
Traces, Places and Belonging

We start our discussion on community-conscious theatre-making by mapping a number of contact points between theatre and communities and uncovering notions of theatre communities historically, spatially and in a sociocultural context. The writings in this opening section have been selected to highlight the wide meaning this volume wants to give to the term 'community' and its relationship to theatre. Stefan Aquilina writes about amateur theatre in the early Soviet era. It is a case study of the role that theatre, and specifically amateur theatre, had in reshaping communities and using theatre to enable social classes that were previously denied political agency to become important players. The study explores the strategies that were undertaken to enable theatrical activity to happen where there was no infrastructure or where the infrastructure was inadequate. In contrast, Cremona and Borg discuss a territory that is just over 300 km² but, owing to its dense population and a history where community theatre was the major entertainment of the working classes, has inherited a multitude of theatre spaces, many of which are ill-maintained and underutilized. The project they describe had the aim of making these spaces better known outside the immediate neighbourhood, and as a result to bring more performances into them. Zoe Zontou tackles another kind of transformation in her chapter. Applied theatre is a force for change, an 'antidote to the negative excesses of postmodernism' as she writes, quoting Kershaw. The project she discusses helps recovering drug addicts transform their lives, but the focus of the project and the chapter is on the creation of a new community, not of recovering addicts but of theatre-makers.

What is striking in all three chapters is a sense of urgency to expand our understanding of theatre communities beyond the notions of audience and spectatorship. This part makes an attempt to (re)locate theatre communities by tracing some intriguing histories of community-conscious theatre-making, and by looking at the spatial and architectural embeddedness of theatre communities as well as forms of belonging. The three distinct perspectives employed in these contributions allow us to consider the various modalities of constructing theatre communities, being either around shared values, shared spaces or a sense of togetherness. Common to each of this approach is a real commitment for engagement beyond social and economic capital.

Communal Solidarity and Amateur Theatre in Post-Revolutionary Russia: Theoretical Approaches

Stefan Aquilina

Modern theatre and performance in Russia was not only marked by the ground-breaking practices developed by professional practitioners like Konstantin Stanislavsky and Vsevolod Meyerhold. A parallel movement developed within amateur theatre circles that, though at the margins of the scene in turn-of-the-twentieth-century Russia, evidenced a marked increase in numbers and activity after the October Revolution of 1917. Workers, not only in the main cities like Moscow and Petrograd/Leningrad but also across the country, relished the public voice that theatre offered. The inroads that the workers had made by 1922 were proudly and positively trumpeted by Platon Kerzhentsev, a leading figure in early post-revolutionary debates on the nature of proletarian art and community theatre, to which he contributed through several theoretical writings that culminated in the publication and extensive revision of his book *Tvorchesky Teatr* (*The Creative Theatre*) (Keržencev [1922] 1979).[1] A central chapter in this book is 'The results of the new theatre', where Kerzhentsev gives a broad review of the scene while showing a clear and biased identification towards amateur theatre. For example, at one point Kerzhentsev says: 'The experience derived from the past two years [1918–20] has taught us that the revolutionary creativity of the popular masses in the fields of the arts is capable of achieving major victories' (Keržencev [1922] 1979: 97). However, underneath this romantic championing, one can find a number of examples that shed light on the practices adopted by the workers in creating their theatre pieces. One such description of an amateur production runs as follows:

> A dramatic text that treated the theme of the revolution was collectively created by the workers, the majority of whom had never set foot in a theatre before. One particular scene depicted the workers bringing down a wall that represented

the old times. As the actors onstage shouted and hurled themselves against the wall, the spectators instinctively stood up as one from their seats to help the actors in their struggle. The victorious notes of the Internationale were played when the wall was destroyed, to which the whole hall participated.

(Keržencev [1922] 1979: 97)

A danger when studying amateur theatre in post-revolutionary Russia is to draw general statements and conclusions on a movement that was marked by endless diversity. Performance forms like revolutionary melodramas, concert-meetings, living newspapers and agit-trials were at different stages, in the late 1910s and throughout the 1920s, among the most popular examples of amateur practice. However, two qualities do emerge from Kerzhentsev's example that recur in both the literature of the time and more recent secondary studies, to the extent that they can be treated as characteristic features of the scene.[2] First, amateur theatre can be seen to have developed in communities localized around spaces like the workplace (e.g. a factory), entertainment and pedagogical environments (i.e. the workers' clubs) or neighbourhoods. Tangible space, therefore, was an important contributor in the creation of theatre communities.[3] Kerzhentsev described this theatre as 'a theatre of the proletariat' rather than 'a theatre for the proletariat', a theatre in other words that not only sought to stage themes of interest to the workers but which was also 'built on the creativity of the nation's lowest strata' (Keržencev [1922] 1979: 35), with actors who tended their machines during the day and created theatre in the evening. Second, amateur theatre workers relied on their own collective creativity and ingenuity as a substitute for the most basic theatre resources like light, stage, formal texts, costumes, scenery and so on, resources that they often lacked. This practice was common enough to give post-revolutionary amateur theatre the title of *samodeiatel'nost teatr*, i.e. 'do-it-yourself theatre'.[4]

This essay has two tightly connected aims. First, it analyses post-revolutionary amateur theatre as a form of community theatre, one that was as much about the broader (revolutionary) context as it was about local situations, and in which public and private political spheres intertwined in an act that, even and particularly so in Russia, was always kept under the authorities' vigilant eyes. Such a composition of seemingly binary elements (public/private spheres, individual/group and control/creativity) nods towards the second aim of the essay, which tackles how recent and contemporary historiographical approaches are articulated as a tension between concrete archival research and that which is seemingly its opposite, i.e. the imaginative interpretation of the scholar. The essay will place critical theory at the intersection between historiographical rigour and imagination, and will offer one case study of such theoretical application, namely how Michel de Certeau's theories on 'strategies' and 'tactics' facilitate our understanding of post-revolutionary amateur theatre. I will attempt this theorizing by referring to Lynn Mally's seminal work on post-revolutionary Russian amateur theatre (Mally 2000). I will discuss methods that Mally uses to support her argumentation and draw attention to a particular moment when de Certeau's theories would have supported her interpretation of the political significance of amateur theatre.

Aesthetics and Production Processes of the Amateur Theatre

The 'strength' of amateur theatre in post-revolutionary Russia can be located in the collective practices used to make do with a general lack of resources: in the words of one contemporary writer, amateur theatres 'did not have a tenth of the resources of the high theatrical culture, of the technique, craftsmanship or finance which had been at the disposal of the old timers' (Rudnitsky 1988: 46). Similarly, contemporary chronicler Nina Gourfinkel emphasized in her account on the scene the crude but often ingenious practices of amateur actors.[5] One example she gives revolves around a collective piece titled *Lenin*, staged in 1926 by a group of workers who called themselves The Ship. Four main scenes, each representing an episode from Lenin's life, were presented. These were: (1) Lenin's arrival to St Petersburg; (2) the taking of power; (3) acts of aggression against Lenin and (4) the music of the Soviets. Means were scarce, and Gourfinkel noted how the production budget was only of 50 roubles (Gourfinkel 1979: 127–29). The illumination of the performance was a major problem as even the most basic light rigs were not available. Consequently, the actors held electric lamps in hand through which they illuminated their bodies and faces. Various parts of the stage were lit in the same way. Gourfinkel described the clever creation of the following scenes:

> *At the office.* Six participants are standing, while another two are sitting in the background. The latter are bare-chested, and are moving in rhythm to a workers' song which the actors are singing themselves. The lamps are only illuminating the heads and upper parts of their bodies, highlighting their well-built torsos. The lighting created a series of unsymmetrical shadows; it gave the impression of moving machines, of rotating wheels, and of a great number of workers.

> *The 1905 shooting.* The workers are illuminated only for an instant, which gives the impression of people being shot and, consequently, falling to the ground. The stage was pitch-dark, while a pile of bodies were placed in a barely lit spot. One of the workers, the only one who was properly illuminated, detaches himself from the group and continues the action.
>
> (Gourfinkel 1979: 128)

Musical effects were created through the use of a piano, harmonica and drums. A series of plates, brooms and paper sheets augmented these instruments. For example, the brooms were used to create the sound effect of a train entering a station, while the Aurora's cannon shot was recreated through a strong drum hit. 'Finally', Gourfinkel wrote, 'the resources used to create these various effects were put together to create the music of the Soviets' (1979: 129).

What transpires from this example is that the community of 'The Ship' called upon their ingenuity and collective creativity to overstep the limited resources that were at their disposal. Even The Leningrad Theatre of Young Workers (TRAM), which was considered as a large-scale amateur group, showed a 'lack of pretension, simplicity and unambiguous clarity of the theatrical form' (Rudnitsky 1988: 204). This was most characteristic of their amateur years.[6] For example, in *Work Days* (1926) actors performed on a tiny stage, wearing everyday clothes, and using very simple props such as a guitar, a bed, a table and a chair. Simple flats were used as a backdrop (see image in Mally 2000: 120). A bigger stage was used for *The Thoughtful Dandy* (1929), which was however conspicuous by its austerity (Mally 2000: 134). A similar austerity is to be noted in the production of *The Shot*, where simple wooden and unpainted flats represented a house; another scene only featured six ladders (see image in Rudnitsky 1988: 244).

Space offered similar challenges, and amateur theatre was to be found less in conventional theatre spaces and more in communal and shared spaces like street corners, squares, public gardens and the workers' clubs. Huntly Carter mentions the improvised play *The Mangy Dog*, which he saw performed in a dark and stuffy cellar. This setting, however, did not stop the performance from making an impact on him (Carter 1929: 133). The lack of a fixed space allowed the groups to play on a newfound responsibility of bringing the theatre to the people, often performing on the same level of the spectators and choosing material shared by both actors and spectators. Gourfinkel gives the following example of street theatre:

> [In 1920] an original experiment was attempted. Power cuts were common that year, and every time the power returned it was met by a widespread outburst of joy and cheering. Twelve trams travelled across the city through half devastated streets. They were equipped with open air platforms, and decorated in drapes and with painted canvas. They were transformed into mobile theatres. During the frequent power cuts, the actors, who had changed in the tram, took to the stages and gave short presentations of ten to fifteen minutes.
>
> These experiments were developed in the subsequent years; in Leningrad alone, one could count three hundred mobile companies. A part of these companies travelled the city and mingled with the crowds. They either used platforms

which had been prepared beforehand or acted on the streets or pavements, circled by the spectators. Other companies occupied the platforms more permanently. Trucks were used.

(Gourfinkel 1979: 125–26)

A similar spatial spontaneity is seen in many of the spaces used for indoor performances: the amateur groups performed in bars, tea-rooms, halls, basements and in any other space where political instigation was deemed necessary (Mally 2000: 26–27).

The communal dimension of amateur theatre emerges again in the practice known as 'collective dramaturgy', a form of group-work to create performance scripts (Gourfinkel 1979: 137–38). Collective dramaturgy was managed through the appointment of a facilitator, whose main responsibility was to introduce the theme. The workers then fleshed up this theme by recalling their own life experiences and examples that they might have read about or seen at the theatre or cinema. The following are two such scenarios:

> A working-class family. A father and his son work at a factory, while the daughter is engaged to another worker. There is a strike which is followed by all members of the family. However, the daughter's fiancé chooses to distance himself from the strike, and, consequently, the girl renounces the love of this class traitor.

> The following is another theme. An old man has two sons. The elder has a college education. He is an intellectual, a sweet human being with strong ideals. The second son is a worker and Bolshevik. The two fall in love with the same girl. She prefers the older one, who exhibits good manners but reacts to the events of the civil war in a cowardly and fearful way. On the other hand, the Bolshevik dies as a hero. The girl collects the Red flag which has slipped from the hand of the young man and pushes the workers forward for another attack.

(Gourfinkel 1979: 138–39)

It is important to note that even the theme had a strong communal dimension about how to live with one's fellow man. The relationship between any individual man and the Revolution was envisaged as too complex for the common man to understand. Indeed, the whole idea of the 'individual' was itself considered as counter revolutionary (Hellbeck 2006: 121, 131–34). Conflicts of 'a social nature were much easier to grasp and more politically correct' (Gourfinkel 1979: 138), which explains the working-class background in the social dramaturgies above.

21

A sense of community is fostered when groups of people bind together over common goals, a practice that underlines theatre work in general and amateur theatre in particular. Apart from the desire to produce the best possible theatre with the scarce means in hand (and to become known for it), the amateur actors in the examples above came together to carry out an endeavour that had collective authorship at its core. The communal DIY practices, spaces and themes served to 'fill [actors but also spectators with] proletarian solidarity and comradeship' (Stourac and McCreery 1986: 43), defining social factors within a context that promoted group-work as a way out of the stagnation in which the country had fallen. Amateur theatre in post-revolutionary Russia, therefore, connected both 'inwards', with the experiments in form that marked a lot of modern theatre and performance, and 'outwards', with the broader cultural experiment to create a society based on equality and collectivity.

Application of Theory to Historiography: Amateur Theatre as an Act of Resistance

The above accounts of amateur practice can be seen to have tackled five out of the six questions that theatre historian Thomas Postlewait uses to frame convincing historical research, namely the 'who', 'what', 'where', 'when' and 'how'. These frames facilitate reconstructions of theatre events, but it is the sixth interrogation, the 'why', which interprets the historical data (Postlewait 2009: 1). By using post-revolutionary amateur theatre as an example, I will now move to propose critical theory as a tool that facilitates historical interpretation. In this way, I will suggest that the ad hoc practices of amateur theatre contained the seeds of political resistance because they fit in with difficulty in the surrounding context as it was developing in the 1920s. Reference will be made to Lynn Mally's account on post-revolutionary amateur theatre, titled *Revolutionary Acts: Amateur Theatre and the Soviet State, 1917–38* (2000), which I consider to be the most comprehensive book in English on the subject.

The use of theory in historical studies has given rise to recent debate, and there is no agreement between historians on its validity, or on the extent to which it should be used in historical studies. Consequently, while several sources on theatre historiography do hint at the application of theory in the study of theatre history, few go to Jackie Bratton's extent of advocating for a 'theorised theatre history' (Bratton 2003: 4). Instead, relevant sources make reference to broad and vague categories of thought which only seem to suggest theoretical engagement. Examples of these include Gilli Bush-Bailey's statement that we can 'connect with the past through *present consciousness*' (Bush-Bailey and Bratton 2011: 107, emphasis added), or Christopher Balme's assertion that 'we can only have access to it [a historical phenomenon] via *conceptual constructs*' (2008: 101, emphasis added). These are in my opinion less loaded terms and appellations for theoretical frameworks. Similar instances include the following:

- Postlewait's and Sušec Michieli's reference to 'multiple *interpretive tactics and strategies*' (2010: 243, emphasis added);
- Postlewait's awareness of the practice that 'adopt[s] and appropriate[s] *analytical models* from scholarship in the humanities and social sciences [...] [which include] defining concepts of gender, race, class, and ethnicity' (2004: 182, emphasis added);
- Ron Vince's consideration on '*methods of interpreting* [theatre history] and to the *metaphors* by which we construct our hypothesis' (1989: 13, emphasis added).

The substitution of the word 'theory' with subtler alternatives marks a certain ambivalence in the application of theoretical frameworks to theatre historiographical studies. Perhaps this is a symptom of what Mark Fortier described as 'a degree of resistance' to the encroachment of theory in academic disciplines because, 'for some, theory is too abstruse, too jargon-ridden, too divorced from practicality [and] [...] contemplative' (Fortier 2002: 2–3). Theoretical application to historiographical research has indeed been critiqued and its potential dangers exposed. Therefore, while Jim Davis unequivocally asserts that one cannot expect historiography to be 'theory free' and that it is '[f]ar better to acknowledge the ideas that are influencing one's own opinions rather than to assume naively that one is untouched by theoretical positions' (Davis 2011: 92), other authors expound on how theory can suffocate historical analysis. For example, Postlewait is critical of historiographical studies that are excessively rooted in theoretical frames, where theory becomes an all-too-restrictive channel that binds rather than informs the study, making 'events [...] formulaic illustrations of a system or theory' (Postlewait 2009: 10).

Mally does give a theoretical framework to her analysis (2000: 18–19), and she contrasts 'aesthetic drama' to Victor Turner's concept of 'social drama' to discuss how both actors and spectators 'are altered through the process [of doing and seeing theatre]' (Mally 2000: 18). Apart from this brief theoretical input, however, it is clear that her work is rooted in archival reconstruction where it is the material unearthed that advances the narrative forward. One approach that she uses to support her argumentation is by drawing broad and general conclusions on the scene, which she then backs up by making reference to single and specific examples. The following instances are representative of this approach:

> State cultural *bureaucrats* charged with supervising *theatres* worried about their ability to channel this frenetic activity that was only nominally under their

control. As *one* high ranking central official wrote with some despair about amateur stages, 'As yet, we know very little about them'.

(Mally 2000: 18, emphasis added)

Many different *organizations* were responsible for club formation. *One* short list of clubs in a Petrograd newspaper identified sponsors ranging from the local Communist party, regional city soviets, individual factories, and trade union organization.

(Mally 2000: 25, emphasis added)

[T]he majority of new *centres* founded after the revolution were opened in urban environments designed for other functions. Not only did they lack auditoria, they had no dressing rooms, space for props, or comfortable seating for the audience. Even when a club boast an adequate hall for performances, many different groups laid claim on the space. [...] This meant that *theatre groups* had to discover other rooms – or hallways – for rehearsals. *Some groups* moved often to search for better accommodations. *One* Petrograd circle changed quarters four times in a two-year period.

(Mally 2000: 27, emphasis added)

In these instances, it is clear how Mally seamlessly shifts from the plural to the singular cases and from specific examples to the scene in general. This approach has the advantage of indicating the size of the scene – one source says that amateur theatres 'sprang up everywhere like mushrooms after rain' (Rudnitsky 1988: 44) – but it also raises questions over the extent to which general statements on a scene can be discerned from singular examples. On the other hand, Mally is very strong in the reconstruction of the Worker-Peasant Theatre, a division within the Narkompos (the equivalent of the Ministry for Education) that was tasked in early 1919 with the creation of a popular theatre for the workers and peasants. Mally's exposition on the Worker-Peasant Theatre is thorough because she makes reference to a variety of different sources, seven, in fact, over the space of just two pages (Mally 2000: 21–22).

The exposition on the Worker-Peasant Theatre paves way for the following statement:

With its connotations of autonomy and self-expression, *samodeiatel'nost* ['do-it-yourself theatre'] carried a potential threat to higher authorities. State leaders wanted to encourage the ambitions and talents of the lower classes, particularly the working class, on which they based their legitimacy. These new historical actors needed to be able to 'do things themselves.' But what would happen if they acted in ways that offended or challenged the new government? What if their creative work proved difficult to guide and control? The possibility that self-activity might turn into dangerous spontaneity was a constant worry for early Soviet leaders.

(Mally 2000: 24)[7]

Mally's point here is that the workers-actors' reliance on their own ingenuity and creativity brought them in conflict with the government's strive to control and direct every sphere of the emerging Soviet life. The evidence for this statement is less concrete. There are, for instance, no examples or quotes from amateur actors asserting their creative freedom, while the footnoted references in the quotation relate to conflicting meanings of the term *samodeiatel'nost* and the place of spontaneity and consciousness in Bolshevik political theory, material, therefore, that is tangential to Mally's interpretation.

It is specifically the interpretive statement that amateur theatre conflicted with the surrounding political regime that would have gained potency had it been framed around de Certeau's theories on the practice of everyday life. De Certeau formed part of a group of French theorists – which also included Henri Lefebvre – who tackled everyday life not as a locus of trivial and repetitive actions but as a field of critical knowledge that speaks about the creativity of human nature.[8] As Lefebvre writes: 'it is in everyday life and starting from everyday life that genuine creations are achieved, those creations which produce the human and which men produce as part of the process of becoming human' (2008: 45). De Certeau's contribution to the discourses on everyday life underlined daily life's significance as a seat of political action, within the tension generated between two forces that he called strategies and tactics (de Certeau 1988). These two forms of social action expound on ways in which power is not only imposed but also resisted. In brief, a strategy is any entity or system that seeks to exert control over people, while tactics are the covert, rather than in-your-face, actions through which the ordinary users of a system resist being controlled. Workplaces like factories are built along strategic lines because they operate through clearly defined structures that include clear-cut hierarchical roles (director, manager, shift leader, operators, etc.), well-defined rules and regulations that are often written down and disseminated (such as production quotas, shifts, attire, etc.) and, most importantly in de Certeau's eyes, the appropriation of a tangible and visible space that serves as a seat and manifestation of power. In fact, strategies are defined by the 'colon[isation] of a visible, specific space that will serve as a "home base" for the exercise of power and domination' (Gardiner 2000: 172). Permanent space as a metaphor for the permanence and timelessness of the entity becomes imperative, and strategic players 'open' their space to 'users' in view of affecting control over them.

Ordinary users of a system, in this case the workers, rarely have the resources to formally oppose the strategic power in a face-to-face confrontation and, therefore, more indirect, inventive and subliminal forms of intervention called tactics are used. De Certeau stresses that many everyday practices (reading, cooking, walking, narrating stories, etc.) are tactical in character and that this tactical character is a requisite to shed off the trivial connotations of everyday life (de Certeau 1988: 30). For example, reading offers tactical space within the strategic organization of the words on a page by allowing the reader to attach his own memories and images to the text. Reading, in other words, transports the reader: 'to read is to be elsewhere, where *they* [the readers] are not, in another world' (de Certeau 1988: 173, original emphasis). Tactics can appear insignificant when transferred to the workplace, such as when a worker writes a letter on company time and using company material, or when he or she counters the routines at the factory through an imaginative suspension of time and space. These actions, however, are elevated into acts of resistance when performed within a community of users who experience the same authoritarian drive of a strategy. In his analysis of the functioning of everyday life, de Certeau primarily talks about actions that are individually authored. In fact, his case studies are about the reader, the walker and the narrator, all in the singular. However, the repercussions of these actions go beyond the individual into the group of which the individual is a member. As de Certeau says:

> In the very place where the machine he must serve reigns supreme, he [the worker] cunningly takes pleasure in finding a way to create gratuitous products whose sole purpose is to signify his own capabilities through his work and to confirm his solidarity with other workers or his family through *spending* his time in this way. With the complicity of other workers (who thus defeat the competition the factory tries to instill among them), he succeeds in 'putting one over' on the established order on its home ground.
>
> (de Certeau 1988: 25–26, original emphasis)

Tactics, therefore, exhibit an inventive nature that recalls timely acts of intervention, concealment, veiled disruption and secretive jest. They are in the paradoxical position of operating within a strategy but only to interrupt, albeit briefly, the system's operations. Moreover, tactics necessarily exist because of the controlling drive generated by their 'mother' strategy, in the sense that tactical manoeuvres emerge as a reaction to strategic frameworks and cannot exist independently of them. There will be no need for tactical manoeuvre in a context that is liberating rather than oppressive and authoritarian.

The relationship between the emerging Soviet system and the amateur theatre can be organized on the strategies-tactics model. That the Bolshevik Party itself was organized on strategic lines is seen in Vladimir Lenin's words, who advocated for 'the painstaking establishment of accounting and control, [...] [because] the strictest organization and labour discipline [...] will lead us to socialism. Without this there is no socialism' (Lenin 1974: 297). Soviet strategies had to function 'like clockwork' and give the semblance of 'business like models' (Lenin 1974: 213). Strategic elements that facilitated this organization and control included, among others: the appropriation of large and visible spaces as headquarters; the Soviet-ization of public spaces through the erection of Soviet symbols and monuments; the creation of larger than life characters as examples to follow; the setting up of an over-bearing bureaucracy that, from as early as January 1918, enfolded every aspect of life[9]; and crucially, the constant stream of written material that was produced to articulate the Party's ultimate authorship of Soviet reality:

> The Bolshevik leaders had assumed power in an armed uprising that had deposed a state structure that had stood for centuries. They had never been elected by democratic process. Hence the regime's claims to legitimacy were largely grounded in a claim to cherishing and realizing more closely than might any rival the principles of the belief system – a secondary justificatory line of argument being improvements in the national economy and the material well-being of the citizens as indicators that they were progressing along the 'road to Communism'. As a consequence, written texts assumed enormous importance in the political life of the country. In the Soviet Union writing had such an authoritative status because it was felt it would establish the truth of the order to be found in Bolshevik experience. Writing was a means for promulgating the Party's ultimate authorship of Soviet reality.
>
> (Clark et al. 2007: xii)

Similar actions to transform the arts into a strategic field were made. In a letter to the Politburo (June 1922), Leon Trotsky suggested the creation of a list of young writers, complete with a dossier on each entry. In this way, the Party would know exactly who the writers were, what their style was, their political affiliations and so on. Such a strategy would regulate future output and also facilitate censorship (Clark et al. 2007: 34). Amateur theatre was similarly kept an eye on. Worker-actors who participated in amateur theatrics were often affiliated with such strong spheres (i.e. strategies) as the Red Army, the Baltic Fleet or the trade unions. In these spaces, the government's regulatory hand was at its strongest. These affiliations made it easier for the Party to present official repertoire guidelines and training programmes, as well as make other official interventions (Mally 2000: 34). Repertoire guidelines proved a particularly significant tool for the Party to oversee amateur work. Early repertoire guidelines relied mostly on the classics, particularly on Ostrovsky's plays, but these were eventually extended to include foreign works (such as Shakespeare, Emile Verhaeren and the Greek classics), as well as a number of contemporary names (Keržencev [1922] 1979: 73–85).

In this context, amateur theatre's more do-it-yourself approaches were elevated from theatre practices to tactical actions. There are several reasons why amateur theatre can be read as a tactic: that in relation to the skill, resources and visibility of the professional companies and their 'monumental theatres' amateur actors adopted a much cruder aesthetics that chimes with de Certeau's formulation of strategies being 'strong' and tactics being 'weak' (de Certeau 1988: 34); or that amateur theatre's more spontaneous practice produced timely but ephemeral commentaries on their immediate context rather than declarations intended for longevity. Most pertinent to the discussion about theatre communities, however, is the 'communal solidarity' that de Certeau identifies as a necessary condition for tactical play and that amateur actors embodied through the collective work undertaken and the consequent shared ownership that such work engenders. In contrast to the government's 'agenda [...] to expand Communist control over economy, education, and culture [with the aim of] [...] recasting the entire society' (Brovkin 1998: 21), an amateur theatre that was rooted in what a community of workers could achieve together by pooling resources became an activity laden with political significance and elusive of strategic systematization in the form suggested by Mally. Gourfinkel's examples given above can be therefore interpreted as follows: while the themes of the performance by The Ship (a celebration of Lenin and the Revolution) fit well within the political needs and discourses of the time, the way that the staging process relied on the participants' ingenuity contrasted with the regulatory hand of the government and made the piece elusive of the latter's strategic and controlling impulse. The reactionary potential of amateur theatre emerges again in the example of collective dramaturgies: while the themes did indeed support the ideologies of the new status quo, the practices that engendered them, rooted as they were in discussion, improvisation and the existence of alternative and optional possibilities, clashed with the larger context whose agenda was the systematic, and, in de Certeau's terminology, strategic, organization of life.

Conclusion

In this essay I attempted a reconstruction of some post-revolutionary amateur theatre examples. Considering the vast tapestry of theatrics that were staged by worker-actors in the early 1920s, such a reconstruction will always remain partial, especially within the context of a relatively short book chapter. Consequently, in my reconstruction I have sought to emphasize the do-it-yourself ethic that worker-actors adopted and the potential that amateur theatre has in nourishing theatre communities. It is this do-it-yourself ethics that makes a study of early post-revolutionary amateur theatre relevant to contemporary community-conscious theatre discourses. While statements about the Revolution, the plight of the workers and future socialist utopias were strongly rooted in the ideologies of the time, and consequently, context-based, the act of coming together to create theatre by pooling from the group's immediate skills and resources reads strongly as an early example of what today we would refer to as devised theatre. Communities in the twenty-first century are not only defined by the tangible space they inhabit, but more and more by shared needs and aspirations, similar to the way that amateur actors gravitated together to play a political role through theatre.

In my account I also discussed how Mally's interpretation of amateur theatre as a political act that had the potential to elude the Government's drive for control finds resonance with de Certeau's theories on strategies and tactics. My methodology relied on the qualification of early post-revolutionary Russia as a strategy and of amateur theatre as a tactic. These qualifications establish a relationship based on power between the government and amateur theatre to support the interpretation that the worker-actors communal and do-it-yourself practice bordered on 'dangerous spontaneity'. Beyond such a case-specific example, however, my application of de Certeau also argued in favour of using critical theory as a historiographical tool. It draws attention to the fact that archives are never the depository of complete and neutral material, and that equally important in the construction of theatre and performance histories is the individual point of view and background of the scholar.

REFERENCES

Aquilina, Stefan (2013), 'Transforming everyday life: The political struggles of amateur theatres, Meyerhold, and Stanislavsky', unpublished doctoral thesis, Malta: University of Malta.

Balme, Christopher (2008), *The Cambridge Introduction to Theatre Studies*, Cambridge: Cambridge University Press.

Bratton, Jacky (2003), *New Readings in Theatre History*, Cambridge: Cambridge University Press.

Brovkin, Vladimir (1998), *Russia after Lenin: Politics, Culture and Society, 1921–29*, London and New York: Routledge.

Bush-Bailey, Gilli and Bratton, Jacky (2011), 'Case study 2: Memory, absence and agency: An approach to practice-based research in theatre history', in B. Kershaw and H. Nicholson (eds), *Research Methods in Theatre and Performance*, Edinburgh: Edinburgh University Press, pp. 98–107.

Carter, Huntly (1929), *The New Spirit in the Russian Theatre*, Worcester: Ebenezer Baylis and Son Limited.

Certeau, Michel de (1988), *The Practice of Everyday Life* (trans. S. Rendall), Berkeley, CA: University of California Press.

Clark, Katerina, Evgeniĭ, Dobrenko, Artizov, Andrei and Naumov, Oleg (2007), *Soviet Culture and Power: A History in Documents 1917–1953*, New Haven, CT: Yale University Press.

Davis, Jim (2011), 'Research methods and methodology', in B. Kershaw and H. Nicholson (eds), *Research Methods in Theatre and Performance*, Edinburgh: Edinburgh University Press, pp. 89–98.

Fortier, Mark (2002), *Theatre/Theory: An Introduction*, London and New York: Routledge.

Gardiner, Michael E. (2000), *Critiques of Everyday Life*, New York: Routledge.

Gourfinkel, Nina (1979), *Teatro Russo Contemporaneo* (trans. M. Turano), Roma: Bulzoni Editore.

Hellbeck, Jochen (2006), *Revolution on My Mind*, Cambridge, MA: Harvard University Press.

Highmore, Ben (2002), *Everyday Life and Cultural Theory*, London and New York: Routledge.

Keržencev, Platon [Kerzhentsev] ([1922] 1979), *Il Teatro Creativo* (trans. E. Casini Ropa), Roma: Bulzoni Editori.

Lefebvre, Henri (2008), *Critique of Everyday Life,* vol. 2 (trans. G. Elliot), London: Verso.

Lenin, Vladimir (1974), *Collected Works*, vol. 27 (ed. R. Daglish, trans. C. Dutt), Moscow: Progress Publishers.

Mally, Lynn (2000), *Revolutionary Acts: Amateur Theatre and the Soviet State*, New York: Cornell University Press.

Markov, Pavel (1934), *The Soviet Theatre*, New York: G. P. Putnam's Sons.

Matthews, Mervyn (ed. and trans.) (1974), *Soviet Government: A Selection of Official Documents on Internal Policies*, London: Jonathan Cape Ltd.

Postlewait, Thomas (2004), 'Theatre history and historiography: A disciplinary mandate', *Theatre Survey*, 45:2, pp. 181–82.

—— (2009), *The Cambridge Introduction to Theatre Historiography,* Cambridge: Cambridge University Press.

Postlewait, Thomas and Sušec Michieli, Barbara (2010), 'A transnational community of scholars: The Theatre Historiography Working Group in IFTR/FIRT', *Theatre Research International*, 35:3, pp. 232–49.

Rudnitsky, Konstantin (1988), *Russian and Soviet Theatre,* London: Thames and Hudson.

Sheringham, Michael (2009), *Everyday Life: Theories and Practices from Surrealism to the Present*, Oxford: Oxford University Press.

Stourac, Richard and McCreery, Kathleen (1986), *Theatre as a Weapon,* London and New York: Routledge and Kegan Paul.

Tyson, Lois (2014), *Critical Theory Today: A User-Friendly Guide,* London and New York: Routledge.

Vince, Ron (1989), 'Theatre history as an academic discipline', in T. Postlewait and B. McConachie (eds), *Interpreting the Theatrical Past: Essays in the Historiography of Performance*, Iowa City, IA: University of Iowa Press, pp. 1–18.

Editors' Note

Aquilina's opening chapter in this volume not only links us back to post-revolutionary Russian theatre, but also offers some important considerations towards understanding contemporary devised theatre. Mirella Schino's *An Indra's Web* (2018: 216–54) gives a good background to the political, social and economic situation for the Russian theatre discussed by Aquilina. Further on this, please see Senelick and Ostrovsky (2014), especially the Introduction. Natalia Murray's article 'Street theatre as propaganda: Mass performances and spectacles in Petrograd in 1920' (2016: 230–41) discusses some of the performances dealt with in this writing and includes a striking photograph of a tram platform performance. For an in-depth analysis on the histories and diverse impact of amateur theatre on local and national environments, please see Nicholson et al. (2018). Emma Govan, Helen Nicholson and Katie Normington provide a comprehensive introduction to the theory, history and practice of devised performance in their book *Making a Performance: Devising Histories and Contemporary Practices* (2007). For a history of devised theatre, see also Milling and Heddon (2015).

Further reading

Govan, Emma, Nicholson, Helen and Normington, Katie (2007), *Making a Performance: Devising Histories and Contemporary Practices*, Abingdon: Routledge.

Milling, Jane and Heddon, Deirdre (2015), *Devising Performance: A Critical History*, rev. ed., Basingstoke: Palgrave Macmillan.

Murray, Natalia (2016), 'Street theatre as propaganda: Mass performances and spectacles in Petrograd in 1920,' *Studies in Theatre and Performance*, 36:3, pp. 230–41.

Nicholson, Helen, Holdsworth, Nadine and Milling, Jane (2018), *The Ecologies of Amateur Theatre*, Basingstoke: Palgrave Macmillan.

Schino, Mirella (2018), *An Indra's Web: The Age of Appia, Craig, Stanislavski, Meyerhold, Copeau, Artaud*, Holstebro: Icarus Publishing Enterprise.

Senelick, Laurence and Ostrovsky, Sergei (eds) (2014), *The Soviet Theater: A Documentary History*, New Haven, CT: Yale University Press.

NOTES

1. This essay uses an Italian translation of the fourth edition of Kerzhentsev's book, originally published in 1920. All translation from this and other sources in Italian are mine.
2. My focus will be on the earlier part of the post-revolutionary scene. For a list of sources that tackle the post-revolutionary amateur scene, see the References.

3. On how specific communities gave rise to amateur theatre groups, Pavel Markov wrote: 'Every district, every army unit, every factory had its own "theatre-circle," watched over and developed with the greatest care and attention' (1934: 137). See also Mally (2000: 24–29).

4. On the different appellations given to the post-revolutionary amateur theatre movement, see Mally (2000: 20–24).

5. Gourfinkel's account is unavailable in English translation, and I draw attention to a number of passages from it in order to also underline its value as a primary source on the scene. The version that I used is similarly available in Italian translation.

6. The group heeded the instigation of the authorities and turned professional in 1928 (Rudnitsky 1988: 204).

7. See at least two other instances where Mally reiterates the same point on the political and resistive potential of amateur theatre: 'It was precisely the homemade, unpredictable quality of amateur work that concerned Soviet regulators. [...] State cultural bureaucrats charged with supervising theatres worried about their ability to control this frenetic activity that was only nominally under their control' (Mally 2000: 15, 18).

8. Introductory sources on the critical domain of everyday life that reference de Certeau, Lefebvre and others like Mikhail Bakhtin, Agnes Heller, Roland Barthes and George Perec include Sheringham (2009), Highmore (2002) and Gardiner (2000).

9. See the official decree 'The structure of local government' in Matthews (1974: 22–27). For a more extended discussion on the strategic organization of the Soviet world, see Aquilina (2013: 62–70).

Theatre in Malta:
Which Spaces Does the
Community Occupy?

Vicki Ann Cremona and Ruben Paul Borg

Introduction

This chapter focuses on the development of a methodology for the appraisal of theatre spaces and presents an exercise in identifying such spaces in the Maltese Islands. However, the research conducted is based on a methodology that may be adapted and applied to small states or regions where resources for theatre and the arts, as well as financial gain from these, are limited. In smaller countries, theatres are situated within smaller communities and have less possibilities of professionalization, yet they are particularly close to the social structures of the community, such as cultural centres, local culture groups or religious institutions. Small communities producing theatre often do not envisage the possibility of touring with their productions because there is a perceived impression either of lack of theatres to go to, or lack of interest from other communities. Our research has brought to light the fact that even in smaller states and regions, there may be a more significant presence of theatre spaces than one would expect, and that it is useful to identify them in the effort to establish more national or regional programmes that imply cultural communication and exchange at the level of smaller communities.

Little is known about theatre spaces in Malta before the building of a *teatro pubblico* in Valletta in 1732, on the footprint of two demolished houses, which is known today as the Manoel Theatre. Today, the theatres that come immediately to mind are the ones situated in the capital cities of the two islands; however, theatre buildings spread beyond the capitals in the late nineteenth and early twentieth centuries, practically at the same time as the development of band clubs. Their architecture and location within the village and town communities, as well as their ownership, patronage and spectatorship indicate not only the evolution of scenic space, but also the theatres' role and importance in community life. The run-up to Valletta as the European Capital of Culture (ECoC) in 2018 created new interest for theatres and theatrical spaces. The organization of events for Valletta ECoC 2018 created the need for more theatre spaces besides those located in Valletta itself. This was also due to the involvement of all 68 local councils in the country, which supported Valletta's bid on the condition that, given the small size of the islands, the concept of Capital of Culture be extended to the whole of the two main islands. A national project, entitled 'Cultural Mapping', gave rise to an online interactive map and two publications about culture in Malta (Cremona 2016, 2017). This, and erroneous public perception about the lack of theatres in Malta, led us to embark on research concerning theatre spaces across the Maltese Islands.[1] Our aim was to identify the relationship between theatre spaces and the community, particularly in small nation realities, by examining the theatrical spaces available across the islands of Malta and Gozo.

The methodology and results of this research created the premise for envisaging community theatres as cultural poles, due first and foremost to the fact that in people's minds, they are still seen as places of culture. Identifying these places and making known their characteristics, is one way of attracting more cultural activity to them, and consequently more interest. This, in turn, may contribute to more intense exploitation as well as conservation of the buildings themselves, even if this often implies total refurbishment. Such a study also brings to light hidden architectural jewels, which are often little known or appreciated by the local community.

The Theatre

The word 'theatre' encompasses a variety of spaces that may be used for the performing arts. In small communities, the variety and number may be more restricted according to the importance and investment attributed to theatre. Malta offers a range of spaces, predominantly frontal theatres with a proscenium arch stage, often built in the late nineteenth or early twentieth centuries. During this period, many theatres were developed, generally, but not always, linked to church and parish institutions as well as schools. Theatre spaces evolved into cinemas with the ever-increasing popularity of this new form of entertainment. Theatres also became focal places for political activities, particularly in the 1950s and 1960s. A number of important theatres were built during or after the 1960s, including the largest theatres on the Maltese Islands: the one at the Mediterranean Conference Centre in Valletta, the two main theatres in Gozo and the theatre at Ta' Qali, which is built on the concept of the Ancient Greek theatron; some were restructured, such as the Manoel Theatre and the University of Malta theatre in Valletta, known as the Valletta Campus Theatre (the latter was transformed into a black box theatre in the late 1980s); others were abandoned or changed use. Today there are very few black box theatres or theatres in the round and no multimedia and multi-space theatres. Certain theatre spaces are also adapted to cater for other community needs.

In assessing a theatre, a number of key principles must be taken into account. General aspects include not only the theatre location itself, and the theatre's size, layout, design and services, but also issues such as accessibility, fire safety and building sustainability. The different spaces forming the theatre building are connected to different uses – such as front of house, dressing rooms, backstage etc. The complexity of a theatre building is reflected in the hierarchy of spaces it contains, and the components of each space. The quality of a theatre is also determined by the use and functionality of the different spaces, and the versatility they offer to the community that uses them.

The Community

Theatres are privileged public areas because of their size, and often, their location. In an epoch where social media creates virtual networks of people, but does not privilege direct physical encounter, community spaces become essential for individual and social interaction, and may offer attraction to different age-groups. Currently, one serious problem that is being faced in Malta and elsewhere is how to attract young people to the theatre, both as consumers and as creators of and participants in the arts. Many community theatres lack actors, stage managers, backstage etc. It has been claimed that 'family and social environment are fundamental elements in encouraging cultural participation' and that not enough studies have been conducted on evaluation by young people themselves of the cultural offer, opportunities and expectations in cultural participation (Interarts 2010: 14). Given that theatre is run mostly on an amateur basis, it is not seen as a lucrative pastime, and is often ignored. However, an existing building in close proximity to one's place of residence may provide attraction and will 'usually have some following within the community, even when it has been closed or in other uses for many years' (Strong 2010: 181). Nostalgia and fidelity can be exploited to attract new generations to the theatre; spatial refurbishment and partial new builds can also contribute to creating a new theatre community.

This has been the case with two theatres in Valletta, namely St. James Cavalier and Pjazza Teatru Rjal. The first, originally a historical gunpowder and arms depot, contained a water reservoir. The whole building was remodelled into a cultural

35

centre as one of Malta's millennium projects, with various spaces including exhibition halls, a cinema, a music room and a café; a theatre was built inside the old reservoir. The transformed space has attracted a whole new clientele, made up both of older and younger people, who frequent its different spaces, especially the theatre, thanks to the versatility of the space-in-the-round and its exploitation for a variety of activities. Pjazza Teatru Rjal is an open-air theatre built on the site of an opera house that was destroyed during World War II and that is situated in the heart of the city. Although the theatre initially caused much public controversy, it has found its place in the island's cultural calendar, particularly during summer when it hosts a variety of performances that appeal to different age groups. This theatre has inserted performance within the space of the community, even simply by the fact that what is happening inside may be heard beyond and attract attention.

Our research brought to light the fact that there are far more theatres in Malta and Gozo than one would think a priori, and many of these are underexploited. This realization made us surmise that clearer knowledge of the various theatrical spaces existing across the island might encourage more cultural networking, with productions visiting different localities and thereby attracting diverse audiences, many of whom are no longer in the habit of frequenting theatrical and artistic productions. This possibility may give rise to more economic feasibility of a diversified range and quantity of artistic productions, given that currently, the number of performances of a single production are very limited, and many of these performances deserve to be more fully exploited.

In light of this, in order for community theatres to survive, these spaces have to be envisaged in such a way as to be accessible and exploitable spaces for the community even when theatre is not occurring. Therefore, in conceiving their development, their use for the community has to be taken into account as they are places of community interaction through encounter or through collective activity.

Research Objectives

The study was guided by the following objectives:

a. The promotion of decentralization of theatre spaces beyond the capitals Valletta and Rabat in Gozo, through the rediscovery and recovery of little-known community theatres spread throughout the Maltese Islands;
b. The exploration of the possibilities and limits of these spaces, as well as their potential for improvement, refurbishment and development;
c. The elaboration of a methodology for the assessment of different typologies of theatre spaces;

d. The creation of an improved and more exhaustive list of theatres in the Maltese Islands, given that the existing official list of theatres was found to be incomplete and included spaces that cannot be classified as theatres, nor are they used for this purpose;

e. The creation of the first catalogue of theatres in the Maltese Islands;

f. The development of theatre spaces as a lasting legacy of Valletta Capital of Culture 2018;

g. As a long-term objective, the creation of a network of theatre spaces in the Maltese Islands, which would enable companies to tour around the country, allowing their performances to reach wider and more diverse publics.

Research Methodology

Our starting point was a study carried out by the National Statistics Office (NSO) published in an NSO Newsletter dated 19 November 2013 that listed 72 theatres across Malta and Gozo. It specified that 492 productions had been staged the previous year, reaching a total audience of 293,772 persons, an impressive figure if one considers that the total population of Malta is about 460,000. The NSO methodology referred to a theatre survey across Malta and Gozo covering all established theatres and community spaces that may be used as theatres, including parish, school and community halls. The methodology did not appear to distinguish between a community hall and a building that is solely intended and exploited as a theatre. Consequently, the list included a significant number of multi-purpose halls that could be adapted to host theatrical events, but missed important theatres in the Maltese Islands. Neither did it define the type of theatrical event that could be hosted in the halls. It was beyond the scope of the NSO survey to supply any data that could be exploited by persons in the sector with regard to possibilities of staging their performances, but the necessity to address this lacuna was felt by the theatre community. While the main purpose of the first stage of the research was intended to lead to the development of a quality assessment tool for theatre spaces to assist in defining priority areas for intervention, it was also considered necessary to compile a proper list of theatre spaces. This led eventually to the definition of an assessment methodology in the first stage and was followed by the compilation of the first catalogue of theatres in the Maltese Islands, supported by relevant information on key indicators.

During the compilation of the catalogue, not only was the quality of the space assessed on the basis of its attributes, but the space examined was evaluated in such a way as to determine whether it could be truly considered as a theatre.

Taking the NSO study as our starting point, a pilot study was launched with the development of a quality assessment methodology, focusing on eight theatre spaces situated in the capital, Valletta, its suburb Floriana, and in Rabat, the main city of Gozo (Borg 2017a). These spaces comprised public theatres, community theatres and one theatre belonging to the University of Malta. The study focused on quality assessment of the theatres and was articulated around the following attributes: policy and planning; technical theatre aspects; infrastructure; architecture and space; accessibility; structure; services, energy efficiency, building physics; health and safety; social and cultural aspects; management aspects; financial aspects.

A set of sub-indicators was linked to each of these attributes; these included stage dimensions, stage architecture, accessories, equipment etc. Grading criteria were used to evaluate each of the attributes and were organized as follows: new/functional and operational; old/functional but requires maintenance and repair; present but not functional; not present; could not be verified.

Theatre spaces were classified according to spatial disposition: backstage, stage, house, front-of-house and external space. In order to provide a comprehensive picture of quality assessment of these spaces, the data gathered was organized in a matrix enabling the classification of attributes. The information gathered and classified contributes to identifying critical areas for intervention on the buildings themselves, as well as indications for refurbishment and upgrade.

The methodology elaborated in the pilot study was refined and applied to a limited set of theatres beyond the geographical limits of the first study. This methodology revealed the necessity to embark on the next stage of investigation, which took into account a much wider spectrum of theatres across the Maltese Islands. Furthermore, the objectives of this investigation were to focus on specific indicators that would allow for the exploitation of the theatres by performing arts companies, which would render them more relevant for the community and would bring in new financial resources. For this reason a four-person multidisciplinary team was appointed, with expertise in building materials, civil engineering and architecture, services engineering, theatre history and technology, theatre entrepreneurship and community theatre. The experts were responsible for the preparation of a strategy that was targeted to identify the theatres and to gather data concerning these spaces through desk studies, site investigations and interviews. Once gathered, the data was to be organized in a coherent manner, analysed and the findings made accessible to the general public.

The necessity for a range of theatre spaces for the activities organized for the Capital of Culture led to the elaboration of a simple methodology that allowed for consistent collection of data by non-experts. Thanks to this, data could be compiled in the shortest time possible while ensuring that the core criteria for addressing the professional needs of users would be accurately registered. A first list of theatres was compiled, which included the ones listed in the NSO survey as well as others that had been omitted. The experts used this methodology on 80 theatres in Malta, with the aim that it would continue to be adopted for theatres that had not been included in their list, and which could be the object of an ulterior survey in the future. The team visited and inspected the theatres listed to carry out an appraisal and collect the material data between 2015 and 2016.

In order to render these spaces more visible for the industry and the findings available to the general public, it was decided to publish an online catalogue of the theatres examined, showing a selection of core indicators (Cremona et al. 2017). The rationalization of the attributes reflected the needs and expectations of the professionals in the performance sector. The catalogue supplied information concerning the type of stage; the dimensions of the stage and auditorium; stage equipment; technical information concerning lighting and sound; availability of dressing rooms; audience capacity and comfort; state of maintenance of the building; access; and additional features including administration and ownership, and contact details of the theatre.

Challenges of the Study

This study has not been able to examine the social characteristics of the potential audiences who would be more susceptible to frequenting particular theatres rather than others, either because of distance, the productions on offer or the type of relationship that is established between the managers of the space and the community. An essential factor to keep in mind was that 'a simple calculation based on a catchment area (defined by the number of people living within a certain distance of a proposed building) does not indicate the correct potential for participation' (Appleton 2008: 13); however, heightened awareness of a space and of the potentialities for its enhancement may prove to be an important factor of cultural attraction. The type of audience also determines the type of facilities that should be included in a theatre, such as bars, restaurants, foyer as well as the type, amount and level of stage equipment to be invested in. Social characteristics of audiences also help to determine the type of performances that are more susceptible to attract audiences and participation, and is an essential component in the programming of a theatre. Programming strategies must take into account an audience's cultural interests and development, as well as its cultural heritage. In Malta, certain specific local traditions in theatrical productions still predominate, such as Passion plays that are staged during the Lenten period. This type of performance must be catered for, from the point of view of both space and equipment, in the same way as exposure to new cultural opportunities or educational programmes. Local cultural appeal constitutes, therefore, an important factor in the kind of marketing strategies that should be deployed to bring people to community theatre.

The study has not delved deeply into the administrative aspect of the theatres examined; it has simply limited itself to essential points such as ownership of the theatres and contact details. Given that most theatres in Malta are run on a voluntary basis, or their use is incorporated within the pedagogical exigencies of schools, we did not examine the administrative and personnel realities of those entities who have full-time employees dedicated to the theatres' administration, nor did we go into volunteer management of the spaces. These aspects went beyond our remit, but deserve a separate study as they can throw more light on community involvement in the promotion and development of Malta's cultural capital.

Although the study has taken into account elements such as the size and format of the various auditoria, it has not traced the reasons for the physical size of the various community theatres, nor did it delve deeply into the materials used and the finishes added to embellish the space. Moreover, much more archival work needs to be done about the theatres themselves, and more research into their building structure and fabric, design, layout and planning must be conducted also in relation to the period in which they were built and to other architectural typologies that were contemporary to them both in Malta and beyond. The state of repair of the buildings requires more thorough examination. These aspects, particularly the latter, would feature in a detailed study that aims at refurbishment or regeneration of these theatre spaces.

Discussion

The methodology developed in the initial study was applied to theatres that are considered as prominent theatre spaces in the country in Valletta, its suburb Floriana and Rabat, Gozo. The scope of the first assessment exercise was to elaborate a methodological instrument that would lead to a more comprehensive multi-criteria assessment tool that could be applied to theatres over the entire Maltese territory. This quality assessment tool was intended to assist experts in their evaluation of the state of the theatres, taking into account the needs of the different users, and allowing for the determination of priority areas for intervention or refurbishment. The data collected for each individual theatre was presented in a data matrix that provided quantitative and qualitative information as determined by the various indicators. The quality assessment highlighted the wide-ranging needs of the spaces analysed. The data collected may serve as a basis to elaborate a deeper investigation into theatre buildings, their role within the community and possible approaches towards refurbishment and restructuring of these spaces.

In the second stage, the methodology was refined and applied to a limited set of theatres beyond the geographical limits of the cities. This led to the third phase of the research, with the compilation of a list of theatres throughout the Maltese Islands and their assessment.

The tangible result of the three-phase study that was carried out was the publication of the first catalogue of theatres in Malta. This catalogue should not be seen as an ultimate product, but as an initial step for much deeper research into theatre spaces in Malta and Gozo. Many additional spaces have come to light after the catalogue was published and deserve to be included in an exhaustive national catalogue of theatres. Besides providing a list of spaces with information that may be of interest to theatre entrepreneurs, work on the catalogue has brought to light certain factors that shall be discussed below.

Architectural Heritage

Cataloguing theatres provided the opportunity to become aware of and draw attention to spaces that had never really been taken into consideration beforehand, some of which were not even listed by the NSO. Some of these theatres constitute veritable heritage monuments of twentieth-century architecture. This is either due to the persons who designed and constructed these spaces, such as the Maltese artist Emvin Cremona or the past prime minister, Dom Mintoff, who as an architect was responsible for a number of theatres after World War II; or because they provide certain architectural features that are almost unique in Malta, such as the Blue Arena Theatre in Zabbar, which offers a fine example of art deco theatre architecture. Up to now, no theatre built in the first half of the twentieth century has been scheduled as a historical monument, a situation that is also true of other countries; in fact theatre experts who are interested in historic and old buildings have lamented the interventions of architects in the 1950s and 1960s who in modernizing the theatres did not sufficiently take into account 'the architectural and theatrical potential of the traditional proscenium arch playhouse' (Mackintosh 1993: 79). Conversely, this significant historical value presents limitations to adaptability and substantial challenges with regard to refurbishment. Moreover, a preliminary look into the materials and structural systems used for the construction of these theatres has shown that a whole range of types and qualities of materials and structural elements were used, which were also dictated by the prevailing materials and technology at the time of construction. This allows for the understanding of specific methods of construction as well as for the types of refurbishment and restoration that should be planned.

41

The diminished value of certain theatres, due to the fact that they could not keep up with developing technology or resist degradation due to the rising costs of refurbishment, was also noted. In fact, this negative factor also proved positive in preserving certain equipment that otherwise might have been lost. From a contemporary perspective, equipment cannot simply be removed even if obsolete by today's standards. It requires study as to its rarity, its intrinsic worth and its value in relation to the context in which it was used.

It was noted that in certain cases, the lack of a theatre within the community was felt, and that a theatrical space, re-appropriated by the community, could provide an important cultural focal point. Success stories in this regard point to the underlying potential of these spaces in developing community life. Such has been the case, for example, with the restoration and rehabilitation of the Salesians' Theatre in the seaside town of Sliema, where a theatre that at the beginning of the twentieth century was considered prestigious enough to be decorated by Giuseppe Calì, one of Malta's foremost artists of the time, was almost abandoned by the 1990s, until a substantial bequest provided enough money for a thorough refurbishment. The theatre has now become a cultural hotspot and an alternative to the Valletta theatres, also thanks to a cultural cooperation agreement with Arts Council Malta.

Modernization

Refurbishment today has to take note of all the latest technology, which, however, has to fit into theatrical spaces that were not necessarily originally designed in a way to allow for such installations. In these cases, refurbishment also means transformation. Unfortunately, this is all too often carried out in ways that do not respect the traditional, historical structure and fabric because of the generally high costs of modernization, given that when operating in existing buildings, especially those that have been standing for a relatively long time, budgets have to account not only for refurbishment, but most of all for restoration, which may reveal layers of the past through previously unrecorded features. Moreover, modernizing a building to allow it to cater for current needs, without betraying its original characteristics, represents an onerous challenge, as well as a technical and logistical one.

The list of theatres to be catalogued also allowed for the penetration of spaces hidden within schools, few of which are actually exploited for public use, beyond that of the schoolchildren and their teachers. These theatres have the potential to be transformed into veritable cultural centres, given the right management of the space. This type of transformation was effected with regard to the Don Bosco theatre in Rabat, Gozo that belongs to the Catholic Church. The building houses a whole complex of spaces that are exploited for various cultural activities, such as cinema, theatre, dance etc. and has become a focal point for the local community.

Many theatre spaces may, with some refurbishment, be exploited for other uses besides artistic performances. These theatres, which usually constitute one of the largest exploitable spaces within a community, could be used as multi-purpose halls housing different activities that would attract the community. A number of church-owned theatres are already being used in this way, with moveable seating and multi-purpose lighting. However, physical flexibility needs to be supported by adequate cultural management of the spaces, that cultivates a broad outlook on the different dimensions and expressions of spectacle, entertainment and cultural activity in general,[2] and a desire to network more intensely with other cultural spaces across the islands and even beyond. This type of cultural undertaking could effectively contribute to developing a more intense cultural life within the community itself, as well as opening it up to other cultural possibilities that would serve to enrich its cultural capital and contribute to the country's cultural wealth.

Key Issues within Theatre Spaces

Accessibility to and within theatres is a preponderant factor that is presently being taken more and more into consideration. Our study examined the factor of accessibility, and though it was noted that many theatres provide accessibility for spectators, things become more complicated when artists' spaces are taken into consideration. It is generally more difficult for people with disabilities to access a stage area and find adequate dressing rooms and bathrooms in the actors' area.

Safety considerations are essential in a modern theatre, and current safety standards imply radical transformations in some theatres, which are not always possible due to historic architectural restrictions. In fact, an association of historic theatres in Europe called Perspectiv was set up to a few years ago; one of its initial objectives was to justify the reasons for the impossibility for certain historic Renaissance and Baroque theatres to apply certain EU safety norms that would have spoilt their historic fabric.[3] However, hazardous materials such as asbestos are still present in some theatres and their removal, although urgent, poses many problems. Further assessment of the structural integrity of theatres, in particular that of older structures, is necessary. One of the most serious concerns in theatres is fire, given that many theatres contain a preponderant amount of wood in order to improve acoustics. Modern building regulations in European countries specify various safety measures to ensure a variety of features that address fire hazards, such as fire doors, evacuation routes and the use of non-flammable materials. During our site visits, we examined fire safety precautions within the theatres and found that although all theatres had fire extinguishers, very few were actually equipped with fire hydrants, and a very small number had fire curtains on the stage. Moreover, non-flammable seating and soft furnishings were not present in most theatres due to the high costs that such refurbishment would involve. Fire retardant coatings had been applied to stage curtains and in quite a few cases, to seating upholstery. An important measure in combating fire is rapid evacuation. This implies not only clear signposting of exits, but multiple exits allowing people to escape. This aspect had been clearly addressed in certain theatres, especially those in schools.

Theatre equipment is another important issue to consider. Contemporary performance makes great use of technology requiring sophisticated equipment, which entails heavy investment. Maltese theatres generally have a good basic level of equipment, but it is more difficult to find more complicated apparatus, which are normally hired for specific productions. Moreover, no theatre has multiple revolving platforms, multiple screens that are permanently installed, which limits the creation and development of highly technological contemporary productions that have become characteristic in certain European capitals.

Climatic control of the environment within a theatre is often very limited in the theatres investigated. Ventilation often relies on fans and, in some cases, on architectural features such as high-level windows and openings along the sides of the auditorium, which also double up as emergency exits. Although some theatres are equipped with cooling systems, they do not have heating systems.

The Catalogue

As stated previously, the catalogue was a good initial exploratory step into the research of theatre spaces in Malta and Gozo. However, eventually a more exhaustive study should be conducted, and should be approached in phases. A first phase would enable the examination of all theatre spaces in Malta and Gozo, through a multi-criteria assessment process. This would be followed by an evaluation of the different buildings in order to grade them not only according to historical interest, but also their current overall state. This grading would allow to determine the level of need for intervention, and help establish a timetable of interventions that would be staggered in time and that could be funded through public-private initiatives. Determining the type of intervention necessary should not be limited only to the exterior features that render a theatre more beautiful and attractive, but must go into elements that, though less obvious, are essential and often costly features related to restructuring and restoration. Detailed plans of stages and auditoria, including lighting plans, should be professionally drawn up. Very often, these plans are missing or, if available, lack many important details.

Although the catalogue provides a quick overview of each theatre's characteristics and qualities, theatres are dynamic spaces that change in time according to new technological and social developments. Therefore, a catalogue can only remain valid if it is constantly updated and expanded. Previous versions will constitute the history of the evolution of these spaces. It is therefore important that renewal and conservation of data are taken very seriously.

As a first catalogue of theatres in the Maltese Islands, the document has the potential to serve as the reference database by national authorities in scheduling properties and in defining the assets offered by the building in both historical and social terms for the community.

Future Needs

This study has focused on the identification and possible uses of community theatres in a small island state, but it has provided an example of possible studies in similar small community frameworks. The running of theatres in a small country like Malta cannot be compared to that of theatres in the large capitals across the world. As in other small states, Malta cannot aspire to stage some of the huge productions requiring enormous resources in money, professional personnel and equipment. However, the compliance of spaces to standards and regulations, in particular with regard to safety, is a critical factor in the monitoring of theatres as well as in establishing priorities for refurbishment. Moreover, it is essential to keep abreast of and invest in new staging technologies and methods, as well as continue to undertake research in acting and staging techniques that may also derive inspiration from what is happening elsewhere. Internet technology has helped create more awareness of theatre developments abroad, both with regard to content and staging; and this has opened new horizons for Maltese theatre-makers. Thanks to local and European funding, international collaboration, cultural exchange and diplomacy, Maltese publics have the opportunity to watch foreign productions and have begun, albeit timidly, to export local productions to other countries. These new developments and exchanges may be of benefit to theatre in the community, because they will certainly help raise standards and nurture professionalism. Quality theatre can in turn be a way of attracting publics and safeguarding theatre spaces for future generations, as well as attracting the necessary funding for their conversion into veritable community reference points. The assessment of the quality of theatres and the elaboration of a catalogue of theatres are necessary to define the needs of future development and to set strategies at the local and national level for intervention that will improve the theatrical experience, not only for the audience but also for artists and performers. The ultimate goal is to strengthen culture within the community.

REFERENCES

Appleton, Ian (2008), *Buildings for the Performing Arts: A Design and Development Guide*, Oxford: Architectural Press.

Borg, Ruben Paul (2016), 'Quality assessment of culture space: The theatre', in V. A. Cremona (ed.), *On Culture, Mapping Valletta 2018*, Malta: Midsea Books, pp. 32–45.

—— (2017a), 'A methodology for the quality assessment of the theatre', in V. A. Cremona (ed.), *Capitalising on Culture: Malta and the European Capital of Culture*, Mediterranean Studies Series, no. 1, Malta: University of Malta Publishing, pp. 77–96.

Cremona, Vicki Ann (2016), 'Introduction', in V. A. Cremona (ed.), *On Culture: Mapping Valletta 2018*, Malta: Midsea Books, pp. vii–xv.

—— (2017b), 'Introduction', in *Spazji Teatrali: A Catalogue of Theatres in Malta and Gozo*, Malta: Valletta 2018 Foundation and Arts Council Malta, https://valletta2018.org/wp-content/uploads/2017/03/Spazji-Teatrali-A-Catalogue-of-Theatres-in-Malta-and-Gozo.pdf. Accessed 5 March 2019.

—— (2017c), 'Mapping culture and cultural interaction in view of Valletta 2018 European Capital of Culture (ECOC)', in *Capitalising on Culture? Malta and the European Capital of Culture*, Mediterranean Studies Series, no. 1, Malta: University of Malta Publishing, pp. 1–13.

Cremona, Vicki Ann, Borg, Ruben Paul, Chetcuti, Keith and Buhagiar, Sean (2017), *Spazji Teatrali: A Catalogue of Theatres in Malta and Gozo*, Malta: Valletta 2018 Foundation and Arts Council Malta, http://valletta2018.org/wp-content/uploads/2017/03/Spazji-Teatrali-A-Catalogue-of-Theatres-in-Malta-and-Gozo.pdf. Accessed 13 November 2017.

Interarts (2010), *Access of Young People to Culture: Final Report*, EACEA/2008/01 (OJ 2008/S 91-122802), http://www.interarts.net/descargas/interarts1834.pdf. Accessed 21 October 2017.

Mackintosh, Iain (1993), *Architecture, Actor and Audience*, London and New York: Routledge.

National Statistics Office (2013), *News Release*, 19 November, https://nso.gov.mt/en/News_Releases/Archived_News_Releases/Documents/2013/News2013_223.pdf. Accessed 15 September, 2015.

Strong, Judith (2010), *Theatre Buildings: A Design Guide*, Abingdon and New York: Routledge.

Editors' Note

Theatre and architecture represent a growing field in theatre and performance studies. Theatre buildings and performance spaces are important markers on the national and international cultural landscape, playing a central part in cultural, but also social ecologies. Architectural aspects in the area of theatre and performance draw increasingly on community perspectives, since serving the needs of diverse communities is key to the design and sustainability of a theatre as an arts institution. Juliet Rufford gives a good introduction on the dynamic relationship between theatre and architecture in her *Theatre and Architecture* (2015). In her recent monograph, *Event-Space: Theatre Architecture and the Historical Avant-Garde* (2018), Dorita Hannah has drawn on both performance studies and architectural studies to argue towards 'performative architecture' and the built environment of theatre and performance as event-space. Cathy Turner's *Dramaturgy and Architecture: Theatre, Utopia and the Built Environment* (2015) critically looks at the social and aesthetic aspects of theatre and architecture, challenging the way we think of buildings and spaces. For further reading on the latest developments in theatre spaces and contemporary practices, see also Arnold Aronson's *The History and Theory of Environmental Scenography* (2018).

Further reading

Aronson, Arnold (2018), *The History and Theory of Environmental Scenography*, 2nd ed., London: Methuen.

Hannah, Dorita (2018), *Event-Space: Theatre Architecture and the Historical Avant-Garde*, London and New York: Routledge.

Rufford, Juliet (2015), *Theatre and Architecture*, Basingstoke: Palgrave Macmillan.

Turner, Cathy (2015), *Dramaturgy and Architecture: Theatre, Utopia and the Built Environment*, Basingstoke: Palgrave Macmillan.

NOTES

1. This study was supported by Valletta 2018 Foundation and Arts Council Malta.
2. Although censorship with regard to the content of theatrical performances was abolished in 2012, by a law expressly granting freedom of expression, ownership may, indirectly, lead to certain forms of censorship. It is obvious, for example, that the Church cannot allow anything that goes expressly against its doctrine, beliefs or teaching to be shown in its precincts.
3. Perspectiv has also developed into a collaborative network for touring productions.

Performance, Dislocation and Spirituality: *Adrift Together*

Zoe Zontou

The concept of emotional dislocation is a phenomenon that has become relevant in contemporary Europe. The economic crisis has led to an alarming increase in mental health issues, homelessness, drug addiction and suicides (Martin-Carrasco et al. 2016). Subsequently, these issues have brought to the surface the need to re-emphasize notions of belonging and spirituality, in a quest for meaning and hope, in a fast changing political and economic landscape (Bauman and Raud 2015; Hancock et al. 2012). Problem drug users, the 'addicts', have been histori-cally depicted as a symbol of the crisis of consumption and dislocation, a symbol of a fragmented society (Brodie and Redfield 2002; Milhet et al. 2011). As Diehl points out, 'our shared cultural understandings of addiction are shaped largely by a metaphor of waste. Within this metaphor, the addict is identified as "[s]omething wasted or destroyed," as "refuse matter"' (2015: 15). By using the metaphor of waste Diehl reveals the many and complex connotations between addiction, culture and dislocation. In his renowned book, *The Globalisation of Addiction: A Study in Poverty of the Spirit,* Bruce Alexander (2008) echoes Diehl (2015) when he argues that addiction is the result of prolonged feelings of dislocation and unworthiness. It is the result of emotional and social disconnection. In order to conceptualize this phenomenon he coined the term *dislocation theory of addiction* that broadly refers to 'an enduring lack of psychosocial integration' (Alexander 2008: 59). Dislocation in this context is being used in its broad sense and detached from its association with geographic displacement. It indicates psychological and social separation from one's social environment that frequently results in alien-ation and emotional distress. In relation to problem drug users, dislocation is a crucial barrier to recovery and social reintegration.

In the United Kingdom, as the geographical location of this study, it is esti-mated that over 371,279 or 9.16 per 1000 inhabitants aged 15–64 are addicted to one or more substances (Crawford et al. 2016). The recent shifts in drug policy, particularly in terms of the treatment of people in recovery from alcohol and other drug dependency, have increased the gap between people in recovery and the wider society. Despite the fact that there is an overreaching emphasis on recovery, with the introduction of the recovery capital agenda (HM Government 2010); the 'Broken Britain' rhetoric that has been introduced by the UK Coalition government followed by the Big Society agenda contributed further to the demonization of people in recovery (Hancock et al. 2012). People in recovery from addiction have been further ostracized. This is due to the fact that the policy placed emphasis on individuals' responsibility to recover instead of supporting the idea of recovery as a collective process, contributing to a greater sense of loneliness and social isolation. Consequently, the demonization of problem drug users has increased their social exclusion and operates as a crucial barrier in accessing public drug treatment services, education, employment and culture. A 2015 study by Creative Future, which examined barriers to arts access and participation for marginalized adults, highlighted some of the financial and social barriers (e.g. prohibitive travel/ admission costs, health problems, low confidence) that act as crucial barriers to access cultural activities in addition to the fear of discrimination, prejudice and stigmatization (Potter 2015). This contributes to their exclusion from mainstream popular culture and highlights the pitfalls of accessing cultural activities. However, as Buchanan and Young (2000) remind us, a great number of problem drug users were socially excluded prior to initiating their drug habit. In fact, drug use has been seen in these cases as a coping mechanism that these individuals implement in order to manage in a hostile environment. To this end, emotional dislocation is not the result of addiction per se, but rather the consequence of social inequality. Alexander (2008) makes the recommendation that addicted people can best be helped by restoring their place in a functioning community. Hence, psychosocial integration is the reconciliation of the individual with their ultimate need for social belonging, autonomy and sense of worthiness and achievement. It is precisely Alexander's argument on the importance of psychosocial integration that is going to operate as the focal point for my argument. This volume is concerned with explorations of theatre communities and community-conscious theatre-making, and in this chapter I reposition the role of performance and personal narratives of vulnerability at the centre of the debate, in examining the role of applied theatre in contemporary culture. I propose that participation in performance-making can play a significant role in enhancing the individual's notions of connectedness. In doing so, this chapter seeks to explore the work of Fallen Angels Liverpool Performance Group (henceforth Fallen Angels). Fallen Angels is a peer-led dance theatre group of adults in recovery from addiction. Their current project *Adrift Together* reflects on their personal narratives of addiction and recovery through movement and drama. Members have demonstrated a passion, commitment and additional interest in developing dance theatre skills. They have received funding from the Big Lottery Fund to enable the group to hold weekly sessions in Liverpool, UK. Developing on from previous activity, the group is now established, and has developed a strong interest in dance theatre as a form of advocacy. They are now in a position to reach out to support others to access the group and benefit from the group's activities. Working with local Liverpool service users of recovery groups, Fallen Angels have used their personal stories of addiction and recovery as stimuli to create a digital storytelling dance theatre piece.

I have worked with the group since their establishment in 2012, as researcher in residency and as a creative consultant. I am responsible for monitoring and evaluating the projects as well as designing and delivering a series of participatory workshops on personal storytelling and theatre. The methodological framework of this chapter is a synthesis of reflective ethnography, practice-led research and qualitative modes of enquiry. During an ongoing reflective evaluation in March and April 2016, in which I conducted a series of interviews with the participants, the recurring theme of spiritual performance emerged as the main concept that defined their experience of the project and has driven my inquiry. The way that the participants related their experiences to notions of spiritual performance raised many and complex questions regarding the connection between spirituality and applied theatre. In this chapter, I argue that applied theatre has a particularly prominent role to play in revitalizing our understanding of the power of arts to act as a catalyst in the efforts to reconstruct our notions of self-representation, belonging and interaction with others. That is to say, I am not going to make large claims about theatre's transformative powers. Instead this chapter offers an exploration of some potential connections between disciplines that could supplement our understanding of the links between psychological integration and theatre practice, particularly in terms of how applied theatre responds to the growing number of individuals who lack social connectedness. I will discuss these concepts in further detail in the following sections.

Dislocating Belonging in Applied Theatre

Bauman asserts that we live in a 'liquid', modern, individualized society of consumers in which globalization, individualization and a spineless way of living has led us to experience astonishing feelings of loneliness, insecurity and uncertainty. Yet the consumerist markets' 'ephemeral and evanescent armistices' (Bauman and Raud 2015: 48) alongside new technological inventions have caused rapid change in our way of living and raised fundamental questions about autonomy and self-representation. These new approaches to belonging challenge the way that we understand our human subjectivity and subsequently our position in this world. They have placed an overreaching emphasis on reconsidering our understanding of belonging, in order to encompass the uncertainty and ephemerality of relationships. As Bauman asserts, 'the enmity of "belonging"' (Bauman and Raud 2015: 48) relies on our readiness to breaking out from these relationships and start all over again. The multiplicity and circular pattern of belonging is conditional and rooted on dissonance and dislocation. The fluidity and flexibility of belonging has been captured well by Vikki Bell (1999). Drawing from Judith Butler's (1999) influential work on performativity in gender studies, she proposes that belonging is performative. She argues,

> taking the temporal performative nature of identities as a theoretical premise means that more than ever, one needs to question how identities continue to be produced, embodied or performed, effectively, passionately and with social and political consequences.
>
> (Bell 1999: 2)

The ambivalence of belonging as an identity construction devise can be further problematized when it is discussed in reference to marginalized and stigmatized groups as in the case of people in recovery from addiction. Initially, people who consume drugs seek membership to the subculture out of the need to find mutual support and share common experiences with regard to their common habit. They also have a strong need to become part of a group as a means of obtaining recognition, and for collective justification. The performative aspects of belonging are manifested, in this case, through the ritualized acts of injecting, smoking or snorting substances. The spiritual and ritualized aspect of drug-taking formulates the symbol of belonging and operates as a cultural signifier. This ritualized, performative aspects of belonging is embedded in the 'addicts' identity. Therefore, recovering from addiction means obtaining new ways of producing, embodying or performing their identities and therefore their desire for belonging. The importance of a ritualized, performative approach to constructing a non-addict identity has been recognized in many health and educational settings, as in the case of self-help support groups such as Alcoholics Anonymous (Galanter et al. 2013; Sremac 2010). In this spiritual-based mutual support context, narratives of identity are being deconstructed and performed in the secrecy of the meetings. They provide a ritualized framework for the desire for belonging to be reconsidered and performed. Hence, belonging is the effect of the performative nature of the narratives of self, and not vice versa: it is a performative achievement. This chapter will push this form of argument further by exploring the ways in which autobiographical performances produced by recovery addicts manifest the complex incorporations between problematic senses of belonging and applied theatre.

FIGURE 1: Fallen Angels member, *Adrift Together*, Liverpool 2015. Photo credit: Andrew Millar.

It starts with the recognition that applied theatre is a practice embedded in problematic notions of belonging. It is in itself a theatre practice 'outside' the mainstream, hence out of place. Frequently, it takes place outside theatre buildings and engages with individuals or communities that are affected by dislocation and share a troubled sense of belonging. Historically, applied theatre has been regarded for its potential to address questions on belonging, an assumption that was based on the fact that theatre is an activity that involves the qualities of collaboration, solidarity and affiliation. In an updated second edition of *Applied Drama: The Gift of Theatre*, Helen Nicholson (2014) addresses the complexity of belonging and its relationship to applied theatre. As she argues, applied theatre practice is 'intimately tied to politics of context, place and space' (Nicholson 2014: 129). Therefore working in applied theatre brings into focus questions of dislocation, identity and belonging. In this sense, it ought to be concerned with empowering the participants by constantly reconfiguring their meaning of belonging. Nicholson problematizes notions of belonging in relation to space and place and in reference to globalization, mobility and the hybridity of space. This echoes Sally Mackey (2016) who discusses belonging in relation to geographical dislocation and in reference to refugees and asylum seekers. As she asserts 'our practices can trouble the meanings of place, destabilizing suppositions of locality, dwelling, inhabitation, territory, indigeneity, community, residence, belonging, connection and ownership' (Mackey 2016: 107). I am interested in applying Mackey's arguments to my analysis of applied theatre and psychosocial integration, and in the case of individuals who have been affected by emotional dislocation and exclusion from their communities. As a result their sense of belonging has been numbed. I suggest that applied theatre is a form of practice that reaffirms our desire for connectedness and belonging, which can be stimulated by the experience of working with others. As Baz Kershaw suggests, applied theatre 'potentially provides the most powerful antidote to the negative excesses of postmodernism' (Kershaw 1998: 67), which as I argued earlier are strongly related to feelings of loneliness and dislocation.

By taking into consideration the above arguments, I pose the following questions: can applied theatre play a role in dislocating and re-inventing meanings of belonging? Finally, how can the investigation of theatre projects with people in recovery from addiction (as the cultural symbols of emotional dislocation) supplement our understanding of the possibilities of applied theatre with other social groups that face similar issues? This mode of enquiry coincides with Anatoli Vassiliev's (2016) message for the World Theatre Day 2016 in which he asks 'do we need theatre'? His provocation comes at a moment of ideological crisis in the cultural sector, in which the political instability and funding cuts forced many artists and organizations to reconsider their ethos and reposition themselves in

FIGURE 2: Fallen Angels member, *Adrift Together*, Liverpool 2015. Photo credit: Andrew Millar.

relation to the marketization of the arts, in addition to the instrumentalization of cultural policy to meet neo-liberal agendas (Harvie 2013). This political and economic situation has reinforced a problematic notion of belonging within the art sector itself. Therefore dislocating the meaning of belonging in arts and well-being has become a new paradigm. Without dismissing the ambiguity of belonging as I discussed above, I am interested in teasing out to what extent applied theatre can address questions of belonging in contemporary liquid culture.

Adrift Together: *The Quest for Spirituality*

> In addiction we feel alone, adrift and isolated; if we find recovery we realise that it bonds us together.
>
> ('Chris' 2015)[1]

The project *Adrift Together* reflects on the recovery journey through the darkness and isolation of addiction to a place of spiritual togetherness, which is the bond shared by addicts in recovery. Having participated in a series of introductory workshops, Fallen Angels members came up with the theme of *Adrift Together*, as a starting point to create movement and a poetic imaginary related to it. The theme of adrift emerged as a response to the participants' reports that they are frequently experiencing feelings of dislocation and loneliness as a result of addiction. This project has allowed them to work closely with other people from the local area, exploring themes around notions of self-presentation, autobiography and tackling stigma as well as exploring their potential future. The group met weekly in a local studio in Liverpool. The workshops were led by Paul Bayes Kitcher, the artistic director of Fallen Angels. During each session a ceremonial space was created that allowed the participants to open to each other. The session began with open discussion in which everyone had the opportunity to talk about their feeling in the present moment. This was an opportunity to talk to each other, share their stories, news or even just express their feelings. These introductory discussions aimed to assist the participants to express themselves in an open and safe environment, connect with each other and focus on the here and now of the workshop. It set up the ground for the workshop as often the participants were asked to reflect through movement on a specific area of their life story, or events and feelings that were shared at the start of the workshop. Following this, the workshop began in which the participants were moving from verbally expressing their emotions to creating movements and routines as a means of articulating specific moments of their lives or feelings. The routines often symbolically depicted an impression of a specific life moment related to addiction that can be imagined in dance theatre.

It was about the expression of certain feelings associated with various stages of their recovery journey, moments of feeling adrift and isolated. Rather than chore-ographing something very specific and structured, the group was engaging in expressing their narrative recovery journey, with its many twists, turns and chal-lenges to overcome. Working solo or in pairs, the participants created a sequence of improvised movements. Selected phrases and signature movements that meta-phorically described different aspects of their personal journeys: frustration, chaos, connection, disconnection, despair, serenity and every emotion in between. The transition to a non-verbal, embodied language capable of expressing emotions and experiences that are difficult to articulate in words allowed the participants to connect with themselves and others spiritually. Movement has become the meta-phor of their life stories and an opportunity to revisit them from an artistic point of view. This nonlinear, highly creative way of exploring life experiences creates a space to focus on the embodied experience of addiction and its many different parameters. As 'Linda', a Fallen Angels member maintains:

> To express emotion through movement is a freedom unparalleled by words. It is to reach into the unconscious and connect with the soul, a way of getting in touch with pain and being able to release it. It is a celebration of hope and a joining together of kindred spirits.
>
> ('Linda' 2016)

'Linda' highlights the significance of embodiment as a full experience of the senses that enables one to appreciate the aliveness that is surging through the body. Performing autobiography in this ritualized context allows a re-imagining of iden-tity. The significance of finding freedom of expression as a way of cultivating their personal life story trajectories and reconnecting with themselves and others was one of the main components of the project. By working with movement, symbol-ism and personal storytelling the participants deepened into the physical and emotional aspects of addiction recovery. This was an opportunity to find integrity in the way they move their bodies and reshape their stories into an artistic form. These moments of performance-making were significant as they created spaces to work creatively with past traumatic experiences, tap into the unconscious and connect with their inner selves. Returning to Bell's concept of the performativ-ity of belonging, I argue that in the process of creating and sharing their autobi-ographical routines, the participants were reconfiguring their own subjectivity and hence their position in the world. It was through these embodied perform-ative self-narratives that they were simultaneously inscribing their definitions of belonging. This was further evidenced during the reflective evaluation session in which the participants were asked to reflect on their experiences of the project.

When I asked them to comment on what it means for them to dance their stories, they connected it to moments of spirituality. They asserted,

> We have been into darkness and are looking for *spiritual connection* […] it's therapeutic to put movement to our past, it's a release, it helps us to make sense of our stories rather than running them around our heads all the time.
>
> ('John' 2016; 'Nick' 2016, emphasis added)

> The project has helped me a lot to connect more with the people, and learn how to express myself through dance and movement. I feel I belong to something special and the atmosphere is so *spiritual* it uplifts and leaves me feeling amazing each week, one big family x.
>
> ('Jane' 2016, emphasis added)

As an applied theatre practitioner and researcher working in the field of addiction recovery for over a decade, I am a little suspicious and wary of the term 'spirituality' and find it a problematic term that tends to imply religiosity, New Age or other

FIGURE 3: Fallen Angels members, *Adrift Together*, Liverpool 2015. Photo credit: Andrew Millar.

forms of transcendence. Initially, I did not feel entirely comfortable with the suggestion that spirituality and applied theatre are connected. As far as I was concerned, spirituality is a complex concept that means different things in different contexts.

My scepticism in referring to spirituality in my analysis of Fallen Angels' project echoes the views expressed by Sarason (2001). Although, he is arguing this point from the position of community psychology, I believe his concerns are relevant here:

> There is an understandable defensiveness in using concepts like spirituality, religiosity, and transcendence. They smack of the supernatural, the non-operational, the irrational. We know (at least I do) that when we use those and similar concepts the eyes of our listeners take on a glaze and their facial expression takes on a quizzical, challenging cast. It does not take long before we and our listeners are engaged in a semantic struggle at the end of which no one has convinced anybody of anything.
>
> (Sarason 2001: 599–600)

By taking the above into consideration, it is necessary to clarify that I am not yet convinced that applied theatre leads to spiritual connectedness. Instead, I endeavour to respond to the participants' comments and conceptualize how participating in performance-making might have an affirmative impact on their journeys to recovery, particularly in terms of fostering psychosocial integration and desire for belonging. Moreover, I am fully aware of the imperatives of a participant-driven research project and I am keen to understand what they mean by 'spirituality' and how it connects with their experiences of creating a dance theatre piece about their lives. To this end, I am using the group's own definition of spirituality by which they refer to opportunities to be themselves, to be with others, to feel connected and to be able to express themselves freely in a non-judgmental environment ('Amanda', 'Neil' and 'Phil' 2016). The participants frequently mentioned feelings of alienation from mainstream culture and a strong desire to belong. In the dance theatre group they found an experience of community that is often underlined by using words such as 'family'. This was immediately evident in 'Ben''s response,

> The project has helped me to express my feelings by dancing. The connection with the group is like family and you always come out the session feeling complete.
>
> ('Ben' 2016)

There was further acknowledgement that a person's spirituality extended their potential and capacity for growth and change, their desire for connectedness and their search for meaning. While the connection between performance and spirituality is not an uncommon practice (see, for example, The Institute of the Study of Performance and Spirituality, Mindfulness and Performance, and Movement Medicine), the dimensions of spirituality central to the dance theatre project with people in recovery from addiction suggested that there was a new field of study. Further explorations on the various definitions of spirituality brought into light that practices as, for example, showing appreciation for the arts or participating in creative activities were regarded as spiritual (Delle Fave et al. 2011; Gilbert and Nicholls 2003). In relation to Fallen Angels, spiritual performance has given them the opportunity to get in touch with the momentum of the workshop and find affirmative ways of connecting with themselves and others. In turn, these moments of connection generate a sense of meaning that is translated to personal change and connectivity. This is significant to people in recovery from addiction as it foregrounds their previous experience of spiritual experience that were mostly triggered through substance misuse (Grund 1993). In her analysis of Movement Medicine, Kieft (2014) draws a powerful distinction between dance spirituality and other forms of spirituality like meditation and contemplation. She maintains that working on autobiographical experiences through movement and creativity is a unique medium in activating an embodied, lived spirituality. This type of spirituality encompasses past and present experiences, and grounds the individual in the present moment. Kieft's definition is essential here as it demonstrates the subtle imbrications of spirituality and performance. Nevertheless, I am adding another dimension to this argument by connecting the above with spirituality in addiction as the cultural symbolism of disconnection. I argue that participants' quest for spirituality through performance manifests their need for community and belonging. I foreground Bell's (1999) argument that belonging is performative, in order to suggest that belonging is generated in dialogue with others, and through a deeper appreciation of the individuals' common experiences. The spiritual performances are important tools to initiate the ritualized process of belonging and to signify the passage from the addictive body to becoming other. The vulnerability of the performing body is in a precarious position in-between and betwixt the two cultures, the culture of addiction and the culture of recovery. This moment of flux or in-betweeness is manifested through their shared sense of vulnerability and a recognition that their bodies matter, and are not 'wasted', 'destroyed' or a 'refused matter' (Diehl 2015: 15). This resonates with Turner's (1969) concept of liminal performances, which as Schechner explains is a temporary 'state of extreme vulnerability where they are open to change. Persons are stripped from their former identities and positions in the social world' (Schechner 2002: 66). Engaging in different forms of liminal performances capable for reconfiguring life experiences and expressing them as such through performance is considered necessary for finding collective ways to re-imagine identity and belonging. This engagement in a spiritual embodied storytelling indicates a transition between different parts of the individual's life story, but also a movement from the present towards the future. Bridging together these paradoxes increases the individuals' self-awareness and generates a sense of being part of something creative and affirmative. It enables the participants to access an 'other' form of knowledge beyond their rational thinking, capable of offering new insights about their life stories and how they have been written and manifested through their collective memory.

Turner's liminality appears to be a useful context for conceptualizing the moment of embodying unity and spirituality among the Fallen Angels participants. They have often described their experiences of dance theatre with phrases such as being 'wholly present in the moment, a sense of reaching out and expansion into the cosmos' ('Jane' 2016; 'Ben' 2016; 'Nick' 2016). Hence, these momentous experiences of collective community might be regarded as a form of spiritual awakening. Therefore, through externalization and embodiment of past and present experiences, as well as dreams and future wishes, I argue that a quest for spirituality and belonging might take place. In my view, participation in performance-making might be able to assist the individual not only to experience moments of belonging and spirituality, but also to rediscover meaning and connectedness to others. This can be made possible by allowing the participants to be simultaneously creators

FIGURE 4: Fallen Angels member, *Adrift Together*, Liverpool 2015. Photo credit: Andrew Millar.

FIGURE 5: Fallen Angels members, *Adrift Together*, Liverpool 2015. Photo credit: Andrew Millar.

and participants in moments of instant belonging. Hence, I suggest that applied theatre's strength lies in its ability to provide an immediate experience of belonging and spirituality. As Lewis suggests, people on the path to recovery 'need to be able to see their own lives progressing, moving from a meaningful past to viable future. They need to see themselves as going somewhere, as characters in a narrative, as making sense' (Lewis 2015: 204). It is Lewis' idea of moving to viable cultural narratives that, as I demonstrated, projecting their experiences through drama and movement, allowed them to conceptualize their futures and also to convey new meanings – perhaps more positive ones – out of their past experiences. Therefore, a closer examination of their responses and the material produced during the somatic and drama improvisations operates as an indicator that these individuals are in constant conflict between harmony and dissonance, which, as I described, is frequently symbolized in the solo or pair routines of falling, trembling and rising.

This point has been clearly illustrated in 'Ben's' response during the reflective session in which he wrote this poem:

> I will dance my story,
> But not for glory,
> I dance like it is my last,
> I dance from my past,

I dance like it's my first
Dance quenches my thirst,
Dance to my emotion,
Dance is my potion

('Ben' 2016)

Lewis' (2015) reference to the importance of seeing themselves as going some-where, and making sense of their past connects with 'Ben's' views of dance as an opportunity to retell his story 'not for glory' but for 'potion'. It is in this idea of potion that I find the links between applied theatre, the recovery process and the individual's imperative to belong. I believe that the provision of the appropriate environment for both expressing and performing their desire for belonging is of primary concern in applied theatre. In the case of Fallen Angels the usage of move-ment and personal storytelling as an effective means of exploring past experience was a potentially useful strategy. Despite the emphasis on the autobiographical experience, the creation of a safe, spiritual and creative space for these engage-ments to occur provides the platform to conceptualize what life might be like, and creates possibilities for a better future. These conceptualizations are essential in developing the individual's sense of self and motivating them to produce changes in their lives. It was an opportunity to visualize their lives without drugs, and in ways that contradict the dominant cultural narrative of addicts as 'waste'.

Conclusion

Rosi Braidotti suggests that what is needed is an 'affirmative politics' that is 'rooted in the micro practices of everyday life' and 'express[es] the multiple ecologies of belonging' (Braidotti 2013: 192–93). In these micro practices of everyday life the individuals have the opportunity to liberate and rediscover themselves. To this end, this moment of practice can be interpreted as a need for collective sharing, mutual support and acceptance regarding a common issue of concern in their current reali-ties. Although this chapter is careful not to make any larger claims about the trans-formative power of dance theatre, it suggests that participation in theatre activities can make a small contribution in supporting people in recovery from addiction to feel, perhaps only momentarily, a sense of belonging and a sense of place. In turn, the process of telling and retelling their personal experiences and translating them into performance helps them to construct a chaotic, painful past into a meaningful, affirmative dance story. By means of redemption this further enhances the concept of self-representation and enhances self-acceptance and belonging. Overall, this chapter proposes an overarching emphasis on the importance of living in the present and the need to find ways to reconcile past experiences with the present through performance.

Dislocating notions of belonging in applied theatre through the lenses of a dance theatre project with people in recovery from addiction makes me reconsider my personal sense of belonging and agency within the context of a liquid consumerism culture, especially, in terms of how the project offered an alternative way of reconfiguring belongingness. I argue that experiencing profound moments of togetherness and spiritual connectedness can be regarded as a motivational force to foster our quest for spirituality and belonging. To this end, applied theatre might be offered as an antidote to emotional dislocation.

REFERENCES

Alexander, Bruce (2008), *The Globalisation of Addiction: A Study in Poverty of the Spirit*, New York: Oxford University Press.

'Amanda' (2016), interview with Zoe Zontou, Bluecoat Arts Centre, Liverpool, 13 July.

Bauman, Zygmunt (2011), *Culture in a Liquid Modern World*, Cambridge: John Wiley & Sons.

Bauman, Zygmunt and Raud, Rein (2015), *Practices of Selfhood*, Cambridge, MA: Polity Press.

Bell, Vikki (1999), 'Performativity and belonging: An introduction', *Theory, Culture & Society*, 16:2, pp. 1–10.

'Ben' (2016), interview with Zoe Zontou, Bluecoat Arts Centre, Liverpool, 13 July.

Braidotti, Rosi (2013), *The Posthuman*, Cambridge, MA: Polity Press.

Brodie, Janet F. and Redfield, Marc (eds) (2002), *High Anxieties: Cultural Studies in Addiction*, Berkeley, CA: University of California Press.

Buchanan, Julian and Young, Lee (2000), 'The war on drugs: A war on drug users?', *Drugs: Education, Prevention and Policy*, 7:4, pp. 409–22.

Butler, Judith (1999), *Gender Trouble Feminism and the Subversion of Identity*, 10th ed., New York: Routledge.

'Chris' (2015), interview with Zoe Zontou, Bluecoat Arts Centre, Liverpool, 5 December.

Crawford, Catherine, Lombardo, Silvia, Thomson, Fay, Visintin, Cristina and Wright, Craig (eds) (2016), *United Kingdom Drug Situation: Focal Point Annual report 2015*, London: Focal Point at Public Health England, https://www.researchgate.net/publication/301199121_United_Kingdom_Drug_Situation_2015_EDITION_UK_Focal_Point_On_Drugs/download. Accessed 5 March 2019.

Delle Fave, Antonella, Massimini, Fausta and Bassi, Marta (2011), *Psychological Selection and Optimal Experience Across Cultures: Social Empowerment through Personal Growth*, Dordrecht: Springer Science+Business Media B.V.

Diehl, Heath A. (2015), *Wasted: Performing Addiction in America*, Farnham and Burlington, VT: Ashgate Publishing.

Galanter, Marc, Dermatis, Helen, Post, Stephen and Sampson, Cristal (2013), 'Spirituality-based recovery from drug addiction in the Twelve-Step fellowship of Narcotics Anonymous', *Journal of Addiction Medicine*, 7:3, pp. 189–95.

Gilbert, Peter and Nicholls, Vicky (2003), *Inspiring Hope: Recognising the Importance of Spirituality in a Whole Person Approach to Mental Health*, London: National Institute for Mental Health in England.

Grund, Jean-Paul C. (1993), *Drug Use as a Social Ritual: Functionality, Symbolism and Determinants of Self-Regulation*, Rotterdam: Instituut voor Verslavingsonderzoek.

Hancock, Lynn, Mooney, Gerry and Neal, Sarah (2012), 'Crisis social policy and the resilience of the concept of community', *Critical Social Policy*, 32:3, pp. 343–64.

Harvie, Jen (2013), *Fair Play: Art, Performance and Neoliberalism*, Basingstoke: Palgrave Macmillan.

HM Government (2010), *Drug Strategy 2010: Reducing Demand, Restricting Supply, Building Recovery: Supporting People to Live a Drug Free Life*, London: Home Office, https://assets.publishing.service.gov.uk/government/uploads/system/uploads/attachment_data/file/98026/drug-strategy-2010.pdf. Accessed 5 March 2019.

'Jane' (2016), interview with Zoe Zontou, Bluecoat Arts Centre, Liverpool, 13 July.

'John' (2016), interview with Zoe Zontou, Bluecoat Arts Centre, Liverpool, 13 July.

Kershaw, Baz (1998), 'Pathologies of hope in drama and theatre', *Research in Drama Education: The Journal of Applied Theatre and Performance*, 3:1, pp. 67–83.

Kieft, Eline (2014), 'Dance as a moving spirituality: A case study of Movement Medicine', *Dance, Movement & Spiritualities*, 1:1, pp. 21–41.

Lewis, Linda (2016), 'Risen dance theatre', 22 August, https://risendance.wordpress.com. Accessed 12 January 2017.

Lewis, Marc (2015), *The Biology of Desire: Why Addiction is Not a Disease*, New York: PublicAffairs, U.S.

'Linda' (2016), interview with Zoe Zontou, Bluecoat Arts Centre, Liverpool, 13 July.

Mackey, Sally (2016), 'Performing location: Place and applied theatre', in J. Hughes and H. Nicholson (eds), *Critical Perspectives on Applied Theatre*, Cambridge: Cambridge University Press, pp. 107–26.

Martin-Carrasco, Manuel, Evans-Lacko, Sarah, Dom, Geert, Christodoulou, Nikos G., Samochowiec, Jerzy, González-Fraile, Eduardo, Bienkowski, Paul, Gómez-Beneyto, Manuel, Dos Santos, Maria J. H. and Wasserman, Danuta (2016), 'EPA guidance on mental health and economic crises in Europe', *European Archives of Psychiatry and Clinical Neuroscience*, 266:2, pp. 89–124.

Milhet, Maitena, Bergeron, Henri and Hunt, Geoffrey (eds) (2011), *Drugs and Culture: Knowledge, Consumption and Policy*, Farnham: Ashgate Publishing.

'Neil' (2016), interview with Zoe Zontou, Bluecoat Arts Centre, Liverpool, 13 July.

Nicholson, Helen J. (2014), *Applied Drama: The Gift of Theatre*, 2nd ed., Basingstoke: Palgrave Macmillan.

'Nick' (2016), interview with Zoe Zontou, Bluecoat Arts Centre, Liverpool, 13 July.

'Phil' (2016), interview with Zoe Zontou, Bluecoat Arts Centre, Liverpool, 13 July.

Potter, Susan (2015), *Fair Access to the Arts: Investigating the Barriers to Accessing Main-stream Arts Opportunities for Disabled and/or Marginalised Artists and Writers*, http://www.creativefuture.org.uk/wp-content/uploads/2015/12/CF-Report-DIGITAL.pdf. Accessed 3 September 2016.

Reynolds, James and Zontou, Zoe (2014), *Addiction and Performance*, Newcastle: Cambridge Scholars.

Sarason, Seymour B. (2001), 'Concepts of spirituality and community psychology', *Journal of Community Psychology*, 29:5, pp. 599–604.

Schechner, Richard (2002), *Performance Studies: An Introduction*, New York: Routledge.

Sremac, Srdjan (2010), 'Addiction, narrative and spirituality: Theoretical-methodological approaches and overview', *Religija I Tolerancija*, 8:14, pp. 255–73.

Turner, Victor W. (1969), *The Ritual Process: Structure and Anti-Structure*, London: Routledge and Kegan Paul.

Vassiliev, Anatoli (2016), *Message of World Theatre Day 2016*, http://www.world-theatre-day.org/pdfs/WTD_Anatoli_Vassiliev_English.pdf. Accessed 7 July 2016.

Editors' Note

In 2017 *Performance Research* dedicated a section of a special issue on drug use to the value of performance in recovery from addiction. Besides an article by Zoe Zontou on the substitution of substance addiction to an addiction to performing, the section also includes a contribution by James Reynolds 'Outside Edge's theatre for recovery' in *Performance Research* (2017), which discusses the work of Outside Edge, a London-based company doing work that is comparable to Fallen Angels'. For a comprehensive analysis on the role theatre and performance have in relation to health and wellbeing in diverse communities, please see Baxter and Low (2016).

Further reading

Baxter, Veronika and Low, Katharine E. (eds) (2016), *Applied Theatre: Performing Health and Wellbeing*, London: Bloomsbury.

Reynolds, James (2017), 'Outside Edge's theatre for recovery', *Performance Research*, 22:6, pp. 73–82.

NOTE

1. I have obtained written permission from participants to use quotes from the interviews I conducted as part of this study. The participants' names have been changed to protect their identities.

PART II

Performing Communal Identities:
Ethics, Politics and Affect

Following on from the opening section that situated theatre communities within performance histories, applied theatre and architectural and spatial perspectives, this part deals with the ethical and political perspectives inherent in contemporary theatre's engagement with different communities. The contributors to this part cover several different theatrical scenarios across Europe and India. Maria Elena Capitani explores recent reworkings of classical Greek and Roman tragedies by contemporary playwrights for British audiences. If tragedy is no longer meaningful in the urban western world, what kind of performance will elicit a response that is comparable to the effect that tragedy would have had in the ancient world? The discussion becomes mainly one of ethical, rather than aesthetic issues. Ethics is also the fulcrum around which the practice that Pujya Ghosh discusses. For the theatre practitioners in rural Bengal that she studies, engaging in theatre means creating a lifestyle that many readers familiar with the New Testament or the theatrical communes of early twentieth-century Russia will find intriguingly similar. The playwrights discussed by Capitani take on the task of addressing an audience base that is temporally removed from that for which the source material they use was written for, and the search for relevance creates texts that are completely new. Likewise, performances discussed by Ghosh destabilize texts that for centuries had been used to legitimize a socially unjust system. If contemporary British playwrights are forging classical texts anew to speak to their audiences, the Indian theatre-makers discussed in this section are forging both the text and the audience. In contrast, Galea's contribution discusses different efforts to create a theatre that speaks to a nation (albeit a very small nation) as a community. For this to happen, the cultural and political establishment should engage in a meaningful discussion around the diversity of identities, issues of representation and the role of heterogeneous communities.

Drawing on ethical qualities, political and ideological aspects of community-conscious theatre-making, all three chapters in this part ultimately point towards issues of identity. What are the possibilities of establishing communal identities in contemporary theatre and performance? And what kind of performative means are employed in such theatre practices? Both the questions and the variety of examples presented in this part are becoming increasingly important and pressing amidst recent shifts in global politics and economics.

The Politics of Spectatorship:
Community, Ethics and Affect
in Contemporary British Rewritings
of Ancient Tragedies

Maria Elena Capitani

In his seminal *The Death of Tragedy* (1961), George Steiner solemnly declares the demise of the noblest genre, stating that this elitist and non-negotiable literary form originating from the cradle of western civilization, in its highest rendition, no longer exists (or – at least – is extremely rare). However, the recent proliferation of translations, adaptations and appropriations of ancient tragedies on contemporary western stages suggests that this dramatic archetype is a more permeable and protean template than critics and spectators tend to think. Indeed, thanks to its inherent capacity to be rewritten, restaged and re-interpreted across different centuries, the malleability of the tragic structure and the permeability of its dramatic and theatrical borders seem to be stronger than the perishability of this well-established genre. In this regard, it is important to observe that the 'built-in' tendency to renovate itself across centuries is not exclusive to tragedy. Rather, this transformative potential is typical of the theatrical art form in general, as Margherita Laera affirms:

> Theatre returns, it always does. [...] Theatre also rewrites. It constantly does. [...] Above all, theatre repeats, and incessantly so. It repeats itself and the act of returning and rewriting, as though it were struck by an obsessive compulsion to reiterate and re-enact, again and again, the vestiges of its past.
>
> (Laera 2014: 1)

The natural resilience of theatre and the particularly fluid essence of tragedy are even enhanced by this transmigration crossing temporal, spatial, linguistic and cultural boundaries. In Sarah Annes Brown's terms: 'The persistence of tragedy may in part be ascribed to its capacity to be adapted and transformed across periods and cultures, indeed to be enriched by such displacement' (2007: 1). If, on the one hand, the persistence and self-reiteration of this genre should be associated with 'a dynamic of transition' (Brown 2007: 1) and self-reinvention, on the other, it is worth pointing out that tragedy in revised form seems to have been reinforced and promoted by moments of historical transition and crisis, holding a highly revealing mirror to cultural, social and political changes.

Although contemporary spectators may a priori be suspicious of such a prestigious genre and consider this dramatic pattern obsolete and disturbing, in a unique way, the tragic mirrors the zeitgeist of our 'age of angst', and its theatrical impact powerfully elicits a network of ethical and affective reactions from those who experience it. As Jennifer Wallace argues, '[i]f tragedy is deemed to be a matter of response, rather than purely aesthetic structure, then it immediately has implications for ethics' (2007: 5).

Focusing on some of the most stimulating rewritings of ancient tragedies written and produced in England – Sarah Kane's *Phaedra's Love* (first performed in 1996) and Martin Crimp's *Cruel and Tender* (2004a) – and Scotland – Liz Lochhead's *Medea* (2000) and David Greig's *The Bacchae* (2007) – between the 1990s and the first decade of the new millennium, this chapter aims to show how the tragic arena, by conjuring up ethical issues in the presence of spectators who face actors dealing with death, loss and extreme suffering, becomes a locus of testimony permeated by 'affective intensities' (Gregg and Seigworth 2010: 10–11). This deeply emotional experience in which performing bodies are witnessed by spectatorial bodies raises some urgent questions about the ongoing dialectics between personal and communal identity in late-capitalist western societies. Examining their re-appropriation of pivotal elements of tragic language such as the *ostension* (Elam 2002: 26–27) of the body and the representation of the chorus, this study explores how a number of present-day British playwrights reassess spectatorship and community and stage the fruitful intersections between politics, ethics and affect.

Before examining the above-mentioned British re-interpretations of Greek and Roman tragedies, it is indeed worth pointing out that contemporary rewritings of ancient (hypo)texts not only compel critics and spectators to reconsider a canonical genre but, at the same time, develop new strategies to investigate today's understanding of concepts such as community, spectatorship and participation in theatre practices, thus fostering the debate informing this book. Indeed, appropriating and transferring a dramatic artefact based on a mythical narrative from antiquity to contemporaneity implies and encourages an active process of individual and communal re-figuration that goes beyond the traditional idea of reception, frequently laden with passive overtones. As Laera observes, '[t]he notion of myth (or mythology) is key to the understanding of community. Every community has its own myths, which enable mechanisms of cultural identification and a degree of social cohesion to take place' (2013: 16). If mythologies are 'narrative systems which produce, support and validate social customs and cultural beliefs' (Laera 2013: 17), it can be argued that the deconstruction and re-vision of these discourses via the use of the tragic body and the device of the chorus reframe the idea of community and, as a consequence, of community-conscious theatre-making, throwing light on its political and ethical echoes.

The first of the plays that will be examined in this chapter is Sarah Kane's radical and palimpsestic re-interpretation of the Phaedra myth, loosely based on Seneca's tragic hypotext as well as on modern European sources, such as Bertolt Brecht's first full-length drama, *Baal* (written in 1918), and Albert Camus' debut novel, *L'Étranger* (1942). A short piece divided into eight brief scenes and directed by Kane herself, *Phaedra's Love* was first staged at the Gate Theatre, London, on 15 May 1996, exactly sixteen months after *Blasted*, the (in)famous debut play of the *enfant terrible* of British theatre. In this contemporary appropriation, which was commissioned by the Gate, Kane dislocates the ancient tale of Phaedra and her stepson Hippolytus from its classical context and relocates it to Cool (or – more appropriately – Cruel) Britannia.

As some critics have noted, the polysemy of the title generates ambiguities: *Phaedra's Love* can indicate both love in an abstract sense and, more concretely, Hippolytus, the queen's object of desire (see Nils Tabert quoted in Saunders 2002: 140). In actual fact, Kane wanted to refer exclusively to the male protagonist of the play, who – in her twentieth-century rewriting – becomes a repulsively cynical, apathetic, overweight and promiscuous prince. As a consumerist spectator of his own life living in a 'lethargic state of nonexistence' (De Vos 2011: 94), Hippolytus '[f]ill[s] up time' (Kane 2001: 79) by watching a violent Hollywood film '*impassively*' (Kane 2001: 65, original emphasis), eating junk food, masturbating into a sock '*without a flicker of pleasure*' (Kane 2001: 65, original emphasis) and having sex with women and men. This amoral character seems to be totally unable to feel emotions and prone to hurt other people's feelings and commodify their bodies. Despite all of this, Phaedra adores him. Probably the most tragic figure in this postmodern revision rich in comic and grotesque overtones, the queen hangs herself behind the scenes in the name of her illicit and unrequited love. As Kane herself points out, Phaedra's death constitutes a turning point in the drama: 'her accusation and suicide liberates Hippolytus and sets off the most extraordinary chain of events leading to the collapse of the monarchy' (quoted in Saunders 2009: 72).

First idealized as frequently happens within celebrity culture, Hippolytus' body – the pivot around which the whole play revolves – is subsequently dismembered by the discontent of those who previously idolized it. Towards the end of *Phaedra's Love*, unnamed members of an angry mob, hugely disappointed by Hippolytus' rape charge, wait for him outside the court. The Gate is turned by Kane into a spectacular arena where a heterogeneous and stratified community – formed by ordinary people coming from various parts of the country as well as members of the Royal family (Hippolytus' father, Theseus and Phaedra's daughter, Strophe) – gathers to participate in this public execution. When he finally emerges, Hippolytus '*breaks free from the Policemen holding him and hurls himself into the crowd*' (Kane 2001: 100, original emphasis). At this point, the prince literally offers himself to the hostile men, women and children who are increasingly impatient to inflict violence on his body by strangling, kicking, dismembering and stoning it. In doing so, it might be argued that Hippolytus' body becomes 'a zero, a mere site on which society [...] can inscribe itself' (Rebellato 2008: 195).

This escalation of physical violence is entirely in keeping with the fact that, in 1990s Britain, the body was the vulnerable target of *in-yer-face* dramatists including Sarah Kane and Mark Ravenhill, possibly inspired by Martin Crimp's *The Treatment* (1993), and visual artists such as Damien Hirst and Tracey Emin, whose shocking work was supported by Charles Saatchi: 'Throughout the culture, bodies were under attack: distorted, distended, dismembered' (Rebellato 2008: 194). Deprived of their limbs and organs, mutilated figures such as Hippolytus' grotesque body were far from being meaningless objects. Rather, as *loci* inhabited by a fragmented, postmodern Self entrapped in dysfunctional relationships with the Other, their physical boundaries became more permeable, enhancing the intersections and clashes between the individual and the communal body.

In the original production directed by Kane herself, the audience could be considered part of the riotous mob. The theatrical (and ethical) boundaries between the stage and the spectators were blurred by the playwright/director herself, who placed the perpetrators of violence in the middle of the audience, as Christine Woodworth notes:

> Planting actors in the audience implies that we are not only complicit in the violence enacted before us, but that we participate in it as well. Despite the knowledge that the audience turned mob was planted beforehand, the scene positions the 'real' audience members in the midst of the violence.
>
> (Woodworth 2010: 16)

Therefore, in May 1996, the spectators at the Gate Theatre did not merely attend a shocking and visceral performance staging blood, abuse, violent deaths and physical dismemberment, but also felt part of the angry crowd, the community aggressively reacting against the body of power. In the tiny Notting Hill theatre space, individual bodies intermingled, overlapped and interacted with one another, forming a communal body and generating a complex network of corporeal reverberations rich in ethical and sociopolitical echoes.

In this regard, it is reasonable to draw interesting parallels between the dysfunctional royal family staged in *Phaedra's Love* and the House of Windsor. For Saunders, through the female characters of Phaedra and Strophe, the playwright 'comments upon [...] the British royal family. Both mother and daughter are depicted as outsiders to the royal household, and in a cynical move are brought in by the old order in an attempt to refresh and restore its mystique' (Saunders 2002: 75). After all, in a 1998 interview, Kane herself stated that Seneca's tragedy:

> depicts a sexually corrupt royal family so it's completely contemporary. This was long before Diana [Princess of Wales] died. But there is all that stuff in the last scene of *Phaedra's Love* about the most popular person in the royal family dying and so on. Now would be a really good time for a production here.
>
> (quoted in Saunders 2009: 67)

However, it is important to point out that the politics of Kane's drama is never explicit. In line with other critics, Urban has rightly observed that:

> her work is not political [...] in any traditional sense. No programme is espoused; no solutions are proposed. Characters do not represent any clear divide between good and evil, victim and victimizer; there is no clear message, no commitment to a specific goal.
>
> (Urban 2008: 155)

Crossing temporal and spatial boundaries, *Phaedra's Love* exemplifies this point well: the British dramatist does not write a state-of-the-nation play with a clear-cut political agenda and she never offers easy solutions. Rather, she blurs ethical boundaries, rendering it difficult for us to distinguish clearly between the abused and the abusers. Her Hippolytus, for instance, after abusing his body and his sexual partners' emotions, is in turn physically abused by the social body. This sense of ambiguity does not merely concern the characters of the play, but also the blurred relationship between the onstage and the offstage.

If Kane's *in-yer-face* version of Phaedra has the capacity to 'take [...] us on an emotional journey, getting under our skin' (Sierz 2001: 4), in his *Cruel and Tender*, the English playwright, translator and adaptor Martin Crimp explores the political intersections between community, ethics and affect in different (and possibly more subtle) ways. This early twenty-first-century appropriation of *Women of Trachis*, Sophocles' most neglected tragedy, was commissioned by the Wiener Festwochen, the Chichester Festival Theatre and the Young Vic Theatre Company, and was first presented, in a co-production with the Théâtre des Bouffes du Nord and Ruhrfestspiele Recklinghausen, at the Young Vic Theatre, London, on 5 May 2004. In Mireia Aragay's words, Crimp's present-day retelling:

fractures the classical narrative of Heracles, his wife Deianeira, their son Hyllus and Heracles's prisoner of war Iole, by updating it to the early twenty-first-century context of the global 'war on terror' and by introducing a series of changes to both the characters and the narrative itself.

(Aragay 2011: 76)

Cruel and Tender begins with Deianira's twenty-first-century counterpart, named Amelia, sharing her marital problems with a contemporary chorus, formed by a housekeeper, a physiotherapist and a beautician. The adaptation of classical choruses, one of the key elements of ancient tragedy, poses a thorny problem for today's dramatists, actors, directors and audiences, as Simon Goldhill notes:

> The most distinctive feature of Greek tragedy is also the most vexing for any modern company: the chorus. Every ancient tragedy has its chorus, and every modern production has to face the acute problem of what to do with a group of people onstage throughout even the most intimate exchanges of husband and wife, a group which has long odes in dense lyric poetry to deliver between the scenes of actors acting and events happening. More modern performances fail because of the chorus than for any other reason: if the chorus isn't right, the play cannot work.
>
> (2007: 45)

Crimp's reaction is highly revealing in this regard. On the one hand, the playwright does not seem to be much interested in reworking this theatrical convention: 'We don't really do choruses, or it is not really something that I do or am particularly interested in' (quoted in Laera 2011: 222). On the other hand, he feels both compelled and challenged to reconsider and refashion this classical element: 'So it was something that I obviously had to – I wanted to deal with it, because it is a kind of challenge. I wanted to deal with it in some way or other' (quoted in Laera 2011: 222). His 'contradictory set of ideas about the chorus' (Laera 2013: 61) give us a sense of the commonly ambivalent response to this intrusive feature, perceived as a problematic (and sometimes even intractable) device that, for various reasons, is prone to become awkward, defamiliarizing and disturbing for today's spectators. First, from an aesthetic and strictly theatrical perspective, in a naturalistic production the chorus tends to appear as an artificial and anachronistic element. Second, this ancient convention is permeated with sociopolitical and affective overtones. Indeed, the fifth-century chorus, 'performed by twelve to fifteen citizens singing their lines in unison while dancing to music in the orchestra, the circular area of the stage in Greek amphitheatres' (Laera 2013: 65–66), evoked a strong sense of community: 'The chorus offers a commentary on the action that has happened, and looks forward to the action to come, and it does so precisely from the perspective of its collective identity. That is, the chorus mobilizes the *voice of the community* [...]' (Goldhill 2007: 50, original emphasis). As Crimp's words suggest, this chorality has progressively been lost in our late-capitalist society based on fragmentation and individualism:

> I do think there is an issue about choruses. And I think it is to do with the society we live in, because I think we live in a society of individual units. And I think that we find it harder to accept the chorus.
>
> (quoted in Laera 2011: 224)

In *Cruel and Tender*, Crimp reshapes Sophocles' chorus by adopting 'a problem-solving approach [...], coupled with one's own taste' (quoted in Laera 2011: 222). He decides to replace the original group of young women of Trachis, who empathize with Deianira and wholeheartedly support her throughout, with Amelia's gossipy staff – the Housekeeper (Rachel), the Physiotherapist (Cathy) and the Beautician (Nicola). Despite their vague characterization, these three female characters intervene separately, thus defying the idea of a choral voice speaking in unison. Moreover, Crimp adds a couple of recordings of Billie Holiday singing 'My Man' (1936) and 'I Can't Give You Anything But Love' (1937), 'given that the original chorus danced and sang' (Crimp 2004: n.pag.). Laera suggests that Crimp's contemporary rendition of the chorus aims to familiarize this anachronistic and 'exotic' convention:

> perceived as anti-realistic, to a realist logic, where the collective character becomes either a piece of music played on the stereo or a set of distinct individuals. Verisimilitude is therefore restored and the show can be read as credible by a twenty-first-century audience. The implication of Crimp's choices is that the capitalist logic and the theatrical conventions of realism are irreconcilable with a 'strong' notion of community, one that would allow an audience to understand the chorus [...] as a representative of itself as a collective social entity.
>
> (Laera 2013: 62–63)

It should also be noted that, in the unpublished version of *Cruel and Tender* (modified during rehearsals), Amelia's personal assistants forming Crimp's late capitalist anti-chorus are merely indicated by the numbers 1, 2 and 3, a fact that emphasizes their depersonalization and identification with a subordinate role, as Clara Escoda Agustí observes:

> Identifying them by numbers seems like a more coherent option if one bears in mind Crimp's intention throughout the play to empty these characters of subjective traits. He presents them as depoliticized beings who simply

perform the roles they are ordained, unquestioningly partaking of the values of consumerism [...].

(Escoda Agustí 2013: 238)

Crimp's mixed feelings about this disturbing element perfectly exemplify the ambivalent relation of contemporary playwrights, practitioners and audiences to the chorus, whose unison and homogeneity starkly contrast with the individualistic values cherished by late capitalism in western societies. This disturbing feature – which compels writers and theatre-makers to adopt new dramatic and theatrical strategies to deal with an undeniably challenging device – provokes ambiguous emotions and works, as Laera argues, 'on an affective level, whereby the collective figure, especially if speaking as one, is perceived as awkward, generating a sense of unease, but also as intensely fascinating due to its ability to encapsulate the *vox populi* and the participating *demos*' (Laera 2013: 132, original emphasis).

Crimp's atomization of the tragic chorus differs considerably from Liz Lochhead's appropriation of this theatrical feature in her rewriting of Euripides' *Medea* (431 BCE), which won the 2000 Saltire Scottish Book of the Year Award. First performed at The Old Fruitmarket, Glasgow, on 17 March 2000, this re-enactment of the mythical narrative was one of the three plays commissioned by the director of Theatre Babel Graham McLaren to Liz Lochhead, David Greig and Tom McGrath. His ambitious and provocative 'Greeks' project aimed to re-(en)vision classical tragedies 'in the light of the flourishing of theatre arts in the years before and following devolution and the re-convening of the Scottish Parliament after a gap of almost 300 years' (Hardwick 2003: 80). A major historical and political watershed period, Scottish devolution drew an immediate theatrical response and enhanced what Lochhead defines as 'cultural confidence' (Lochhead 2000: vi). In John Corbett's terms, 'the years after 1997 saw an increasing tendency to rethink Scotland as "the centre," and problematize the issues arising from being more directly in control of one's national destiny' (Corbett 2013: 78). In keeping with this political reconfiguration and (partial) re-empowerment of Scotland, Lochhead – who was disappointed with peripheral and marginalized Medeas speaking Scots – decided to give the tragic heroine an English voice and all the other characters different Scottish accents, '*vary[ing] from Scots to Scots-English*' (Lochhead 2000: 3, original emphasis). As she makes clear in her 'Foreword':

It was only after seeing the play in performance here in Glasgow this spring, that it struck me the conventional way of doing Medea in Scotland until very recently would have been to have Medea's own language Scots and the, to her, alien Corinthians she lived under speaking, as powerful 'civilised' Greeks, patrician English. That it did not occur to me to do other than give the dominant

75

mainstream society a Scots tongue and Medea a foreigner-speaking-English refugee voice must speak of a genuine in-the-bone increased cultural confidence here.

(Lochhead 2000: vi)

By staging this meaningful linguistic (and cultural) shift through a clever use of voices,
Lochhead aims to re-position a devolved Caledonia and to re-figure it as a new nation
with full potential, capable of reconstructing itself and renegotiating its communal identity. However, it should be noted that her depiction of the social texture of the country cannot be considered entirely positive. At the dawn of the millennium, when the
play was written and staged, Scotland still appeared as a reactionary and homophobic
land, torn by dichotomies and inequalities: 'The bigotry which has been exposed by
the furore over the abolition of Clause 28 shows that we are a long way from a truly
tolerant Scots society' (Lochhead 2000: vi). Here, 'in order to prove that intolerance is
still part of Glaswegian society' (Angeletti 2016: 243), the Scottish writer refers to the
repeal of Section 28 of the Local Government Act 1988. More precisely, the amendment
2A – abolished by the Scottish parliament as part of the Ethical Standards in Public Life
Act in 2000 – prohibited local authorities from '(a) intentionally promot[ing] homosexuality or publish[ing] material with the intention of promoting homosexuality; (b)
promot[ing] the teaching in any maintained school of the acceptability of homosexuality as a pretended family relationship' (Local Government Act 1988: Section 28). In
order to examine the social divisiveness and substantial inequalities still present in her
country, Lochhead draws upon the inherent politics of a tragedy reflecting the misog-
yny and racism of the time in which it was written and first performed:

> The Athenian (male) society of his time which Euripides scourged for its smug
> and conventional attitudes of unthinking superiority to foreigners and women
> is unfortunately not totally unrecognisable, quaint or antique to me as I survey
> mine two and a half thousand years later.
>
> (Lochhead 2000: vi)

Thus, Euripides' *Medea* provides the contemporary dramatist with a template
through which the latent aspects of the national subtext emerge and 'the darker
side of Scottish culture is indeed explored and questioned' (Pugliese 2013: 80).

With its specific target and insightful reflections on the idea of community,
Lochhead's version of *Medea* fits the primary purpose of McLaren's Theatre Babel,
that is 'to rearticulate ancient Greek drama for a contemporary Scottish audience' (McLaren 2003: n.pag.) and, at the same time, to create something able to
'move and touch' spectators (McLaren 2003), thus asserting the transformative
power of the theatrical medium and its affective impact. Lochhead's transhistor-
ical and diversified chorus – a group of women *'of all times, all ages, classes and*

professions' (Lochhead 2000: 7, original emphasis) – addresses the audience in unison by using the personal pronoun 'we'. Despite its structural heterogeneity, this chorus formed by 'ladies of all time' and 'ladies of this place / and others' (Lochhead 2000: 9), which intermingles local and global echoes, conveys a sense of cohesion, mutual responsibility and unity in its patent diversity:

> we are all survivors of the sex war
> married women   widows   divorced
> mistresses   wives   no virgins here [...].
>
> (Lochhead 2000: 7)

Through the reiteration of compassionate lines such as 'we are sorry for your sorrow sister' (Lochhead 2000: 7, 9), Lochhead's present-day chorus fosters a sense of universal sisterhood. This female and feminist bonding stressed at the beginning of the play promotes the creation of an inclusive community of women based on testimony and reciprocal understanding, from which men are banned. After regarding the English-speaking Medea with initial suspicion:

> I know you've thought me strange   'standoffish'   'a snob'
> you've said of me   not understanding my shyness
> my coolness merely masked my terror of being snubbed
> no one loves a foreigner
> everyone despises anyone the least bit different.
>
> (Lochhead 2000: 9)

The chorus members seem to empathize with this eccentric character and incite her to violence towards her unfaithful husband Jason:

> we promise you   we are women Medea
> we know men   we know who's in the right
> punish him for us Medea [...].
>
> (Lochhead 2000: 10)

Nevertheless, it should be noted that Lochhead's relation to the idea of female solidarity is not as simple as it seems. Rather, the dramatist problematizes the notion of sisterhood among women. In her essay on contemporary Scottish rewritings of Greek tragedies, Angeletti acknowledges that Medea addresses the chorus 'in words apparently suggesting closeness through shared female experiences'; however, she writes that 'a constant distance remains between them and Medea – between, that is, the Corinthians and the foreign woman' (Angeletti 2016: 242).

'In the stage performance', she adds, 'this distance becomes, as it were, audible: while the Greeks speak with a Scottish accent […], Medea's English is impeccable' (Angeletti 2016: 242).

Restaging a strong female character such as Medea and 're-placing' her within a heterogeneous female community encouraging sisterhood, Lochhead investigates the (ambivalent) relationship between the social body and a foreigner who 'stands out of the crowd'. Oscillating between antiquity and contemporaneity, the local and the global, her Scottish retelling of the myth of Medea and Jason explores the notion of a community crossing historical and national borders, as well as its gender/sexual implications.

Like Lochhead's rewriting, David Greig's powerful version of Euripides' *The Bacchae* (405 BCE) brings the mythical narrative to a twenty-first-century Scottish audience. Based on a literal translation by the University of Glasgow's classicist Ian Ruffell, this co-production between the National Theatre of Scotland and the Edinburgh International Festival (in association with the Lyric Hammersmith) was first performed at the King's Theatre, Edinburgh, on 11 August 2007. Greig's appropriation of the classical hypotext re-articulates the idea of spectatorial (and national) community through a peculiar use of the two essential elements around which this chapter revolves: the body and the chorus.

The most magnetic and expressive body in this tragedy is that of the androgynous god Dionysos, played by the internationally renowned Scottish actor Alan Cumming. As Benedict Nightingale writes in his review, the compelling production directed by John Tiffany – who asked Greig to work on this re-interpretation –

> begins with an upside-down figure being lowered on wires from the flies, its bottom bare, its head concealed by gold cloth and drooping black hair. It swivels, lands, and turns out to be Alan Cumming in a long curly wig and a glistening dress.
>
> (Nightingale 2007: 20)

If Dionysos, defined by the Prince of Thebes, Pentheus, as an 'effeminate foreigner' (Greig 2007: 20), returns to Thebes from exile in order to be acknowledged by the local community, after a long absence, Cumming is back on the Scottish stage, deserving professional recognition in his homeland. Through his seductive use of voice, this histrionic Dionysos interacts with the audience, establishing an 'intimate' relationship with his spectators: 'Highly sexualized, entertaining, playful, unabashed, and camp, he teased and flattered the audience' (Inchley 2011: 78). Addressing individual members attending the performance – 'Man? Woman? – It was a close-run thing. / I chose man. What do you think?' (Greig 2007: 7) – he flirts with the community of spectators, thanks to:

his daring and defiant ability to ad-lib. His vocal style and delivery was designed to enrapture the audience, who [...] would often call out and respond to the actor, expressing their allegiance to him, rather than to the non-interactive and complacent voices of the Scottish powers.

(Inchley 2011: 78–79)

Blurring ethical, sexual, gender and generic boundaries, this ambiguous, protean and highly 'theatrical god' (Greig 2007: 29), who is able to 'twist words cleverly' (Greig 2007: 29), subverts the borders between the I and the Other, the stage and the audience, thus rewriting and restaging the notion of community. Permeated with sexual innuendos, a series of comic interludes and metatheatrical echoes, *The Bacchae* offers a fluid stratification of communal discourse: in the theatrical arena, various kinds of communities merge and interact with each other. A strong sense of female kinship sits at the heart of the chorus of Maenads, played by ten beautiful, scarlet-dressed black 'gospel singers, throaty soul sisters commenting on the unfolding Greek tragedy' (Walker 2007: 9) and simultaneously 'creating an erotic spell of empowered sexuality' (Spencer 2007: 26). Dionysos' followers from Lydia can be juxtaposed with another all-female community, the women of Thebes who, after leaving their families,

> [...] have gone
> To the mountain where they hide
> In the darkness of the pine woods
> Offering themselves –
> To (the supposedly divine)
> Dionysos –
> Whoever he may be –
> With dances.

(Greig 2007: 15)

This community revelling in unleashed passions, amorality and violence is based on a kind of frenzied rituality that enhances the oneness of its members: when the divine foreigner 'enters them' (Greig 2007: 16), the adoring women 'scream / In rapturous communion' (Greig 2007: 16). During these 'drunken rituals' (Greig 2007: 19), as Pentheus terms them before being torn apart by his mother Agave and her Bacchic sisters, the Dionysian worshippers liberate their bodies and minds and, in the blind prophet Teiresias' words, 'become one' (Greig 2007: 18), reinforcing the idea of holism and, at the same time, of commonality.

Although Greig's version remains quite faithful to the source in comparison with the rewritings analysed in this chapter, its original production shows how the subversive potential of the play lies in its corporeal dimension.

As Hardwick writes:

> Apart from the paring down of the mythological family tree and the removal of the specifics of mythological place, Greig's script gives much of the same information as would a scholarly translation. But the idiom and the directness of the diction anticipate aspects of the theatrical experience that the performance offered the spectators, especially the performative and expressive role of the body.
>
> (Hardwick 2010: 197)

In this twenty-first-century revision, the liminal and camp body of Cumming interacts with other acting bodies as well as with the bodies of the spectators, blurring the separation between the stage and the audience through the use of voice. As Colette Conroy puts it,

> The body is a way of thinking about the points of connection between the person and the world. It is a way of thinking about the flesh or matter or morphology or biology of a person, and about how that conflicts with, connects with or constitutes culture.
>
> (Conroy 2010: 32)

After all, in Simon Shepherd's terms, '[t]heatre is an art of bodies witnessed by bodies' (quoted in Freshwater 2009: 18) that create a provisional community of onlookers.

In conclusion, focusing on the staging of the body and/or of the chorus in four British re-appropriations of Greek and Roman tragedies, this chapter has provided an overview of the ethical and affective issues raised by the multi-layered interaction between the spectatorial and the performative community. As a social form of art, theatre enacts ethical questions in front of an assembled group of people, forming a temporary and heterogeneous communal body. Even if we can consider an audience as a single entity, Freshwater stresses that 'there may be several distinct, co-existing audiences to be found among the people gathered together to watch a show and that each individual within this group may choose to adopt a range of viewing positions' (Freshwater 2009: 9–10). Thus, the ethical problem at the core of any performance – and especially of one rooted in the tragic and provoking a visceral reaction – is dramatized in the presence of a diversified community compelled to decipher its codes and simultaneously permeable to its affective reverberations. Compared to other literary and artistic forms, Nicholas Ridout states, theatre provides us with valuable and effective instruments to reflect on ethics in (consciously) social and political ways. As the scholar makes clear:

Theatre inserts its ethical questions into the lives of its spectators in a situation in which those spectators are unusually conscious of their own status as spectators, and thus as people who may exercise ethical judgment. It also takes place in the presence of spectators who are aware of their status as spectators who are engaged in reciprocal spectatorship. We watch ourselves watching people engaging with an ethical problem while knowing that we are being watched in our watching.

(Ridout 2009: 15)

This mutual and palimpsestic gaze and the myriad of reflections and refractions it generates create a web of sensory and intellectual stimuli enhancing the active role of the spectator, who does not limit his/her position to that of a passive recipient but personally participates in the theatrical action. Borrowing the words of David Savran on the work of the New York-based experimental theatre company the Wooster Group, '[a]s each spectator [...] enters into a dialogue with the work, the act of interpretation becomes a performance, an intervention in the piece' (quoted in Freshwater 2009: 18). The idea of an active selection, appropriation and authorial – as well as spectatorial – re-interpretation of classical tragedy takes centre stage in present-day British theatre. Deconstructing and creatively reconstructing the tragic archetype inherited from the ancients, contemporary dramatists such as Kane, Crimp, Lochhead and Greig question and re-articulate the discourses concerning personal and communal identity, eliciting affective responses and encouraging ethical reflections.

REFERENCES

Angeletti, Gioia (2016), 'Rewriting Greek tragedy in contemporary Scottish theatre: Liz Lochhead's *Medea* and David Greig's *Oedipus the Visionary*', in G. Angeletti, G. Buonanno and D. Saglia (eds), *Remediating Imagination: Literatures and Cultures in English from the Renaissance to the Postcolonial*, Rome: Carocci, pp. 237–48.

Aragay, Mireia (2011), 'A mirror of our own anxiety: Civilization, violence, and ethics in Martin Crimp's *Cruel and Tender*', *Atlantis: Journal of the Spanish Association of Anglo-American Studies*, 33, pp. 75–87.

Brown, Sarah Annes (2007), 'Introduction: Tragedy in transition', in S. A. Brown and C. Silverstone (eds), *Tragedy in Transition*, Malden, Oxford and Victoria: Blackwell, pp. 1–15.

Conroy, Colette (2010), *Theatre & the Body*, Basingstoke and New York: Palgrave Macmillan.

Corbett, John (2013), 'Liz Lochhead's drama adaptations', in A. Varty (ed.), *The Edinburgh Companion to Liz Lochhead*, Edinburgh: Edinburgh University Press, pp. 72–85.

Crimp, Martin (1993), *The Treatment*, London: Nick Hern.

—— (2004a), *Cruel and Tender*, London: Faber and Faber.

—— (2004b), 'Sophocles and the war against terror', *The Guardian*, 8 May, p. 35.

81

De Vos, Laurens (2011), *Cruelty and Desire in the Modern Theater: Antonin Artaud, Sarah Kane, and Samuel Beckett,* Madison and Teaneck: Fairleigh Dickinson University Press.

Elam, Keir (2002), *The Semiotics of Theatre and Drama*, 2nd ed., Abingdon and New York: Routledge.

Escoda Agustí, Clara (2013), *Martin Crimp's Theatre: Collapse as Resistance to Late Capitalist Society*, Berlin and Boston: de Gruyter.

Freshwater, Helen (2009), *Theatre & Audience*, Basingstoke and New York: Palgrave Macmillan.

Goldhill, Simon (2007), *How to Stage Greek Tragedy Today*, Chicago and London: Chicago University Press.

Gregg, Melissa and Seigworth, Gregory J. (2010), 'An inventory of shimmers', in M. Gregg and G. J. Seigworth (eds), *The Affect Theory Reader*, Durham and London: Duke University Press, pp. 1–25.

Greig, David (2007), *The Bacchae*, London: Faber and Faber.

Hardwick, Lorna (2003), *Reception Studies*, Oxford: Oxford University Press.

—— (2010), 'Negotiating translation for the stage', in E. Hall and S. Harrop (eds), *Theorising Performance: Greek Drama, Cultural History and Critical Practice*, London: Duckworth, pp. 192–207.

Inchley, Maggie (2011), 'David Greig and the return of the native voice', in A. Müller and C. Wallace (eds), *Cosmotopia: Transnational Identities in David Greig's Theatre*, Prague: Litteraria Pragensia, pp. 66–81.

Kane, Sarah (2001), 'Phaedra's Love', in *Complete Plays: Blasted, Phaedra's Love, Cleansed, Crave, 4.48 Psychosis, Skin*, London: Methuen Drama, pp. 63–103.

Laera, Margherita (2011), 'Theatre translation as collaboration: Aleks Sierz, Martin Crimp, Nathalie [sic] Abrahami, Colin Teevan, Zoë Svendsen and Michael Walton discuss translation for the stage', *Contemporary Theatre Review*, 21, pp. 213–25.

—— (2013), *Reaching Athens: Community, Democracy and Other Mythologies in Adaptations of Greek Tragedy*, Bern: Peter Lang.

—— (2014), 'Introduction: Return, rewrite, repeat: The theatricality of adaptation', in M. Laera (ed.), *Theatre and Adaptation: Return, Rewrite, Repeat*, London and New York: Bloomsbury Methuen Drama, pp. 1–17.

Lochhead, Liz (2000), *Medea*, London: Nick Hern Books.

McLaren, Graham (2003), 'Introduction', in L. Lochhead, *Thebans*, London: Nick Hern Books, n.pag.

Nightingale, Benedict (2007), 'A 2,500-year-old conflict that is with us for ever', *The Times*, 14 August, p. 20.

Pugliese, Marianna (2013), *Rewriting Medea: Toni Morrison and Liz Lochhead's Postmodern Perspectives*, Boca Raton, FL: Universal Publishers.

Rebellato, Dan (2008), '"Because it feels fucking amazing": Recent British drama and bodily mutilation', in R. D'Monté and G. Saunders (eds), *Cool Britannia? British Political Drama in the 1990s*, Basingstoke and New York: Palgrave Macmillan, pp. 192–207.

Ridout, Nicholas (2009), *Theatre & Ethics*, Basingstoke and New York: Palgrave Macmillan.

Saunders, Graham (2002), *'Love Me or Kill Me': Sarah Kane and the Theatre of Extremes*, Manchester and New York: Manchester University Press.

—— (2009), *Kane on Kane: The Playwright & the Work,* London: Faber and Faber.

Sierz, Aleks (2001), *In-Yer-Face Theatre: British Drama Today*, London: Faber and Faber.

Spencer, Charles (2007), 'A knockout of epic proportions', *The Telegraph*, 13 August, p. 26.

Steiner, George (1961), *The Death of Tragedy*, New York: Alfred A. Knopf, Inc.

Urban, Ken (2008), 'The body's cruel joke: The comic theatre of Sarah Kane', in N. Holdsworth and M. Luckhurst (eds), *A Concise Companion to Contemporary British and Irish Drama*, Malden, Oxford and Chichester: Blackwell, pp. 149–70.

Walker, Lynne (2007), 'A triumphant homecoming for Cumming', *The Independent*, 13 August, p. 9.

Wallace, Jennifer (2007), *The Cambridge Introduction to Tragedy*, Cambridge: Cambridge University Press.

Woodworth, Christine (2010), '"Summon up the blood": The stylized (or sticky) stuff of violence in three plays by Sarah Kane', in J. K. Curry and E. B. Wallace, *Theatre Symposium, Vol. 18: The Prop's the Thing: Stage Properties Reconsidered*, Tuscaloosa: Alabama University Press, pp. 11–22.

Editors' Note

Stephe Harrop's recent article 'Greek tragedy, agonistic space, and contemporary performance' published in the *New Theatre Quarterly* (2018) discusses the performance of another adaptation by David Greig of a Greek tragedy in the context of community building. Wider issues of theatre spectatorship featured recently in a special issue of the *Journal of Contemporary Drama in English* edited by Mireia Aragay and Enric Monforte with the theme of 'Theatre and spectatorship: Meditations on participation, agency and trust' (2016). An earlier issue of *Platform: Journal of Theatre and Performing Arts* also gives an important insight into 'Spectatorship and participation' (2011). A topical analysis on affection in recent theatre and performance works can be found in Andy Lavender's *Performance in the Twenty-First Century: Theatres of Engagement*, especially in Part IV: 'On (not) being a spectator' (2016: 133–92) of the monograph. For further reading on contemporary British theatre, please see Angelaki (2013). Two other volumes from Vicky Angelaki also discuss the work of Martin Crimp and contemporary British social and political theatre, please see Angelaki (2012, 2017).

Further reading

Alston, Adam, Hammond, Charlotte and O'Toole, Emer (eds) (2011), *Platform: Journal of Theatre and Performing Arts*, special issue, 'Spectatorship and participation', 6:1, Winter.

Angelaki, Vicky (2012), *The Plays of Martin Crimp: Making Theatre Strange,* Basingstoke: Palgrave Macmillan.

—— (2013), *Contemporary British Theatre: Breaking New Ground,* Basingstoke: Palgrave Macmillan.

—— (2017), *Social and Political Theatre in 21st-Century Britain: Staging Crisis,* London: Bloomsbury.

Aragay, Mireia and Monforte, Enric (2016), 'Theatre and spectatorship: Meditations on participation, agency and trust', special issue, *Journal of Contemporary Drama in English,* 4:1.

Harrop, Stephe (2018), 'Greek tragedy, agonistic space, and contemporary performance', *New Theatre Quarterly,* 34:2, pp. 99–114.

Lavender, Andy (2016), 'Part IV: "On (not) being a spectator"', in *Performance in the Twenty-First Century: Theatres of Engagement,* Abingdon: Routledge, pp. 133–92.

Living and Working in Tepantor: Understanding Political Theatre and the Community

Pujya Ghosh

This chapter offers an examination of a grass-root theatre group called Ebong Amra ('And Us') and their theatre village, Tepantor, situated in a small village in rural Bengal, India. Through writing this chapter I have engaged with the group's work to understand how they push the boundaries of political theatre through their theatre practice and performances that goes beyond being representations for social construction, identity formation and subjective transformation. For about fifteen years, Tepantor has offered a significant opportunity for people of the Bauri community to script power relations on-stage and live new permutations of the same off-stage. Living and working with the community in their space (both the theatre village and the village Saathkahuniya), I have tried to understand how people learn from and live the consequences of on-stage interactions and experiences in their off-stage lives. Their story traces their experience with and commitment to practices of theatre-making unique to the Ebong Amra community as an indication that representations can be an apparatus of change.

Political theatre can be understood as that which emphasizes a political issue or issues in its plot; it can also be defined as exploring themes more universal and central to society itself, but traditionally it has always been understood through its alignment with the history and development of left-wing politics. Piscator used the word political theatre for the first time to describe his efforts to create a theatre that would champion the cause of the proletariat in its battle against the bourgeoisie (see Piscator 1980). Later, many theatre practitioners and writers, from Brecht to Boal have subsequently pursued similar matters and put on discourse different aspects of relations between theatre and politics (see Brecht 2014; Boal 2000). In India, specifically in Kolkata, the Group Theatre movement was synonymous with the development of political theatre and since its inception, was largely driven by left-democratic ideas. It was built into an even stronger movement in the 1960s and 1970s especially in the wake of the Naxalbari movement.[1] The great task started by the Indian People's Theatre Association (IPTA) in the 1940s reached a different, expansive level during that period precisely because the theatre movement created an opposition to the world-view represented by colonial theatre, not through innovation in dance or bodily performance or in abstraction encouraged by institutionalization, but through the concrete notions of political events and performative representations. In the meantime, Bengali theatre became firmly situated as a component of civil society, a space in which political battles would be reflected and new futures dreamt of. There were many instances of brilliant stagecraft and intense depth of production during the decades that reflected democratic politics – with certain groups drifting towards a revolutionary rhetoric – and humane ideals, based on literature drawn from all over the world.[2] Unfortunately, by the 1980s it began to fade away and became vague, since the revolution, supported by the political theatre movement, was incorporated into the state system itself. Post-1980s, instead of revolutionary slogans, impassioned rhetoric and socialist realism, political theatre began to collapse under the weight of its own ideological shortcomings in the face of a very different and less inspiring social reality, which was the Left Front rule in Bengal for 35 years. In the past decade or so in Bengal, theatrical productions reflect a multiplicity of specific-interest issues, moving away from the often didactic, single-issue, class-based forms of political theatre. The connections, sometimes tenuous, sometimes pronounced, with the left-wing have now wilted and many leading theatre personalities, artists and filmmakers have churned out works in an effort to expose the true face of leftist totalitarianism within democracy. New groups of theatre-makers have struggled to move away from a classical Marxist political practice into a space where there is reluctance to talk about political commitment, with politics and its representations confined within political immediacy.

Over time, the term 'political theatre' and the discourses around politics have therefore come to be challenged and that is reflected not only in recent theatre productions but also in recent theatre scholarship. Though the postcolonial history of Indian theatre, especially Bengali theatre, has been that of political theatre, it failed to make any real connection with community building and intervention. Its engagement with the community was limited to getting inspired by, even to the extent of appropriating, the indigenous cultures of a specific community. The 'Theatre of the Roots' programme was launched soon after the country's independence and everyone involved in Indian theatre since the 1960s has been part of it, worked against it, promoted it, criticized it or felt side-lined because of it. It was an attempt by the playwrights and directors, to de-colonize their work, turn to their 'indigenous' roots in religious ritual, classical dance, popular entertainment, martial arts and Sanskrit aesthetic theory to see what they could use to create a modern Indian theatre. In this quest for rediscovering the centuries-old roots, theatre personalities like Habib Tanvir, K. N. Pannikar, Ratan Thiyam, Girish Karnad or Vijay Tendulkar turned to folk theatre for inspiration. The Marxist theatre-maker Utpal Dutt, for instance, showed an abiding interest in the folk form of *jatra* to reach out to the masses. In his forceful defence of *jatra* (in 'In search of form'), Dutt praises *jatra* for having the potentials for a revolutionary theatre (Dutt 2009: 97). Dutt himself experimented with the form in '*jatra-plays*' as he calls them, like *Sanyasir Tarabari* ('The crusade', first performed on 24 September 1972), *Titu Meer* (first performed on 26 January 1978) and the critically acclaimed *Tiner Toloar* ('The tin sword', first performed on 12 August 1971). He even ventured into the direction of Shakespeare's *Macbeth* (performed throughout 1954 in villages of Bengal) in a *jatra* style. In each of these cases, it was an instance of borrowing a performance tradition rather than engaging with the community that practices those art forms. There was a reluctance to take 'western' forms of theatre into these communities, in case they contaminate their 'pure' aesthetic traditions.

Therefore, it is important to locate a space where there is intervention – both aesthetic and political, into a specific community and its life. In what follows I will discuss the category of political theatre and its critical potentialities through the work of the theatre group Ebong Amra and a unique concept of space – Tepantor ('Unbound Space'). By discussing Tepantor and juxtaposing it with the Indian political theatre movement of the 1960s and 1970s and its later incarnations, I intend to open issues regarding the intervention into the community imagination to unravel the notion of the group in theatre and how its structural criteria require a potential intervention in terms of economics, social and cultural connotations. I also intend to examine the significance of broadened left-wing politics – including concerns on contemporary caste, instead of previous discourses in Indian theatre that considered theatre as a way to 'de-class' oneself – in the process of theatre-making in this specific setting.

Tepantor: A Study into Socially Engaged Theatre Practice

During the process of my Ph.D. research, I was looking for groups in Bengal whose theatrical works still reflect the left-wing ideology, and then I encountered Tepantor. They turned the category of leftist political theatre on its head and came across to be the only opposition to the existing theatrical norms guiding the state within its current political situation. Tepantor is a theatre space in a village called Saathkahuniya in Bengal, where around 15–20 low-caste and tribal families together make up the group. Sprawling over four acres, Tepantor, according to the group, is a concept of space and desire, a space to tell their story and a desire to be perceived and recognized as human beings.

On my first day, I reached Saathkahuniya and inquired for Tepantor. I saw a group of young kids playing in the dusty and dry field and I asked them for directions. They pointed towards Tepantor and said in unison, '[t]hat way!'; from their faces I knew that it was one of their beloved places. The vastness and the green, and hundreds of chickens in their pens will be the first thing to catch your attention. Then I was greeted by a group of simple, unassuming young men – some of them a little shy and some who were very keen to get to know me. That day I was in for many surprises and very soon I realized that it would be very difficult to leave this place. The group was formed in the early 1990s but Tepantor came into existence only in 2004.

The group Ebong Amra[3] comprises mostly of men from the lower caste Bauri community who are traditionally landless labourers, or work at sand mills or brick kilns. The group was established by Kallol Bhattacharya, who belonged to one of the only five upper caste families in that village. After he finished college in Kolkata, he went back with the hope of doing cinema there. He turned his focus

FIGURE 6: Tepantor: scene from an impromptu play. Photo credit: Pujya Ghosh.

towards theatre when he attended a workshop at the local government headquarters in his village. The workshop was being led by eminent theatre-maker Probir Guha of Alternative Living Theatre, an experimental theatre group, focusing on physical expressions with only limited use of spoken language in their theatrical work. This led him to explore the potential of theatre by employing physical theatre; and with his friends from the village, he started his theatre group Ebong Amra. He envisaged his theatre helping his friends find the kind of voice and opportunity that he got because of his caste and subsequently his class privileges. They started with practising in open fields, in the evening under the light from the lanterns and doing mostly street theatre. Soon he realized that it was getting difficult to sustain the group because his actors would be tired after a day's work at the fields or kilns. They would simply lack the energy to be regularly present and perform. The money they made from doing shows around the district was never going to be enough for them to totally depend on it. No matter how hard he tried their theatre engagement amounted to an amateurish attempt that lacked both content and acting skills. Kallol Bhattacharya needed to develop a theatre methodology suited for his community and friends. That started to form when he conceived of a space similar to Tepantor. Along with the help of the group's members he built the space over six years by taking two days off their work every week. Now the place has a 900 sq ft of open air performance area, rehearsal space, well furnished rooms for guests, two fishing ponds and land to cultivate vegetables and fruits, and they also keep poultry. This structure was created in order to fully sustain themselves without the need to work outside the village, allowing them to dedicate their time to theatre, most of them also living inside Tepantor as an inclusive commune. The group has a manager who looks after the business end of the poultry farming and fishing and the various 'call-shows'[4] they get around West Bengal. Everything in that space, every permanent structure and furniture included has been built and is maintained by members of the group. A typical day at Tepantor would include the members assembling early in the morning around 6 a.m., *Bakul da* (the person responsible for running the kitchen) serves everyone a round of tea, after which they set out to do theatre exercises comprising mostly of voice and movement exercise followed by improvisations. A tea and breakfast break follows and then the members get around to maintenance work of their theatre village. This is also the time when they make sets and props if they have a production coming up. Once done they head back home for lunch and an afternoon siesta, then they assemble again early in the evening. After yet another round of tea, they gather in their rehearsal area to either rehearse an upcoming play or discuss ideas and scripts. If it is winter and they have no plays lined up for a few months, they spend this time reading books and plays; watching recordings of plays and movies, followed by a lively discussion. Around 8–8.30 p.m. they all head home. The land in Tepantor is collectively owned by eleven people who were the original members of the group, not the founder/director, the work and responsibilities are shared equally by all, and the income is partly given to the members and partly spent towards theatre productions and hosting festivals. This restructuring of the economic dimension of theatre is important because it resolves the economic problems as cited by the theatre-makers post-1970s as the single most important reason for moving into cinema or television or bending towards corporate money, diluting their political content in the process – a predicament shared by groups across the urban–rural divide.[5]

Referring to Blau, Stephen Chinna notes that there was 'a radical fault on the radical Left' that was constituted by a 'mean-spirited binary thinking' (Chinna 2003: 104) that refused to differentiate between specifics and stereotypes, reducing the former into the latter and such 'utopian urges and reductive stances betray the similar rigid self-righteousness of much political theatre, in that it presumes it has the right to speak for the other' (Chinna 2003: 104). Accordingly, political theatre should be a framework that is able to offer a space where the social and cultural components of the represented community can be accommodated and

FIGURE 7: Tepantor: the rehearsal space. Photo credit: Pujya Ghosh.

expressed. Hence, it is important that Ebong Amra makes a strong distinction from the theatre of the 1960s and 1970s, primarily because they believe that doing theatre in villages requires telling the stories of the community in their own language. As Parimal Ghosh argued, during the 1960s and 1970s, the so-called progressive theatre of that time was fundamentally the theatre of the urban, middle class, and their productions reflected the romantic fondness of the middle class for revolution, a space where the middle class achieved temporary liberation and attained a theatrical courage (see Ghosh 2012). Therefore that kind of theatre found stability as a middle-class activity, where plays were created by and catered for the middle class, and eventually became surrounded by bourgeois 'theatre' and by 'theatre' for television, both of which were a regression of sorts, and the space for radical theatre begun to shrink.

According to the group, they neither possess the power of verbalization nor are they apt at grasping rhetorical language. For the group, their language is based on communication through the body of the actors, the stains of history on these bodies and articulation through the physical labour of the body, since labouring is what they know. Hence their productions are less dependent on speech and more focused on the use of the actors' body, the fragility of their bodies, markings of hostility on individual lives.

They are also rooted in their culture, music, dance and religious rituals, and they often borrow from that cultural repertoire. They also live in close connection with the Santhal communities and they often collaborate with them for specific productions, and hence their plays often use songs and rituals that are an integral part of both the Bauri and Santhal communities. Their theatre-making not only reflects contemporary subjects, 'focusing on the fragile life of bodies, on threats to the entirety of what is conceived as "natural," hostility to any strict coding of individual life, dissipation of the frontier between public and intimate life' (Badiou 2007: 22) but contrary to what Badiou might argue, they also present a genuine movement of and for (personal) transformation. I will discuss this aspect in the next part of the chapter with a focus on the plays produced by the Ebong Amra group.

Mahakabya er Pore: *The* Mahabharata *Production*

Over the years, the group has performed different genres of plays; from plays based on local issues showing close resemblances with agit-prop theatre, to addressing bigger political debates on communalism or the ongoing *people's war*[6] in different parts of the country, and the larger politics of violence appealing to a global consciousness. The play that I will discuss in detail is entitled *Mahakabya er Pore* ('Beyond the epic'), which was first performed during the summer of 2012.

91

I believe this production will reveal the politics of the group clearly. This is a story from the *Mahabharata*[7] of the tribal boy Ekalavya who wanted to learn archery, the privilege of the *kshatriyas* (the twice born, warrior caste) only. The text as performed by Ebong Amra tells the journey of Ekalavya, the reasons he wanted to learn weaponry, Dronacharya's (the guru of the *Pandavas*) refusal to teach him and finally Ekalavya's mastering war tactics by learning from afar. The core difference in Ebong Amra's take on Ekalavya's tale is Ekalavya's refusal to give his thumb as *guru dakshina*[8] as I will discuss below.

The part of Tepantor reserved for performance and audience seating was brilliantly lit up, surrounded with long poles adorned with bright-coloured banners. Along their already constructed performance area, the actors had dug up trenches to create levels that brought more life to war sequences and simultaneous scenes. The entire place and the stage including all the set and props were made inside Tepantor and by the members of the group. As the audience settled down, we could see the most unassuming and frail man sit at the corner of the stage with varied musical instruments; the actors taking their positions, mostly bare bodied, some had their faces painted and wearing turbans and dhotis. The play began with actors from the Santhal community preparing for a ritual celebration. The scene was bright, musical and well-choreographed and moved on to show why Ekalavya needed to learn how to fight.

This is one of their productions where they collaborated with interested members of the Santhal tribe who are also residents of the same village, Saathka-huniya. The reason behind having both communities represented is dramaturgical and rooted in the background of Ekalavya's story to have two different tribal communities present: 'forest dwellers' and the untouchables. It was the joint decision of the chiefs of the mentioned communities who urged Ekalavya to learn the art of warfare for their own protection from other neighbouring tribes over territorial conflict. An integral part of the scenography was the actors' own voice and bodies. To create the setting of the forest, one could see the actors walking/crawling like animals, making roaring, howling and chirping sounds. The sounds were created in such a way that it could easily have been mistaken for a recorded sound or as if coming from backstage. The fact that the actors have gone through training in Indian martial art forms such as *Kalaripayattu* and *Lathi*[9] was highly visible due to the fact that the production only used minimal dialogues and the story was told through body movements. Learning of martial arts has been a conscious decision of the group's director. Since extensive use of language was not an option, the actors' theatre training had to involve techniques through which they could use their bodies more effectively and with ease. As the play progressed, the narrative which is mostly familiar to the community unfolded easily. Though the acting could be considered amateurish on many levels, one cannot but appreciate the impeccable control the actors had over their bodies and the sound they were making, sometimes in synchrony. The script writer's addition, and a key add-on, in the narrative of Ekalavya, was that of an old wise man. This character, throughout the play becomes the guiding figure, the conscience and even the moral compass of Ekalavya and his people. The 'wise man' never gives them any answers; he just leads them to understand if they want a new beginning for themselves. This new beginning was the simplest twist at the end and yet loaded with radical potential. At the end when Dronacharya realizes that despite his warning to Ekalavya that learning archery was only the right of the Kshatriyas, he had still gone ahead with it – and that Ekalavya had built a statue of Dronacharya, as his symbolic *guru* – he found the perfect opportunity to humiliate him by demanding his rightful *gurudakhina* from Ekalavya. Refusing everything that Ekalavya offered, Dronacharya demanded that Ekalavya cut the thumb of his right hand and give it to him as a gift. As the audience anticipates the enactment of the historic moment, Ekalavya surprises us by declaring that he will not give this thumb; not this time. The gasp of the audience started to subside as Ekalavya launched into a short monologue on how his people have been oppressed for centuries and whenever they tried to stand up with their heads held high, it has always been brutally crushed. His refusal to give his thumb, declared Ekalavya, was the beginning of a series of refusals at accepting discrimination and a pledge to continue the fight for equal opportunities. The play ends with Ekalavya going back to his people, to a scene of celebration as they move forward in their journey.

Although inspired from the *Mahabharata*, the text and its performance presented here manages to bring up issues of class struggle, of war and violence, and most importantly issues of the caste system. Caste as a problem remains conspicuously absent from the theatre of 1960s and 1970s especially in Bengal where class-based theatrical experiments were generally accepted as the principal aspects of reality especially because it reflected the rupture created through the peasant's and worker's struggle during the Naxalbari Movement. Therefore, theatrical performances were marked by revolutionary slogans, impassioned rhetoric of a classless society and socialist realism, and were used as a weapon for de-classing oneself.[10] But in the wake of new political structures and systems of exchange, there has been a shift from class-based political issues to those of gender, caste, sexuality and so forth, which have led to recognition of diverse, specific struggles constrained in particular contexts. In the context of caste, the last couple of decades have witnessed Dalit[11] assertion from all over the country. In Tepantor's version of Ekalavya's story – which was traditionally read as justifying the caste system – the Dalits used the narrative to give their alternate reading as a symbol of dissent. This is reflected in many theatre productions especially from Maharashtra, Haryana and Uttar Pradesh and also in concrete political action. For example, on

24 September 1998 there was a rally of Dalits in Lucknow, Uttar Pradesh where they burned the effigy of Dronacharya after holding a trial for not accepting Ekalavya as his student, finding him guilty and sentenced him to death. This production not only represents the discriminatory history of caste in India and locating one's subjectivity in that history, but rather, advocates for taking concrete steps towards breaking this social structure. Therefore, when Tapas Bauri, one of the actors from the low-positioned Bauri caste stands on the shoulders of Tapas Bhattacharya, a Brahman (the highest caste) actor from a neighbouring village, it is not just a visual spectacle but a strong blow at the notion of 'pollution-purity' in the caste dynamics. Hence, the political potency of this and other similar productions does not just lie in the attempt of bringing caste into the folds of Bengali theatre by directly addressing the related questions, but, since all the actors are from a lower caste, it meant finding their own voice and confronting caste issues directly. They were finally getting a chance to say that even though Ekalavya was once forced to give his thumb and was denied his destiny, his people, his successors will no longer do the same; they will not let their rights be denied. Therefore, the political possibility of this play lies not only in the declaration of these bodies and their fragile subjectivities that they will no longer stay silent, but also, and more importantly, in the newly found political power to refuse discrimination. Hence for the members of the group whose only identity has been of a '*chotolok*',[12] the ability to question their status through theatre offers them the 'logic of resistance', or to put simply, a way for them to tell their stories and to continue their fight for equality.

Concluding Thoughts

In India, the theatre has been used for addressing a multitude of issues, ranging from social problems like violence against women to communal tension, social progress, industrialization and displacement. Theatre for this purpose includes activist groups and grass-root organizations, governmental and non-governmental bodies, as well as socially and politically engaged theatre groups or individuals. The groups working with Dalits, women, children, sex workers, minority communities and other marginalized communities, all qualify as practicing theatre for addressing issues challenging them in everyday life. Theatre groups and activist organizations who have sought to raise social and political awareness through the art form of theatre had to include traditional forms and enlist folk artists, realizing that the masses already had performance idioms used for effective communication or depend on the street theatre, which provided a low-cost and immediate means of reaching the masses in India. While historically relevant theatre groups like IPTA focused on rural performers and performances in a bid to raise consciousness of equality, the Indian government on the other side encouraged communities of folk artists economically or through other forms of patronage to include given social messages such as education for all, family planning, personal hygiene, in their particular repertoires. Tepantor and the Ebong Amra group is an obvious counter-movement against such models of theatre-making, still prevalent in the country and of course on the Bengali stage. They not only counter the prevailing themes of mainstream theatre representations in India, but their work also opposes the dominant theatre aesthetics of contemporary Indian theatre. Ebong Amra, by moving away from the stage and putting the performance in the public space, delineates itself from the confines of the proscenium. Although inspired by Badal Sarkar's Third Theatre,[13] the group managed to create a whole different aesthetic in this respect. Ebong Amra's idea is not to develop theatre suited exclusively for the streets, but to be able to do any type of theatre in the open even if it entails elaborate scenography, creating levels or even including their farms and ponds as part of the set. Through their economic independence and by moving away from the stage and into the public space, the group does not have to depend on renting out private theatres (whose rates are unaffordable by most) or state-owned ones (for which the waiting list is endless) in order to stage their productions. This helps them not to align with organizations such as Natya Sojon, a theatre initiative taken by important contemporary theatre-makers and the state in their quest for encouraging rural theatre and indigenous roots like *jatra* or *chaau*. The above-mentioned theatre organization focuses on establishing people's theatre by giving them funds and spaces to perform, and effectively drawing such theatre into the hands of the people and the state, inadvertently bringing the state deeper into the lives of those who are in fact seeking to distance themselves from it or resist its pervasive power.

The kind of communal living and working that Tepantor advocates is very different from other theatre experiments in Indian theatre, in particular communities like the Chorus Repertory Theatre of Ratan Thiyam.[14] This theatre is located on the outskirts of Imphal, Manipur, and has a two-acre campus that was slowly built to accommodate a self-sufficient way of life, with housing and working quarters for the company and it has now become an important regional and national centre for contemporary theatre. However, the working mechanisms of the Chorus Repertory Theatre can be seen as problematic. The theatre constitues both the community and the state (because the company receives state funding), and it is using a feudal structure with a strong and rigid hierarchy within the group, thriving on the star value of Thiyam (playwright and theatre director). In an effort to be rooted to their culture, the group and its director Thiyam have not been able to critically evaluate their culture and tradition and modify it to be more egalitarian. For instance, the male members have to touch the feet of their master every morning before they start their day. Touching someone's feet, a sign of respect, also signifies a strong hierarchy and is a sign of ancient patriarchal values. As for the female performers, only their leader, the most accomplished performer is allowed to touch Thiyam's feet on behalf of all the other women. This is because not all women are allowed to touch the feet of the grand patriarch in their culture. Tepantor, on the contrary, through its structure, composition and incorporation of multiple and diverse approaches to theatre-making, seeks to intervene into the community to find equality. Here, equality can be described in terms of labour and distribution of resources, offering a political aesthetic that attempts to create a theatre that may reach into and beyond the power of the state and the onslaught of capital.

Tepantor is what I would call an experiment in political theatre. In its humble ways it offers us a potential road map to think in and through the community. The efficacy of political theatre here lies in having the power to create a rupture in social structure. As Janelle Reinelt argues, talking about communities of people is important as there is an acute need to move beyond the individual subjects. As created by neo-liberalism and ideologies of global capitalism and consumerism, the celebration of the individual has become almost unchallenged in popular western culture, and an attempt to offset that atomism is a political aesthetics worth struggling over (Reinelt and Hewitt 2011: 15). It is also important to add that the conspicuously 'revolutionary' Indian plays that formed the backbone of the Indian political theatre, voicing the grievances of the people and indulging in proletarian rhetoric, had a relevant, but restrictive impact on the lives of people. Today what makes a play political is not its fidelity to the Party or to any historically prescribed theatrical model (such as Brechtian theatre), but by its fidelity to the communities of people whose oppression needs to be enacted on stage. As Lara Stevens argues, 'the idea of judging an artwork based on its "productive" merit or its ability to galvanize action is also problematic in the way that it instrumentalizes art and measures it according to late capitalist standards of value' (2014: 35). Therefore, the evaluation of Tepantor and Ebong Amra should not be through its productive value of translating their work into a kind of direct political action but rather through its potential to hark upon a new beginning.

REFERENCES

Acharya, Anil (ed.) (2008), *Shat-Shottor er Chatro Andolon* (*The Student Movement of 60s and 70s*), Calcutta: Anushtup.

Badiou, Alain (2007), 'Theatre of operations: A discussion between Alain Badiou and Elie During', in *A Theater Without Theater*, Lisbon: MACBA and Fundaçao de Arte Moderna e Contemporanea – Colecçao Berardo, pp. 22–27.

Banerjee, Sumanta (1980), *In the Wake of Naxalbari: A History of the Naxalite Movement in India*, Calcutta: Subarnarekha.

—— (2002), 'Naxalbari: Between past and future', *Economic and Political Weekly*, 37:22, 1–7 June, pp. 2115–16.

Basu, Bratya (2006), 'I want to create a Third Cinema', *The Statesman*, 25 May, Kolkata: Natya Shodh Sangasthan Archives, CF/432, Bratya Basu.

Basu, Pradip (2000), *Towards Naxalbari, 1953–1967: An Account of Inner Party Ideological Struggle,* Calcutta: Progressive Publishers.

Boal, Augusto (2000), *Theatre of the Oppressed*, London: Pluto Press.

Brecht, Bertolt (2014), *Brecht on Theatre* (eds M. Silberman, S. Giles and T. Kuhn), London: Bloomsbury.

Chakraborty, Bibhash (1988), 'Theatre depends on society for survival', *The Telegraph*, 24 June, Natya Shodh Sanghasthan Archive, CF/331, Group Theatre (B), History/Articles.

Chatterjee, Partha (1990), 'The political culture of Calcutta', in S. Choudhuri (ed.), *Calcutta: The Living City, the Present and Future*, vol. 2, Oxford: Oxford University Press, pp. 27–33.

Chinna, Stephen (2003), *Performance: Recasting the Political in Theatre and Beyond*, Oxford and New York: Peter Lang.

Damas, Marius (1991), *Approaching Naxalbari*, Calcutta: Radical Impression.

Dutt, Utpal (2009), *Towards a Revolutionary Theatre*, Calcutta: Seagull Books.

Ghosh, Parimal (2012), 'Rise and fall of Calcutta's Group Theatre', *Economic and Political Weekly*, 10 March, 47:10, pp. 36–42.

Menon, Sadanand (2011), 'Badal Sircar (1925–2011): A curtain call for political theatre', *Economic and Political Weekly*, XLVI:22, 28 May, pp. 16–20.

Piscator, Erwin (1980), *The Political Theatre* (trans. Hugh Rorrison), London: Eyre Methuen.

Reinelt, Janelle and Hewitt, Gerald (2011), *The Political Theatre of David Edgar*, Cambridge: Cambridge University Press.

Sen, Kaushik (2005), 'Staging a comeback', *The Telegraph*, 17 April, Kolkata: Natya Shodh Sangasthan Archive, CF/328, Kaushik Sen.

Sinha, Surajit and Bhattacharya, Ranjit (1969), 'Bhadralok and Chhotolok in a rural area of West Bengal', *Sociological Bulletin*, 18:1, March, pp. 50–66.

Stevens, Lara (2014), 'Networks of resistance: Connecting stage, street and social media in Tony Kushner's *Only We Who Guard the Mystery Shall be Unhappy*', *Performance Paradigm,* 10, pp. 35–47.

Editors' Note

A very recent critical analysis by Sharmistha Saha, entitled *Theatre and National Identity in Colonial India: Formation of a Community through Cultural Practice* (2018) discussed 'Indian theatre' practices in colonial India with a special emphasis on national identity and communal belonging. In addition, Sanjoy Ganguly's *Jana*

Sanskriti: Forum Theatre and Democracy in India (2010) looks at theatre practices in India as political practice through a forum theatre initiative in West Bengal.

Further reading

Ganguly, Sanjoy (2010), *Jana Sanskriti: Forum Theatre and Democracy in India,* London and New York: Routledge.

Saha, Sharmistha (2018), *Theatre and National Identity in Colonial India: Formation of a Community through Cultural Practice,* Berlin: Springer.

NOTES

1. The Naxalbari movement was inspired by a revolt in the northern part of West Bengal, India, and in March–April 1967, tribal workers who were mainly landless labourers forcibly took land on tea plantations in the Naxalbari area under the leadership of the local members of the Communist Party of India Marxist (C.P.I [M]). Naxalbari is a police station of 206.7 sq kms in areas of the Siliguri subdivision of Darjeeling district which lies in the northern part of West Bengal known as North Bengal. Naxalbari is situated in the slender neck which is India's only vital land corridor that connects Bhutan, Sikkim and the country's north-east zone. It has two international borders, on the west is Nepal at a distance of four miles and on the east is Bangladesh at a distance of sixteen miles. China-occupied Tibet is only 60 miles away on the northern side. The peasants of this region mainly comprise tribal communities – Santhals, Oraons and Rajbanshis and were heavily exploited by the *jotedars* under the '*adhiar*' system. This movement, as various commentators pointed out, was not a sudden outburst but the result of long-standing political agitations in the region. Communists of Bengal had organized cadres in the region from the 1930s onwards, and could now draw on the experience of various mass struggles, most prominently the Tebhaga movement.

2. Many international writers were translated in Bengali for the stage. Notably were Shakespeare's *Macbeth, Othello, Hamlet, The Merchant of Venice* and *A Midsummer Night's Dream*; Henrik Ibsen's *A Doll's House, Enemy of the People* and *Hedda Gabler*; Maxim Gorky's *Mother*, Bertolt Brecht's *The Caucasian Chalk Circle, Three Penny Opera, Mother Courage, Galileo* and *The Resistible Rise of Arturo Ui* to name a few.

3. Ebong Amra means 'And Us'. According to them, the name suggests that there's everyone else, respected people, and then there's US! Ghosh (2014), interview with Kallol Bhattacharya, Tepantor.

4. 'Call shows' is a colloquial term used in India, predominantly in West Bengal. It refers to shows where a theatre group has been invited to perform at a particular venue, mostly during festive seasons and theatre festivals, for which the theatre group is paid by the organizers.

5. From the 1980s, theatre-makers in West Bengal started to feel the limitations of doing theatre in non-economically viable ways. Eminent theatre practitioners wrote about how the funds from the West Bengal government and the central government were abysmal and doing full-time theatre was becoming increasingly difficult. They of course urged for a total commitment to theatre and even they knew that it was an idealistic demand (see Chakraborty 1988). By the mid-2000s, the new brigade of theatre-makers was opening their doors to corporate funding. To quote contemporary playwright and theatre director Bratya Basu, '[w]e are talking about cultural opportunism. If a branded liquor company gives us money to launch a production, I will grab the chance' (2006). Another eminent theatre-maker of today, Kaushik Sen in an interview said,

    > There was initially certain taboos regarding approaching corporate sectors for funding, but these are slowly crumbling. My own play *Kolkata r Elektra* was sponsored by Hutch and I view this trend of corporate funding as an important step towards promotion of theatre.
    >
    > (2005)

6. During the 1960s and 1970s, insurgency, or 'wars of national liberation', became the dominant form of conflict in the world, and Mao Tse-tung's revolutionary theory of People's War became famous as the doctrine behind this new kind of war. In 1965, Mao – through Lin Piao – proclaimed that People's War was 'universal truth', a model for revolution applicable to any society anywhere. The theory developed over a period of about ten years, from the time in 1926 when Mao first discovered revolutionary potential among the peasants until the spring of 1938 when he completed the last of his major theoretical works. The peasant's and tribal movements that are couched in the Marxist-Maoist ideology also borrow this term to refer to their fight against the Indian State.

7. The *Mahabharata* or *Mahābhārata* is one of the two major Sanskrit epics of ancient India, the other being the *Ramayana*. The innermost narrative kernel of the *Mahabharata* tells the story of two sets of paternal first cousins – the five sons of the deceased King Pandu (the five Pandavas) and the one hundred sons of blind King Dhritarashtra (the hundred Dhartarashtras) – who became bitter rivals, and opposed each other in war for possession of the ancestral Bharata kingdom with its capital in the 'City of the Elephant', Hastinapura, on the Ganga river in north central India. What is dramatically interesting within this simple opposition is the large number of individual agendas the many characters pursue, and the numerous personal conflicts, ethical puzzles, subplots and plot twists that give the story a strikingly powerful development.

8. *Gurudakshina* refers to the tradition of repaying one's teacher or guru after a period of study or the completion of formal education, or to spiritual guide. This tradition is one of acknowledgement, respect and thanks. It is a form of reciprocity and exchange between student and teacher.

9. *Kalaripayattu* is a famous Indian martial art form from Kerala and one of the oldest fighting systems in existence. It is practised in most of the parts of south India. A *kalari* is the school or training hall where martial arts are taught. It includes strikes, kicks and some weapon-based practices. Footwork patterns are of key importance in *Kalaripayattu*.
    Lathi is an ancient armed martial art of India. It also refers to one of the world's oldest weapons used in martial arts. *Lathi* or stick martial art was practised in Punjab and Bengal region of India. *Lathi* still remains a popular sport in Indian villages.

10. *Rajrakta* ('The royal blood') in 1971, by Bibhash Chakraborty, Utpal Dutt's *Teer* ('Arrow') in 1969 and *Dushopner Nogori* ('City of nightmares') in 1974, *Tiner Tolowar* (1971), *Lenin er Dak* ('The call of Lenin') in 1972, Badal Sircar's *Micchil* ('Procession') in 1970, to name a few examples of plays during the period of 1960s and 1970s that carried the message of a socialist idea of change and equality.

11. India's caste system assigns individuals a certain hierarchical status according to Hindu beliefs. Traditionally, there are four principal castes (divided into many sub-categories) and one category of people who fall outside the caste system – the Dalits. Dalits have been oppressed, culturally subjugated and politically marginalized. The principles of untouchability and 'purity and pollution' dictate what Dalits are and are not allowed to do; where they are and are not allowed to live, go or sit; who they can and cannot give water to, eat with or marry; extending into the minutia of all aspects of daily life.

12. *Chotolok* is a derogatory way of addressing the lowly or specifically, people of the lower caste. See Sinha and Bhattacharya (1969).

13. Badal Sircar was an influential Indian dramatist and theatre director, mostly known for his anti-establishment plays during the Naxalite movement in the 1970s and taking theatre out of the proscenium and into public arena, when he founded his own theatre company, Shatabdi, in 1976. He wrote more than 50 plays of which *Ebong Indrajit* (1963), *Basi Khabar* (1979) and *Saari Raat* (1963) are well-known literary pieces, a pioneering figure in street theatre as well as in experimental and contemporary Bengali theatre with his egalitarian 'Third Theatre', he prolifically wrote scripts for his *Aanganmanch* ('courtyard stage') performances, and remains one of the most translated Indian playwrights. His 'Third Theatre' became a protest against prevalent commercial theatre establishment. Often performed in 'found' spaces rather than rented theatre halls, without elaborate lighting, costumes or make-up, where audience was no longer a passive, rather became participatory, it added a new realism to contemporary dramaturgy, retaining thematic sophistication of social committed theatre all the while, and thus started a new wave of experimental theatre in Indian theatre. See Menon (2011).

14. Ratan Thiyam is an Indian playwright and theatre director, and the winner of Sangeet Natak Akademi Award in 1987, one of leading figures of the 'theatre of roots' movement in Indian theatre, which started in the 1970s. Also known as Thiyam Nemai, Ratan Thiyam is known for writing and staging plays that use ancient Indian theatre traditions and forms in a contemporary context.

Bodies without Organs and Organs without Bodies: The Maltese Experience of Creating National Theatres

Marco Galea

Introduction

This chapter analyses the concept of national community with regards to theatre in one of the smaller states of the European Union, which has a combination of characteristics that makes this discourse insightful of the intersection between theatre and nationality. Malta is one of the smallest states in Europe, both by size (316 km^2) and by population (less than half a million). It is also an island, situated towards the southernmost tip of Europe, and relatively close to North African shores. Its history includes centuries of close relations and ties (mainly through occupation, but also, as a result, through cultural influence) with important European powers. However, a long occupation by Muslim rulers in the Middle Ages is generally considered to have created the circumstances that led to the creation of the native language that is used in the country and to other markers of ethnicity.

Malta is therefore an interesting national community primarily because this combination of size, geographic marginality and an overbearing history of colonization has made the local population, or at least those parts of the population that were educated enough to find these preoccupations important, to question and interpret the issue of national identity. At least since the mid-nineteenth century, local politics, as well as culture and the arts, has grappled with the problem of defining the Maltese as a community, especially in relationship to neighbours, colonizers and perceived enemies (see Frendo 2012: 39–72). Defining this identity was considered to be an important step towards self-determination, and as a result, nation builders were very selective in emphasizing those markers of identity that linked the Maltese to a glorious European heritage and minimizing the importance of aspects that seem to contradict this (Mitchell 2002: 7–28).

Having a national theatre was a major dream of the cultured classes in the years leading to independence and remains an issue to this day. This chapter will analyse three models that have been considered or tested in Malta and compare the success or otherwise of creating theatre contexts that speak to the nation as a community and fostering a community that feels that theatre is a part of its life. These three models can be described as (1) national theatre seen as symbolized by and working from a central monumental building, (2) an artist-led theatre that taps into state subsidies to address national issues, and (3) a state-funded setup tasked to create nationally relevant theatre without being constrained by a specific physical space or a permanent group of performers.

In Malta, the concept of national theatre cannot be traced further back than the immediate post–World War II period. Primarily this was due to the late development of a national consciousness among the educated classes, and also because the insularity of Malta meant that local artists and intellectuals could really look only at nearby Italy and the colonizing Great Britain for inspiration. These were two countries where the idea of a national theatre was not strong, in Italy primarily because of the large variations between the different regional realities and the lack of progress in unifying them culturally (Gaborik 2008: 139) and in Britain because the success of commercial theatre, in London at least, and the fear of government control over the arts meant that it was only in 1949 that legislation could be passed to sanction the establishment of a national theatre (Rosenthal 2013: 19–34).

When legislators in Malta first considered the institution of a national theatre, the picture their appointed experts painted according to the brief given to them was that the national theatre would be run by the government under the direction of an honorary board with the following objectives:

1. To promote and maintain the artistic standard of all shows given in this theatre [...]
2. To promote and afford opportunities for the development of local talent in dramatics [...] including playwriting, composition and production
3. To give preference to local talent [...]
4. To establish a Library and Museum containing general literature on musical and dramatic subjects and a record of Maltese composers and playwrights and their works
5. To organize festivals
6. To establish a school of singing, playing, dramatics and ballet
7. To encourage shows for children

(Anon. 1948: 8)[1]

The committee of experts felt that this programme could only be realized if a purposely designed state-of-the-art theatre was built, but as Malta was only in the initial stages of rebuilding its infrastructure after World War II, it felt it could not recommend such a measure, and therefore suggested that as 'an interim measure' the old Manoel Theatre, which had somehow survived the heavy shelling of Valletta, be requisitioned by the government to be used as a national theatre. However, there was already an awareness that a theatre built during the early eighteenth century to cater for a limited elite audience could not fulfil the needs of a national theatre satisfactorily.

The expectations, even at this initial stage of discussion, were for a monumental theatre that would be a beacon for a society intent on restructuring after the devastation of war and hopeful of being able to assert itself politically as a nation in the near future. The concept as described in 1948 and the language used are very similar to how Marvin Carlson defines traditional national theatres:

> The common image of a National Theatre is of a monumental edifice located in a national capital, authorized, privileged and supported by the government, and devoted wholly or largely to the productions of the work of national dramatists.
>
> (Carlson 2008: 21)

The Vessel

The ambitions to create such a national theatre, however, were not matched by the possibilities. Political turmoil meant that the project was shelved for almost ten years and the Manoel Theatre only opened after restoration in 1960 (Xuereb 2011a: 113–18). It was now a publicly owned theatre and administered directly by a management committee appointed by the Maltese government, but the nomenclature 'National Theatre' was totally absent at the time of this re-opening.

Yet, the Manoel Theatre often describes itself as 'officially the country's National Theatre' (Teatru Manoel n.d.). As recently as 2016, in a foreword to a photographic book sponsored by the theatre itself, the minister responsible for culture stated that the Manoel was 'Malta's national theatre' (Bonnici 2016: 11). Opened in 1732, it is certainly a monumental edifice, as it can claim to be one of the oldest, if not the oldest functioning theatre in Europe. It is a very well-preserved Baroque theatre, in the country's capital city, Valletta, and it is one of the few active theatres that are government property and financially supported by the state. However, there is neither a legal framework nor the actual practice to justify the denomination of national theatre.

Nowadays, the theatre receives a budget of just over 1 million euros every year, which is less than half of what is spent on the National Philharmonic Orchestra (Ministry for Justice, Culture and Local Government 2017: 12). The money is spent mainly for wages for management and administrative staff, as well as for maintaining what is a high-maintenance historical building. The theatre has then to ask for separate funding for specific projects, like its side endeavour, the annual Baroque Festival.

The crucial missing piece of the jigsaw is that the theatre does not have its own performing company. In fact, the theatre employs no artists at all. The way that the theatre works is through a management committee that is responsible for creating a programme for the theatre. If there is a project that the theatre is particularly keen on, it needs to be commissioned to people who are not on the theatre's payroll. This possibility has been used less often in recent seasons, with the theatre preferring to collaborate with other organizations to create performances. Although it is never stated what this collaboration consists of, considering the resources available, in general terms the theatre provides the space and front of house services, as well as some publicity. The artistic side of things, including possibly the initial concept, comes from outside. Thus, 'policy-making regarding its programmes is restricted' (Xuereb 2011a: 124).

I like to look at the Manoel Theatre as an empty hull, ready to carry any load that fits. A season's offering might include opera, Baroque music concerts, Christmas pantomime, children's theatre, pop music concerts, premieres of new plays in Maltese and productions of West End hits. The annual programme is completed after a call for interest is issued, and performing companies submit the productions they would like to perform at the theatre. The end result is that every year the Manoel hosts a large variety of performances, from musical theatre to chamber music, from pantomime to contemporary dance. Although the theatre is hired out to producers at commercial rates, there is a lot of pressure from performers to be able to use this space. The general attitude of the theatre is to try to be as accommodating as possible, prompting a local theatre historian to describe the theatre as being 'all things to all men' (Xuereb 2011a: 123). Of course, women practitioners are less visible and certain groups of men are privileged.

To an outsider, the statements that the theatre makes about national identity or national concerns are at best confusing. On one hand, since its reopening in 1960 after state acquisition, the more prominent playwrights in Malta have looked at the theatre as their natural home. Indeed, many of the more significant plays of the latter decades of the twentieth century were premiered here. These included most of the plays of the foremost playwright of post-independence Malta, Francis Ebejer (1925–93; see Galea 2008; Crow and Galea 2003). A new play in Maltese performed at the Manoel immediately acquires a status that plays performed elsewhere do not have. On the other hand, the use of the national language is quite limited. For example, the pride of place in the annual calendar, and perhaps the first one to be pencilled in, is the Christmas pantomime, one of the few theatrical performances that are written locally in English, and a genre that was inherited from amateur English performers of the colonial period (Galea 2016: 127–28). English farces in translation or performed in the original English language are as common as original performances in Maltese. This situation could be as much the expression of an identity crisis that small countries tend to suffer from, as much as reluctance on the part of the theatre to make a clear intervention in the issue. However, for a theatre that makes claims to representing the nation, this position is obviously not helpful or illuminating.

At some points throughout its history, the Manoel Theatre fulfilled some of the aims listed by the committee of experts in 1948. For example, a school of actors was established there in 1977 but soon acquired autonomy and relocated elsewhere (Aquilina 2015: 89–110); for the past few years it has cultivated an interesting programme of children's theatre, and a youth opera company also forms part of the theatre's educational programme. For two decades, the theatre also had its own orchestra, which developed into the National Orchestra of Malta in 1997 and later became the Malta Philharmonic Orchestra. With the exception of the orchestra, which has become a respected professional ensemble, all other attempts tended to be short-lived.

The Wine

In this vacuum, the role of speaking to the community of theatregoers as members of a nation is left to independent theatre-makers who operate as 'content providers' to theatres like the Manoel. Since 1960, there have been many of these theatre-makers who have undertaken the task of providing performances for the Manoel. All have different characteristics. Some, for instance, only perform work in English, others only in Maltese, some choose European classics, others contemporary plays. From time to time, however, individuals or companies take it upon themselves to speak specifically to their audience as a nation-community. At least two short-lived companies have used the word *Nazzjonali* ('national') as part of their name, the Għaqda Nazzjonali Drammatika (National Drama Group), active in the mid-1960s (Xuereb 2017: 17–18) and the Kumpanija Nazzjonali tad-Drama (National Drama Company), active in the mid-1980s (Xuereb 2017: 172–76).

During the past few years, the most prominent theatre-maker who I consider to be consciously and consistently speaking to Maltese theatre spectators as a nation-community has been playwright and director Mario Philip Azzopardi.

Born in 1950, Azzopardi made a name for himself as a young stage and television actor, as well as a filmmaker in the early 1970s, before a play he had written about corruption in the clergy, *Sulari fuq Strada Stretta* ('Building speculation in the red light district) (1977) was banned. He felt he was being victimized and migrated to Canada, where he made a successful career directing films, mostly for television. He returned to Malta around 2008, initially claiming to want to spend six months of each year in the country but eventually settling back in Malta on a full-time basis. Since his return, he has primarily been active as a theatre producer, although he has also been involved in various films, either as director, script-writer or producer. What I am mainly interested in here is his enterprise entitled *Staġun Teatrali Malti*, meaning 'The Maltese theatre season'. Through this vehicle Azzopardi produces from three to four plays every year, mainly at the Manoel Theatre and sometimes in collaboration with it. The structure revolves directly around Azzopardi's persona and his reputation as an artist. This reputation relied mainly on three outputs:

1. A feature film he had made in 1971, *Gaġġa*, based on a contemporary Maltese novel. This was a student film made with amateur actors and amateur equipment on 8mm film. It was restored and re-released in Maltese cinemas and on DVD in 2007.
2. The successful staging of *Sulari fuq Strada Stretta* in 2008. This was the same play that had been banned in 1977.
3. The curriculum that the artist had as a filmmaker in North America, which was impressive by Maltese standards.

Therefore, when Azzopardi declared himself more or less the saviour of Maltese theatre (see Galea Debono 2008: 7),[2] a theatre that is considered to be in perpetual crisis, which is itself not surprising, when you take into account the size of the country, his claims had considerable resonance in artistic circles. He suggested a structure on how to write and perform a new play, which in essence has been used for decades in many other countries but was new to mainstream theatre in Malta. Azzopardi (through his organization) commissions a playwright, experienced or otherwise, to write a play on a specific topic. The playwright is paid for the different drafts that he or she will need to come up with. This is in itself uncommon in Malta, as playwriting is hardly ever remunerated, except through state-sanctioned prizes. The draft is then discussed during readings with actors, the director and the producer himself until a satisfactory script becomes available. Initially the project intended to use independent readers, but apparently the producer decided early on that he would need to take responsibility for most decisions related to content.

One of the important issues related to this process is that it has been heavily subsidized by state funding. There has been funding for scriptwriting and production, unquantified 'collaboration' with the Manoel Theatre as well as commissions from the Malta International Arts Festival. Admittedly, all of the plays performed by Staġun Teatru Malti have been huge box-office successes, one of them even having to be restaged after a few months to accommodate public interest, a situation almost unheard of in Maltese theatre. Quite a few have also been screened by state television.

The commercial success of this enterprise may look surprising. Even the most experienced and successful impresarios draw a blank sometimes, but Staġun Teatru Malti productions have invariably been box-office successes. We have already hinted at the messiah-like reputation that Azzopardi has acquired in many circles, but it is also interesting to look at how the plays themselves have been sold to the public.

Mainstream theatre in Malta, especially original theatre in Maltese, has generally shied away from tackling 'taboo' subjects like sexual orientation or the need for a secular society. Azzopardi appears to be taking on these subjects with particular gusto.

His greatest success so far has been the play *Jiena Nħobb, Inti Tħobb* (*I Love, You Love*) (2014), a play about gay relationships and which also dealt with the issue of surrogacy. The play was soon adopted as a standard-bearer for LGBT rights. However, it is certainly not a coincidence that the play was staged around the time when the Maltese parliament was discussing new marriage laws that would allow legal unions between same-sex couples as well as adoption rights. Although, of course, the play is making strong points on these two subjects, the timing leaves room for ambiguity. The Labour Party now in government in Malta was elected in 2013 and had already promised this legislation. Its huge majority in parliament is such that no laws proposed by government risk being blocked, even the most unpopular. Therefore the play, rather than wanting to influence public opinion, is riding the wave of this liberalization. Other plays like *Ċittadin Vassalli* (*Citizen Vassalli*) (2014) and *Xbihat ta' Xi Wħud li Huma Kattoliċi* (*The Appearance of Certain People Who Consider Themselves Catholic*) (2011) deal with the power of the Catholic Church in Malta. *Xbihat* tries to deal with a historical moment in the country's relatively recent past, a bitter quarrel between the archbishop and the leader of the Labour Party in the early 1960s that forced a huge sector of the population to choose between their deeply felt allegiance to Catholicism and their equally strong sense of belonging to the Labour Party. This issue has never been dealt with properly via literature or theatre in Malta, and though the play left most members of the audience, as well as the critics, dissatisfied with its views (Serracino 2011: 22; Xuereb 2011b: 40), it did make some bold statements about secularism. *Vassalli* is a one-sided fictionalization of the life of a historical figure who had struggled to introduce enlightenment ideas in late eighteenth-century Malta and of course fell foul of the state and the Church.

Perhaps what is most interesting in these plays, other than their subject matter, is the theatrical imagery that is meant to, and generally manages to, attract attention and possibly draw in audiences who would not otherwise be interested. One ploy Azzopardi has used at least twice is nudity, more specifically male nudity, on the island's most venerable stage. This seems to be taken as a sign of transgression and enjoyed as such by audiences. Some of the plays use blasphemy and actions which would be considered a sacrilege by most Catholics as features that stand out in otherwise artistically conventional plays. Other plays, especially those commissioned by the Malta Arts Festival, seem to focus on nostalgia, a measure of which is never refused by another sector of theatregoers. My point is that these plays have managed to create an audience that possibly did not exist and who feel that they are participating in a paradigm shift. This is the line that several reviewers also take (Cassar Darien 2011: 21). I believe, however, that a paradigmatic shift is happening, or might have happened already in Maltese society; hence, this kind of theatre merely reflects on social developments rather than directly fostering such changes. At least this is what the popularity and absence of public controversy surrounding these plays indicate.

The right or indeed the need for such a theatre to exist cannot be disputed. What is more problematic is the belief that this successful (mainly because it is popular) model can become a substitute for a coherent policy regarding the state's intervention or otherwise in supporting a theatre that has something to say about identity. As Benedict Anderson taught us, nations are 'imagined' communities. The big question is who gets to do the imagining. In the nineteenth century, it was the ruling classes who defined nations (Anderson 2006: 83–88). Many of these definitions (for example the emphasis on geographical borders, ethnicity and language) have survived, despite the fact that new realities continually challenge them (see Butler 2007: 30–31). I believe that in the twenty-first century Malta is going through a fundamentally important moment when it is coming to terms with new realities such as secularism, multi-ethnicity, effects of globalization and the disappearance of the geographical landscape that formed part of a romanticized national identity. It needs art, including theatre, that can help it problematize these issues, rather than follow an agenda already established by the political class. Azzopardi currently also occupies the position of artistic director of Valletta 2018, the foundation set up to create structures in preparation for Valletta's status of European City of Culture and to programme and manage activities during the year. While the latter is a public position, the one we have discussed in this chapter is not. The role of artistic director of Valletta 2018 is not a permanent one and depends on possibly fickle political decisions. However his position in the foundation seems very strong as even a public anti-Islamic rant did not diminish the government's support for him.[3] His position at the head of an organization he himself set up is even stronger. It is of course not his fault that he is in this position of almost sole interpreter of nationality in theatre and in a wider cultural context, but the community is poorer because of this fact.

A New Wine?

A recent addition to this theatrical landscape has been the setting up of Teatru Malta, a formation fully funded by the state and defined in all official documentation as a national theatre. This entity was only set up in 2017 and announced its first programme of performances in January 2018 and is therefore still an unknown quantity. My discussion will therefore be based on the way Teatru Malta has been announced to theatregoers and on its planned performances.

Teatru Malta forms part of the Arts Council Malta, which is the state's main cultural agency. Although it is sometimes referred to as a 'national theatre company', this nomenclature is not precise. Like the Manoel Theatre, there is no theatre company to speak of, and none is envisaged. The only employees are an artistic director, an executive administrator and a clerical officer. Teatru Malta has been described, both by its artistic director and the Minister for Culture, as 'Malta's first National Theatre without walls' (Teatru Malta 2018: 4, 8). The inspiration is evidently the contemporary model of national theatres, many of which have been set up since the 1970s, with the primary aim of touring the national territory and collaborating with local artists (Carlson 2008: 29). The term 'theatre without walls' has been used widely for two recent national theatre formations, the National Theatre of Scotland and National Theatre Wales. Both of these companies take pride in not being tied to a central theatre and expecting the audience to come to them, but to travel throughout the country with their performances and work with local artists to create works that are particularly relevant to the community itself (McMillan in Reid 2017: 90 and McGrath in Sedgman 2016: viii). Both touring and collaborating are referred to in Teatru Malta's first published programme (Teatru Malta 2018: 6, 8). In fact, eight theatres are specifically listed as hosting performances during 2018, besides a number of other non-formal spaces (Teatru Malta 2018: 46) and most of the productions in the programme are listed as co-productions or collaborations.

The concept of touring has been emphasized and almost given as the raison d'être by the Minister for Culture. In an article he wrote for a local newspaper, he explained that Teatru Malta exists to challenge the Manoel Theatre by creating theatre that would be closer to the communities and would be outside the capital city of Valletta (Bonnici 2017). In fact, a large portion of Teatru Malta's budget for the foreseeable future will be invested in restoring and modernizing local theatres that would eventually be handed back to the community, which will be expected to make regular use of them. It is beyond doubt that theatres like the National Theatre of Scotland and National Theatre Wales owe much of their success to the way they have created performances for and with local communities. How far such an idea can and will be taken by Teatru Malta still needs to be seen. However, one needs to consider that the geographical realities of Malta are different to those of either Scotland or Wales. The distance between Glasgow or Edinburgh and the Highlands, and the difficulty of access that inhabitants in the islands have to theatres in the larger cities, as well as the cultural variations between the different territories, render performances that are specific to the local communities both desirable and feasible. In Malta, because of the size of the country, distances are not a major problem. Regional variations do exist, but local communities are also very small and exist in proximity to each other. The largest town has a population of less than 23,000, and most are considerably smaller. Valletta itself has a population of less than 6000. It is therefore difficult to envisage a situation where different productions would target audiences according to their connection to a specific geographical area. The fact that local theatres are restored and put back on the cultural map is a positive development. However, the creation of a national theatre has passed by an opportunity to create a landmark space that could be owned by the local theatrical community because it would provide facilities that do not exist in other theatres and cannot be built into any of the local theatres, most of which have significant limitations of size and other physical attributes.

We discussed earlier that already in 1948, the Manoel Theatre was considered to be inadequate as a base for a national theatre for the long term. Post-World War II theatregoers always hoped that the site where the Royal Opera House stood between 1866 and 1942, when it was destroyed by German bombs, would one day host a new theatre. The Opera House itself had after all been built because in the mid-nineteenth century the Manoel was deemed too small. It had remained a gaping hole until 2013, when as part of a larger project commissioned to Renzo Piano, it was reconfigured as an open-air performance space (Cremona et al. 2017: 152). At the time the theatrical community protested that this prime cultural site would have limited use. Thus, considering that Teatru Malta was launched to coincide with Malta's first ever stint, through its capital city Valletta, as European Capital of Culture, which happened at a time when the country is going through an unprecedented economic boom, one would have expected that the state made a statement of intent by initiating a process that would lead to creating a theatrical space that would not only serve the national theatre community, but also leave a legacy for future generations.

As the evidence of the working of Teatru Malta so far shows, more than a national theatre company it is to be a state agency that brings together efforts to cultivate theatre programming that is relevant to as wide a spectatorship as possible, and the main strategy will be to seek out this potential spectatorship. However, a close look at the productions listed for 2018 leaves some doubts whether the effort is as extraordinary as it first seems. Many of the collaborations are with other state-controlled agencies, primarily the Valletta 2018 Foundation, the Malta Arts Fund, Festivals Malta and Teatru Manoel. Prior to the formation of Teatru Malta, many of these agencies were already involved in creating theatre in some way. Teatru Malta's effort (barring the restoration of local theatres, which is an innovative exercise and for which money had never been available with any regularity) seems to be a reconfiguration and amalgamation of previously disjointed efforts.

Conclusion

What these three models have in common is the absence of the actor as a central building block. The Manoel is a working theatre that is run by administrators, Staġun Teatru Malti is a vehicle for an impresario to forward his vision of theatre, and Teatru Malta revolves around the assumption that performers will be roped in when they are needed and let go as soon as they are not. While interesting and successful performances have been conducted by national theatres with amateur actors, it is always assumed that the backbone of a national theatre is a company, or at least a nucleus of professional actors. For some reason (and clearly not a financial limitation, as the country has had a professional orchestra since 1968 and a national dance company since 2015) Malta has never decided to set up a professional theatre company that could engage with the community of spectators with its projects and in time with its identity. In more than half a century of independent existence, the Maltese state has delivered to the Maltese theatre-going public national theatres that are either bodies without organs or organs without bodies. National theatres need politicians to will them. In Malta, it seems, actors are a category of artists that politicians prefer to keep at arm's length.

REFERENCES

Anderson, Benedict (2006), *Imagined Communities*, rev. ed., London: Verso.

Anon. (1948), 'National Theatre in Malta: Committee's report and recommendations', *Times of Malta*, 7 December, p. 8.

Aquilina, Stefan (2015), 'The Manoel Theatre Academy of Dramatic Arts: 1977–1980', *Storja: Journal of the Malta University Historical Society*, 2015, pp. 89–110.

Bonnici, Owen (2016), 'Foreword', in *Teatru Manoel: The National Theatre of Malta*, Malta: Klabb Kotba Maltin, p. 11.

—— (2017), 'Viva t-Teatru', *Illum*, 27 March, http://www.illum.com.mt/kultura/teatru/49257/viva_tteatru#.Wm_6ZainHIW. Accessed 28 January 2018.

Butler, Judith (2007), conversation with G. Chakravorty Spivak, in *Who Sings the Nation-State?*, Oxford: Seagull Books, n.pag.

Carlson, Marvin (2008), 'National theatres: Then and now', in S. E. Wilmer (ed.), *National Theatres in a Changing Europe*, Basingstoke: Palgrave Macmillan, pp. 21–33.

Caruana, Jo (2015), 'The devil you know', *The Times [of Malta]*, 8 February, p. 6.

Cassar Darien, Tony (2011), 'When the absolute truth becomes absolutely false', *The Times [of Malta]*, 2 February, p. 21.

Cremona, Vicki Ann, Borg, Ruben Paul, Chetcuti, Keith and Buhagiar, Sean (2017), *Spazji Teatrali: A Catalogue of Theatres in Malta and Gozo: 2016 Edition*, Malta: The Valletta 2018 Foundation and Arts Council Malta, https://www.artscouncilmalta.org/files/uploads/misc/SPAZJI%20TEATRALI%20-%20Online%20[FINAL].pdf. Accessed 28 January 2018.

Crow, Brian and Galea, Marco (2003), 'The Maltese Janus: Francis Ebejer and his drama', *World Literature Today*, April–June, pp. 24–29.

Frendo, Henry (2012), *Europe and Empire: Culture, Politics and Identity in Malta and the Mediterranean*, Malta: Midsea Books.

Gaborik, Patricia (2008), 'Italy: The fancy of a national theatre', in S. E. Wilmer (ed.), *National Theatre in a Changing Europe*, Basingstoke: Palgrave Macmillan, pp. 138–50.

Galea, Marco (2008), 'Francis Ebejer', in *The Literary Encyclopedia*, https://www.litencyc.com/php/speople.php?rec=true&UID=1382. Accessed 29 January 2018.

—— (2016), 'The pantomime other: Building fences in pantomime performance in Malta', *Otherness: Essays and Studies*, 5:1, July, pp. 113–30, http://www.otherness.dk/fileadmin/www.othernessandthearts.org/Publications/Journal_Otherness/Otherness_5.1/The_Pantomime_Other_-_Marco_Galea.pdf. Accessed 29 January 2018.

Galea Debono, Fiona (2008), 'The obscenity of censorship', *The Times [of Malta]*, 23 January, p. 7.

Martin, Ivan (2014a), 'Minister denounces rant on Islam by V18 director', *Times of Malta*, 28 November, p. 44.

—— (2014b), 'Director's Islamophobic views "distinct from role"', 29 November, p. 3.

Ministry for Justice, Culture and Local Government (2017), *Recurrent Expenditure 2018*, Malta, https://mfin.gov.mt/en/The-Budget/Pages/The-Budget-2018.aspx. Accessed 28 January 2018.

Mitchell, Jon P. (2002), *Ambivalent Europeans: Ritual, Memory and the Public Sphere in Malta*, London: Routledge.

Reid, Trish (2017), 'Theatre without walls: The National Theatre of Scotland', *Journal of Contemporary Drama in English*, 5:1, pp. 86–97.

Rosenthal, Daniel (2013), *The National Theatre Story*, London: Oberon Books Ltd.

Sedgman, Kirsty (2016), *Locating the Audience: How People Found Value in National Theatre Wales*, Bristol: Intellect.

Serracino, Carmel (2011), 'Challenging study in Maltese guilt', *The Times [of Malta]*, 2 March, p. 22.

Teatru Malta (2018), *Programme Brief 2018*, Malta: Teatru Malta.

Teatru Manoel (n.d.), http://www.teatrumanoel.com.mt/?m=content&id=139. Accessed 21 August 2015.

Xuereb, Paul (2011a), *The Manoel Theatre: A Short History*, Malta: Midsea Books.
—— (2011b), 'Feisty, clever but defeated by love', *The Sunday Times [of Malta]*, 6 March, p. 40.
—— (2017), *Curtain Up! Theatre in Malta (1963–2015)* (ed. Marco Galea), Malta: Midsea Books.

Editors' Note

Discussions on the concept, functions and outreach of contemporary national theatres are at the forefront of cultural and theatre debates amidst an ever-growing tension between globalization and nationalism, cosmopolitanism and national protectionism in contemporary societies across the globe. Further to Galea's accurate analysis of the subject matter in the context of Malta, Nadine Holdsworth's *Theatre and Nation* (2010) gives an important introduction to theatre's engagement with national identities. In addition, Holdsworth's edited collection entitled *Theatre and National Identity: Re-Imagining Conceptions of Nation* (2014) provides an extensive analysis on the intricate connections between theatre-making and national identity internationally.

Further reading

Holdsworth, Nadine (2010), *Theatre and Nation*, Basingstoke: Palgrave Macmillan.
—— (ed.) (2014), *Theatre and National Identity: Re-Imagining Conceptions of Nation*, London and New York: Routledge.

NOTES

1. The newspaper was quoting the report presented in the Legislative Assembly by Prime Minister Paul Boffa.
2. John Suda, a veteran actor, is quoted as saying

   Mario has Maltese society and Malta at heart. When I met him in Paris in the early 1990s, […] he confided in me about it and stressed his desire to return to Malta to help breathe new life into the theatre scene.

   (in Caruana 2015: 6)

3. In August 2014, many cultural operators asked for Azzopardi's resignation or dismissal from the Valletta 2018 Foundation after a series of Facebook statements in which he had vented his anger on Muslims and called them 'idiots'. He was however defended by government officials and by the foundation itself. See Martin (2014a: 44, 2014b: 3).

PART III

'Glocal' Representations of Theatre Communities

Having discussed the ethics and the diverse political considerations present in contemporary theatre practice towards communities, this section takes a leap towards hybrid cultural spaces and examines the possibilities of developing theatre communities through transcultural and translocal exchanges. The authors of this part of the book look at theatre communities not only within continuously developing transnational spaces such as international arts festivals, but also within multicultural societies. Arts, or specifically theatre festivals, became important opportunities for theatre-makers to showcase their work to a wider public or even to produce new works aimed at festival audiences. Szabolcs Musca explores the strategies that are employed to cater for the different audiences that attend festival performances and explores the balance that is sought between delivering a performance that reflects the performers' identity and the need to be intelligible and meaningful to a diverse audience. Surtitling and translation are common strategies but adapting performances for audiences in different parts of Europe often also entails other practices. These practices bring about what Musca calls 'translating communities', without whom many theatrical productions would not be able to travel outside the cultural and linguistic context in which they were created.

Evi Stamatiou focuses on the festivals organized every summer in Edinburgh and specifically on the role and status that artists have within these festivals. Stamatiou claims that artists are 'commodities' in the festival business that takes over the city in August. Their belonging to a community of artists is discussed as being problematic, in that the status of artists varies greatly due to the diverse nature of the festivals. The performances, and with them the status of performers, range from the large-budget productions that the festival directors strive to take to the main festival to the fringe and free festivals that offer the artists a much lower level of support. As a result, rather than fostering a community of artists, these initiatives tend to lead to artists competing for attention and for the same audience. Stamatiou's narrative of trying to tell a story in the Edinburgh jungle is marked by the failure of the festival system to provide support, and the artist's own failure to create a more intimate artistic community, but it is also a statement regarding the control that neo-liberal thinking has on individuals (whether they are independent artists or pensioners in cash-strapped Greece) as well as on countries and economic systems.

A more positive narrative emerges from Hasibe Kalkan's discussion of postmigrant Turkish theatre in Berlin, a community which is on the margin of German society, whose members are neither at ease within traditional German society nor within the Turkish migrant community of the city. Lack of trust between ethnic Germans and Germans of recent migrant descent led to tensions and isolation, especially in areas with a high presence of migrant and postmigrant population. Shermin Langhoff's work, to bring together young people from migrant and disadvantaged backgrounds to make theatre that is meaningful to the community, has attracted a lot of attention. This is because what would usually be considered simply as social problems, were successfully forged in this theatre to create performances that were not only relevant, but which also developed a new idiom. This belonged to none of the cultures that fed into the work, but instead was created by the meeting of the different groups and their attempts to find a coherent and comprehensible form of expression.

What transpires from these critical accounts is a rapidly changing theatrical and cultural environment where the interactions and indeed tensions between local and global values, practices and methodologies perpetually form theatre communities across cultural and national divides.

Local and Global Stages: Translating Communities in Hybrid Cultural Spaces

Szabolcs Musca

The last fifteen years have brought significant changes in theatrical systems and structures, at least on a European level, due to economic, demographic and social reasons (see Klaic 2012; Lavender 2016). These changes prompted various responses from theatres, frequently resulting in multilateral exchanges and cooperation. New transnational cultural spaces emerged, created by diverse communities of theatre-makers and audiences. Collaborations beyond national boundaries were part of the theatrical spectrum well before the twenty-first century (see Edinburgh Festival and Avignon Festival, both established in 1947). However, in the past two decades, due to an ever-growing international theatre market, new perspectives emerged. International touring, cross-cultural collaborations and the international festival circuits established hybrid cultural spaces and communities with trans-local and transnational identities. But what are the means of mediation between the different culturally determined knowledges and experiences? In this chapter, I will argue that the cultural identity of these communities of theatre-makers and spectators is constructed through cultural and theatrical translation powered by the collaborative nature of theatre itself.

Festival Circuits and the Creation of Hybrid European Theatrical Spaces

We often encounter theatre productions at international theatre festivals that implement artistic changes usually to position themselves within a predominantly local social environment to address their target audiences by means that are familiar to them in the actual local or national environment. Adaptive elements may occur in the performance text (added local-language sentences), and within performative (the insertion of acts from local artists) and stage arrangements (local product advertisements within the set). The Habima National Theatre of Israel, for instance, made alterations to its production of Shakespeare's *The Merchant of Venice* when it presented it at the Globe Theatre in London. As part of the World Shakespeare Festival (2012), Ilan Ronen's direction inserted English-language improvisations in most of the interactive scenes with the audience, hence addressing the audience directly in English while the performance as a whole was played in Hebrew. In this instance, the adaptive strategies served an artistic aspiration to naturalize (or perhaps assimilate) the production within the actual context. In this theatre's case, the intention was ever more important because of the ongoing protests by pro-Palestinian groups, surrounding the Habima Theatre's presence in London.

In another case, also linked to the umbrella programme of the 2012 Cultural Olympiad, a different, foreignizing or exoticist strategy was used by the Sydney Theatre Company. The Australian company staged Botho Strauss' 1978 play *Gross und Klein* in 2011 and played with the original German title throughout their home and international performances. However, this was changed to the English title of *Big and Small* a few weeks before their performance in London, by the organizers of the London 2012 Festival at the Barbican Centre probably for promotional reasons. Nonetheless, the director, Benedict Andrews, intentionally left the foreign cultural indications in the performance text. The English text created by Martin Crimp kept actual German street names and various German-language expressions (greetings, phrases and so forth) in the dialogues and monologues. Set elements (by Johannes Schütz) such as a German flag and street sign were also reminiscent of 'Germanness' in the performance. These textual and scenic elements must have been constructive in engaging with the audiences at the Ruhrfestspiele in Recklinghausen (Germany) or the Wiener Festwochen in Vienna, both festivals being co-commissioners of the production with the Barbican, London, and the Théâtre de la Ville, Paris. However, this was not the case in London. Audiences were appreciative of Cate Blanchett's acting in the leading role of Lotte, but felt alienated by the German references. As a result, the performance was received as something exotic rather than familiar (see Musca 2012; Ferguson 2012).

As the above examples suggest, festival performances tend to create a common cultural field around themselves that engages with national and cultural differences in reception. Alterations on the production level are created to reach out to the respective target context and to involve audiences in a shared interpretation of the theatrical event. This purpose is also served by multidimensional translation praxis that involves surtitles, simultaneous translation (also called simultaneous interpretation in professional terminology), summarizing translation (printed synopsis) and alternative modes such as translation carriers built into the body of the production (e.g. digital translation running on a set element). As Yvonne Griesel observes in her study on surtitling theatre productions, the difficulty of the practice lies in the fact that in this case the source text is neither the foreign language play-text nor the performance text, but 'the production as a whole that needs to be taken into account when translating' (Griesel 2005: 2). As this type of translation practice happens in real-time, it also needs to follow the temporal framework of the production, depending almost entirely on the 'given situative context' (actors' speech, scene shifts etc.); hence, it is also close to the interpreting process (Griesel 2005: 2). Because the text is projected in sequences, translation is heavily reliant on theatrical or stage mechanisms (e.g. the actors' gesturing) to fill in the semantic gaps in reception. Griesel also acknowledges at this point that the audience's 'cultural memory' is also activated (Griesel 2005: 11). Arguably, such mechanical means of translation as surtitling and simultaneous interpretation do not have the ability to solve the complex issues of cultural transfers.

In a Europe-wide report created as a result of a research project examining the place of arts festivals in the European public culture, Giorgi et al. argue that international festivals 'act as translation spaces towards and for universality' (2011: 9). This sense of universality, however, is created by multilateral translation processes as seen above, in a shared cultural space. The study of *European Arts Festivals: Strengthening Cultural Diversity* further argues that:

> The identities crafted in festivals are not territorialised even if they are closely linked to their local settings or sense of place. They are also not fixed but rather transitory and ephemeral. Accordingly, festival identities are different from national identities which are another important vessel for cultural expression and display. It is this ephemeral and non-territorial aspect of festivals that lend support to the ideas of internationalism, cosmopolitanism and trans-nationalism.
>
> (Giorgi et al. 2011: 8)

I have quoted from this argument at length to point out the main aspects and issues incorporated in the debate on international festivals. On the one hand, festivals establish translocal and transnational identities by encouraging artistic and cultural exchanges. Consequently, they have a development function on artistic, local and national levels, resulting in new artistic methodologies, urban regeneration and national cultural branding. On the other hand, all these outcomes raise concerns and tensions between local and global values and communities. I will now reflect on these three aspects of the festival circuits arguing for the importance of a hybrid European theatrical space and theatrical community acknowledging translation (theatrical and cultural) as one of the most important channels of negotiations, exchange and collaboration.

As Roger Ellis points out, theatre festivals are not just international show-cases, but sites of 'cultural interpenetration' (Ellis 2008: 68). Theatrical and cultural exchanges are encouraged through both the artistic and the associated programmes such as workshops, symposia and other educational programmes closely linked to festivals. Through the establishment of these forums, spectators and theatre-makers can meet and exchange ideas, but also develop new cross-disciplinary approaches and physically engage in performance creation.

For instance, in Cluj/Kolozsvár[1] (Romania) at the first edition (2005) of the MAN.In.FEST – International Festival of Experimental Theatre, two workshop series ran during the time of the festival, a practice that featured in later editions of the festival as well. Both Izumi Ashizawa's Noh Theatre workshops and Joseph Ravens' workshop focusing on contemporary performance art ('happening', 'act' etc.) were open for audience and theatre-makers alike. An informal and welcoming environment was established to introduce new cultural traditions and aesthetic approaches to theatre-making, hence contributing to a quite physical experimentation (via movement workshops) of new theatre methodologies that would potentially reinvigorate theatre practices in a specific theatrical context.

This example also shows another important aspect of theatre festivals, that of bringing together different groups of participants. Social interactions are key to establishing hybrid festival communities and a cultural space for exchange. Festival communities are built on dialogue between individuals with 'shared experience of observing and making and somehow participating in the creative process' (Ellis 2011: 112). Interactive opportunities, public discussions and educational projects are also regularly associated with the main theatre programme at contemporary festivals. For example, the IATC Young Critics' seminar series organized by the International Association of Theatre Critics is mostly linked to international theatre festivals around Europe. Thus, it also stresses the importance of critical inquiry besides 'transmitting ideas of [...] openness, curiosity, [and] cultural diversity' (Giorgi et al. 2011: 68). As Giorgi et al. argue in their introduction to *European Arts Festivals*, festivals are 'sites of transnational identifications and *democratic debate*' (Giorgi et al. 2011: 6, emphasis added). I have emphasized the latter term to signal that festivals are also conductive occasions to discuss cultural issues, such as issues of changing European identity (see also Klaic 2012: 138). As they put it: '[...] festivals constitute sites of cultural expression and performance of relevance for European identity-in-the-making and for the European public sphere' (Giorgi et al. 2011: 6). The notion of public sphere in this account appears to denote a polycentric sociocultural space that brings together 'citizens for discussing issues of common (public) interest' (Giorgi et al. 2011: 69; see also Sassatelli and Delanty 2011: 54). The notion of 'transnational identification' stressed by this report implies a cosmopolitan festival public defined by the diversity of knowledge, experience and exchange (see Giorgi et al. 2011: 68). But what are the means of mediation between the different culturally determined knowledge and experiences?

Interestingly, the report does not give an answer to this rather important question. The authors of this study draw their observations on music, film, literature and multi-art festivals without engaging in debates on cultural translation. This would have been essential to map the patterns of exchange between artists and audience members. Ultimately, the cultural identity of a festival community is constructed through (cultural) translation. A reflection on theatre festivals in Europe is also absent from the study. This would have been beneficial in terms of highlighting the interactive nature of these events. In this respect, theatre represents a collaborative ground by its very definition.

Arguably, theatre translation activates both the creative communities of a production and the much larger communities of spectators/audiences as translating communities; also mediating between these communities. With their goal to create shared meanings (for and with the respective festival communities), festival productions also often implement dramaturgical solutions that address an audience with a different cultural and historical mindset. Here we can emphasize the role of adaptive processes in merging various cultural contexts.

In terms of theatre festivals, another important question arises, as Roger Ellis puts it: 'what kind of work will artists develop specifically for such a heterogeneous international audience?' (2008: 75). In a later study focusing on the audiences and the management styles of three European theatre festivals (Festival d'Automne à Paris; Hellenic Festival, Athens; and Mondial du Théâtre, Monaco), Ellis observes a number of trends in this respect. First, that a large number of productions being presented at these festivals are contemporary experimental work produced via crossovers 'developing hybrid art forms from different cultural traditions' (2011: 110). In Cluj/Kolozsvár more than half of the presented international productions (eight out of fourteen) at the Interferences Festival (2012) were cross-genre performances mixing opera, music, puppetry, dance, film and video art with theatrical performance (Interferences Festival Official Website 2012: n.pag.). Other festivals tend to present and promote regional artists, focusing on the work of nationally important companies or directors. Often though, in Eastern Europe, these two festival directions overlap due to the fact that the festivals are eager to position themselves within the overall European festival circuits after decades of cultural isolation under communist regimes. The Romanian National Theatre Festival in Bucharest for instance has an established international section besides showcasing nationally created work. Of course, this is a beneficial form of national cultural promotion as well, as I will show later on.

Lastly, Ellis observes an emerging tendency in festival circuits, that of commissioning new productions 'specifically designed to tour several European stages each season, serving multiple publics' (Ellis 2011: 110). I will discuss this in the next section of this chapter. Here, I just wish to note that this is another important form of theatrical activity that contributes to an ever-growing international theatre and arts market.

So far, I have looked at international theatre festivals as shared cultural fields where national and cultural differences are negotiated and where cultural value systems interact and are exchanged. I have also highlighted the social function of the festivals as places of debate arguing that sharing knowledge and exchanging experiences inevitably go through a process of cultural translation. Translation is also playing an important part in the creation of a 'global theatrical community' that emerges from international theatre festivals (Ellis 2008: 65). The forming of artistic and translating communities is just one of the outcomes of the developments festivals encourage on an artistic, urban and national promotion scale.

Klaic points out the festivals' development function in introducing 'emerging aesthetics', new professional discourses in the field and new methodologies and skills for actors (Klaic 2012: 138). These artistic developments are often supported by festival managements through various residency programmes where companies or individual artists are invited to participate for an extended period or throughout the entire festival period. During this time the company might present more works, participate in or lead workshops, and generally engage in professional networking, establishing itself within an international theatrical community (see Ellis 2008: 69). Festival presence of course also increases the visibility of the respective production (and the theatre-makers as well), and that might even have a positive effect on performance attendance in their domestic context; or – as Klaic argues – further (public) subsidy might be attracted (Klaic 2012: 139). As Ellis observes: 'Festival organisers, [...] have grown much more familiar with different cultural traditions, new aesthetic approaches, and diverse artistic standards [...]' (Ellis 2008: 74).

This potentially means that a multicultural approach and an awareness of cross-national issues would infiltrate the larger cultural systems of the respective festival-organizing context. Accordingly, festivals can 'stimulate the mobility [...] of artistic concepts and ideas' and obviously the movement of artists and their work (Klaic 2012: 139). In 2007, Sibiu/Hermannstadt, a Romanian city with a strong German-Saxon heritage was named European Capital of Culture. Around 400 cultural projects and more than 2000 cultural events ran throughout the year attracting 2 million visitors to the city of just 150,000 inhabitants (Sibfest Official Website 2007: n.pag.). This major cultural achievement was founded on the theatrical activities in the city, the work of the Romanian and German language theatre institutions and their joint organization of the annual Sibfest – Sibiu International Theatre Festival. In this case, the city's theatre festival launched a complete urban regeneration. As Chalcraft et al. argue in their analysis of festivals as cosmopolitan spaces: '[…] by the influx of festival-goers, the festivals become markers in a cultural calendar that fixes these spaces within a global cultural cartography' (Chalcraft et al. 2011: 27).

The Sibfest itself set off the cultural and economic revitalization of the city well before the European Cultural Capital programme, since its establishment more than two decades ago (1994), driven by intercultural collaborations. By 2007 a large tourist turnover ensured an international visibility. Hence, besides an economic input, a city brand was also created (see Giorgi et al. 2011: 7; Ellis 2008: 67–68). This promoted the city as a home of theatrical innovation and artistic experimentation. Both the festival and the year-long cultural project were arguably enhancing the visibility of the region/country as well. Another important aspect of the developments theatre festivals initiate is national promotion.

Beyond the political and economic impacts that can be generated by establishing a festival with an international outlook, presenting at one can also be beneficial in terms of nation branding. As Ellis asserts, the presence of a production at an international festival can be understood as a 'cultural passport' for a respective nation and is increasingly representing a global export (Ellis 2011: 73). Productions staged by German directors Michael Thalheimer (Deutsches Theater, Berlin) and Thomas Ostermeier (Schaubühne, Berlin), for example, may be seen as national cultural exports. Their frequent participation at festivals is very often supported by the Goethe-Institut, the national cultural institute operating worldwide, promoting German cultural products and facilitating cultural exchange. An extensive visibility guaranteed by such festivals arguably results in further invitations as festival directors, managers, theatre agents and so forth try to secure productions for their theatrical events globally. Hence, national and international tours and various partnerships are negotiated. Thomas Ostermeier's *Hamlet* production is a good example of such an extensive international circulation running for several years. *Hamlet* was co-produced by the Hellenic Festival of Athens and the Festival d'Avignon. Besides these two locations, the production was performed in nearly 30 locations globally between 2008 and 2016.

Reaching out to global audiences, however, raises a series of questions with regards to the translation processes and the aesthetics and ideologies of the production. In Roger Ellis' view, international festivals and touring raise questions regarding the relationship between local and global, regional or national specificity and global homogeneity (Ellis 2008: 71–73). Arguably, theatre productions are often deeply rooted in the correlations of their national or regional cultural systems. The majority of the European international theatre festivals however seem to invite works that show a certain level of 'universality', either in their aesthetics (the dominance of movement and visuals), the genre (opera, musical and cross-genre productions) or the language they speak (dominance of English and French). Productions that were informed and based on local communities or represent a regional or national identity do not travel well. When they do appear in the main programmes of mainstream festivals, they often tend to be presented as exotic shows rather than different segments of a hybrid theatrical landscape. Of course, this is also due to power relations and cultural closeness or distance between nations.

While Hungarian independent theatres circulate well in German-speaking contexts (Austria, Germany, Switzerland and Lichtenstein), Romanian theatres would rarely target these parts of Europe. In rare cases, Romanian theatre-makers found their way to German theatres by the themes they presented in their work. Gianina Cărbunariu for instance staged her play, *Sold Out* at the Münchenner Kammerspiele in 2010 presenting a theme frequently debated in Germany at that time. The production thematized the selling of the German-Saxon population of Transylvania by the Romanian communist authorities to West Germany during the 1970s and 1980s. Here, cultural relevancy was given by an ongoing cultural debate on this issue following the awarding of the Nobel Prize for Literature to Herta Müller in 2009, Müller herself being of German ethnicity from Romania, settling in Germany in 1987 after refusing to cooperate with the communist regime.

What this example demonstrates is that production mobility, relocations, transfers, international touring and the reception of these productions in a target context are very much affected by wider cultural, ideological and political discourses. Beyond the mainstream festivals, regional and local theatre festivals frequently present work specifically created with a community in mind. As Dragan Klaic rightly observes: 'Festivals with strong local anchoring [...] can be temporary platforms of resistance to globalisation with a capacity to integrate global issues and local circumstances, needs and aspirations' (Klaic 2012: 137).

The Reflex International Theatre Biennale, taking place in Sepsiszentgyörgy/ Sfântu Gheorghe (Romania) bi-annually, represents a new cultural and theatrical initiative, in the sense that it showcases the theatrical products of a geographical region (Central Europe) with a rather specific cultural identity. This festival has also established strong links with its local community. Regular post-show discussions with the different productions' crew mostly manage to go beyond the strict boundaries of a professional debate and addressed and engaged the general public as well, keeping in mind both the invited theatre professionals and the local community. Reflex invited in rather than ignored (as so often happens in the case of oversized theatre festivals all around Europe) the local community and theatre-goers, and generated a number of opportunities in order to reflect on both singular productions and the tendencies in contemporary theatre-making. Besides regular talks and discussions, two important platforms were introduced, an English-language workshop and a daily radio programme running on the local radio station discussing events and productions. While the radio programme connected thea-tregoers and theatre-makers through the online sound wave, the workshop series 'In/Between Reflex(ions)' was addressed to both national and international theatre students and was designed to help establish a new generation of theatre profes-sionals in Romania. By creating various platforms and opportunities to meet, share ideas and discuss trends and the diversity of contexts in contemporary theatre-making, the festival fulfilled its role to develop a wide range of responses to the performances seen. By definition, reflex means an automatic response to a stimulus; in this case, Reflex meant a conscious response involving curious obser-vation and creative rethinking of theatrical works and trends.

Roger Ellis concludes his argument on the contrasts between local and global within the international theatre circuit by pointing out a parallel existence where: '[...] both types of theatrical communities will coexist on world stages: the local with its specific regional or national concerns, as well as the global [...] with more universal, *supra-national* or *aesthetic* interests' (Ellis 2008: 74, emphasis added).

I have emphasized the terms 'supra-national' and 'aesthetic' in Ellis' argument to highlight that both terms are highly problematic with regard to theatre transla-tion. Both terms are used here to suggest a form of theatre-making that transcends national theatre traditions and conventions. But is such a level of 'universalism' really possible? And how do specific linguistic, cultural and theatrical communities integrate in this global structure?

Clearly, the role of theatre translation and translating communities is consid-erable due to the factors outlined above. Arguably, translating communities are involved in a mediating role between local and global within the hybridized cultural spaces created by international theatre festivals and other forms of cross-cultural collaboration. Also, translating communities are an indispensable element of emerg-ing new modes of production and forms of dissemination in the changing theatrical environment. In the case of jointly created performances, for instance where thea-tre-makers are representing different cultural backgrounds, translation processes would be active in channelling individual contributions to the overall dramatur-gical landscape of the performance, hence establishing a multi-layered, but inte-grative semantic landscape. In multilingual works, translation would also act as a dramaturgical mean. It creates the (theatrical) links between various linguistic elements within the production in order to generate meanings in reception. As multilingual works are often destined for international stages, it is important that the productions create an interpretative matrix that can be 'read' by different audiences.

As the examples so far have emphasized, theatre translation needs to accommodate cultural, theatrical as well as linguistic processes within its remits in order to be able to respond to such artistic and cultural developments.

Translating and Negotiating within a
Pan-European Theatrical Network

In this final part of the chapter, I will outline some important considerations regarding cross-national partnerships to show that translating communities often function as cultural agencies negotiating between different theatrical systems.

As raised previously, theatre partnerships became frequent theatrical activity in the past two decades, establishing expanded cultural networks across national borders throughout Europe. However, as Dragan Klaic points out, sustaining theatre partnerships on a creative level is rather difficult to attain because of the long-standing dominance of the dramatic mode of theatre-making (Klaic 2012: 140). That, of course, also implies that the European stages are specified by the language they use in their devising practices and performances. Although such dominance of language is constantly challenged by new forms of theatre-making (intermedial, movement-based etc. performance) and dissemination (e.g. via surtitles), monolingualism remains a main challenge in artistic partnerships today. Nonetheless, cooperations are more complex operations and involve artistic, financial, organizational negotiations as well as ethical dimensions. As Klaic argues:

> In a cooperation venture [...] much effort is inevitably required to sustain commonly agreed artistic objectives, keep the initial division of responsibilities among the partners and guard their mutual synergy, cope with the individual, group and institutional dynamics of change [...].
>
> (Klaic 2012: 141)

Changes in the artistic (workshops, trainings, devising, textual and performance processes) and organizational, logistic structures of partnerships are frequent. These projects tend to run typically over two or more years, depending on subsidy, so the initial artistic considerations rarely remain intact; on the contrary, they are constantly altered and amended. Also, cooperative projects tend to go beyond theatrical means and often create various platforms for learning and discussions in order to share and disseminate cultural values with members and audiences within and beyond their realm. The cultural products emerging from such partnerships also often address a diverse public: scholars, students and various other groups of the respective society.

The Union of Theatres of Europe (UTE) for example regularly initiate theatre projects designed to reflect on contemporary societal issues in the widest forms possible and involving theatres from several European regions. One of its latest projects, entitled TERRORisms was inaugurated in 2013 and ran until 2015 with partnership between theatres from seven countries. The participating theatres were: Staatsschauspiel Stuttgart (Germany), National Theatre of Oslo (Norway), Jugoslovensko Dramsko Pozoriste, Belgrade (Serbia), Habima National Theatre Israel (Tel Aviv), Young Vic Theatre London (UK), Shiber Hur Company (Palestine) and Comédie de Reims (France). As its title suggests, the cooperative project was focusing on terror and violence in all its forms; terrorism and the communities affected, the effects on public feelings (fears and confidences) and ultimately, the ways terrorism(s) can be performed in contemporary theatre (see Union of the Theatres of Europe 2013: n.pag.). The project is also designed to reach out, far beyond the stage and potentially beyond the two-year framework. For this goal, several outcomes were planned and realized. The project encouraged new writing, as all productions were based on new texts created specifically for TERRORisms by contemporary European playwrights. The Schauspielhaus Stuttgart premièred the first play, *5 Morgen,* written for the project by Fritz Kater and directed by Armin Petras (26 October 2013).[2] The project was also framed by two conferences bringing together theatre-makers, scholars and researchers to discuss topics related to the theme. One of these took place in September 2013 in Oslo, while a closing conference took place in Stuttgart in June 2015 together with an international theatre festival where all the works were performed. In addition, English and German translations of the plays were also developed as part of the project (see Union of the Theatres of Europe 2013: n.pag.).

This theatrical cooperation worked on three interlinked cultural levels. Conferences, round-table discussions etc. analysing the proposed theme, the newly created theatre texts gave textual (literary) appropriations, while production processes and exchanges gave performative approaches and created new cultural understandings on the subject matter. The festival on the other hand attempted to disseminate outcomes in an international reception context. Arguably, such a multilateral artistic scheme is conditioned by textual, performative and cultural translation processes. Bridging between cultural, theatrical and literary networks, translations as both processes and products are constructive in creating new meanings (and potentially canonizing them via drama translations) and facilitating intercultural dialogue. Consequently, translation functions as an interface between different networks, but also between the cultural products and the target public.

In Klaic's view, cross-national theatre partnerships contribute to the creation of an 'integrated European cultural space' (Klaic 2012: 144). As he rightly emphasizes, integration, however, does not mean cultural homogeneity, but is understandable rather as: 'A widening of opportunities to explore and engage cultural diversity and create *new cultural values* in the interaction of cultural traditions, habits, values and features' (Klaic 2012: 144, emphasis added).

I have emphasized Klaic's phrasing above to note that in the series of cultural and social interactions new values are also constructed. I would argue, however, that their integration (back) into the national cultural systems and canons often seems difficult and faces strong resistance. This is because cultural values in such artistic cooperations are created in a quasi-hermetic medium. The creative sphere here is artificially operated by various agreements, having its own unique logical structure and ways of responding to new ideas. In the cultural and social systems prevailing in contemporary societies, a more complex historical, social and political architecture exists that might not be responsive to such new cultural values (e.g. in societies that are still largely mono-cultural). Klaic's view is that such cooperations should be 'public project[s], supported by public authorities' because of their social functions (Klaic 2012: 144).

Rimini Protokoll's documentary theatre project entitled *100% City: A Statistical Chain Reaction* (2008–present), for example, builds on the theatre's social function to create new layers of understanding on the social reality and the mechanisms and dynamics of life in specific urban spaces. Helgard Haug, Stefan Kaegi and Daniel Wetzel's concept was first created in 2008 in Berlin (*100% Berlin*) and later redeveloped in cities around the world, often changing cultural contexts, creating a wave of performances: *100%-London* (2012), *Vienna* (2010), *Melbourne* (2012), *Tokyo* (2013), *Gwangju* (2014), *Vancouver* (2011) and so forth. The theatre recruited 100 individuals representing various social, cultural, religious, age and other groups from the respective cities, each of them representing 1 per cent of the inhabitants. The *100% City* performances create a playground with various group situations in which the participants form hybrid communities. The aim of the production is to give individual faces to statistical data and to show 'ephemeral portraits of belonging and antagonisms' (Rimini Protokoll Official Website 2013: n.pag.).

In Klaic's understanding, such cross-cultural and national theatre projects are effective ways of challenging 'deeply entrenched prejudices and stereotypes' and in approximating different cultural positions, developing common viewpoints. As he points out: 'Such artistic endeavours reduce the cultural distance [...], affirm cultural diversity as a common asset and teach audiences how to appreciate cultural differences rather than be intimidated by them or prompted to reject them as strange, incomprehensible and menacing' (Klaic 2012: 144).

International cultural collaborations and festivals would certainly develop their specific cosmopolitan audiences who are appreciative of such diversities. But how can international festivals and partnerships reach out to wider levels of the social spectrum and avoid frequent allegations of elitism? (See Harvie 2003 on this issue.) Various examples discussed in this chapter show that community theatre initiatives are very effective ways to discuss differences, integrate viewpoints and build shared cultural identities. Nevertheless, such theatrical and cultural processes involve complex negotiations both within and outside the creative process.

The examples discussed show an emerging international theatre market and a global web of theatrical communities that are involved in theatrical and cultural exchange worldwide via tours, partnerships, educational programmes, debates and so forth. I have argued that developments on artistic, reception and structural levels evidently expand the borders of theatre translation to a multidimensional textual, performative and cultural practice, and that this enables the creation of translating communities that function as an interface between theatrical and cultural networks. As I see it, translating communities are creative communities. They either work on theatrical creation (via staging a foreign play in translation, or working in collaboration with foreign artist[s] on theatrical project[s]) or as spectators, they become part of the translating community not only by receiving and responding to the productions via acts of further reflection and interpretation, but also by reviewing, commenting and various other ways of art criticism. Similarly to Stanley Fish's 'interpretive communities', translating communities are determined by shared knowledge created by dynamic cultural transfers. The meanings and interpretations are created on the shared basis of agreement, negotiated by the parties involved and situated within a sociocultural and aesthetic structure also created by the community (see Fish 1980: 303–21). The meanings generated by the translating communities in a certain cultural and theatrical context are created in a specific language. Nonetheless, they have meaning outside the larger community mainly because of the very nature of theatre as a creative medium that builds on different kinds of communication instances in its overall interpretive landscape: textual, visual and auditive.

REFERENCES

Chalcraft, Jasper, Magaudda, Paolo, Solaroli, Marco and Santoro, Marco (2011), 'Music festivals as cosmopolitan spaces', in L. Giorgi, M. Sassatelli, M. Santoro, G. Delanty, J. Chalcraft and M. Solaroli, *European Arts Festivals: Strengthening Cultural Diversity*, Luxembourg: Publications Office of the European Union, pp. 25–37.

Ellis, Roger (2008), 'Globalism and the festival circuit', *Grand Valley Review*, 34:1, pp. 65–76.

—— (2011), 'Serving publics: International theatre festivals and their global audiences', *International Journal of Humanities and Social Science*, 1:14, pp. 110–17.

Ferguson, Euan (2012), '*Big and Small (Gross und Klein)* review', *The Guardian*, 15 April, https://www.theguardian.com/film/2012/apr/15/big-small-gross-klein-review. Accessed 20 November 2017.

Fish, Stanley (1980), *Is There a Text in This Class?*, New York: Harvard University Press.

Giorgi, Liana, Sassatelli, Monica, Santoro, Marco, Delanty, Gerard, Chalcraft, Jasper and Solaroli, Marco (2011), *European Arts Festivals: Strengthening Cultural Diversity*, Luxembourg: Publications Office of the European Union.

Griesel, Yvonne (2005), 'Surtitles and translation: Towards an integrative view of theatre translation', in *MuTra 2005 – Challenges of Multidimensional Translation: Conference Proceedings*, Saarbrücken: Saarland University, http://www.euroconferences.info/ proceedings/2005_Proceedings/ 2005_Griesel_Yvonne.pdf. Accessed 8 January 2014.

Harvie, Jen (2003), 'Cultural effects of the Edinburgh International Festival: Elitism, identities, industries', *Contemporary Theatre Review*, 13:4, pp. 12–26.

Interferences Festival Official Website (2012), 'Performances', http://old.huntheater.ro/interferences/eloadas.php. Accessed 5 June 2019.

Klaic, Dragan (2012), *Resetting the Stage: Public Theatre between the Market and Democracy*, Bristol and Chicago: Intellect.

Lavender, Andy (2016), *Performance in the Twenty-First-Century*, London and New York: Routledge.

Musca, Szabolcs (2012), 'Liebe, liebe Lotte', fidelio.hu, 19 May, http://fidelio.hu/szinhaz/kritika/liebe_liebe_lotte. Accessed 1 July 2012.

Rimini Protokoll Official Website (2013), '100% City Project Description', http://www.rimini-protokoll.de/website/en/project_6337.html. Accessed 10 February 2014.

Sassatelli, Monica and Delanty, Gerald (2011), 'Festivals in cities, cities in festivals', in L. Giorgi, M. Sassatelli, M. Santoro, G. Delanty, J. Chalcraft and M. Solaroli, *European Arts Festivals: Strengthening Cultural Diversity*, Luxembourg: Publications Office of the European Union, pp. 47–57.

Sibfest Official Website (2007), http://www.sibfest.ro/general/en-editions. Accessed 20 March 2014.

Union of the Theatres of Europe Official Website (2013), 'TERRORisms project description', http://www.union-theatres-europe.eu/UNIQ139472972125425/terrorisms. Accessed 3 March 2015.

Editors' Note

Festival studies and international theatre festivals in particular is a relatively new area of study. Keren Zaiontz's recently published *Theatre and Festivals* (2018) provides a good overview of recent development in this field and especially on collective/community aspects of arts festivals. Although not within the immediate geographical context of Musca's chapter, Christina S. McMahon's *Recasting Transnationalism Through Performance: Theatre Festivals in Cape Verde, Mozambique and Brazil* (2014) looks at theatre festivals as sites of cultural dialogue amidst a global arts market. For further reading on cross-cultural performance and cosmopolitanism, also see Gilbert and Lo (2009).

Further reading

Gilbert, Helen and Lo, Jaqueline (eds) (2009), *Performance and Cosmopolitics: Cross-Cultural Transactions in Australasia,* Basingstoke: Palgrave Macmillan.

McMahon, Christina S. (2014), *Recasting Transnationalism Through Performance: Theatre Festivals in Cape Verde, Mozambique and Brazil,* Basingstoke: Palgrave Macmillan.

Zaiontz, Keren (2018), *Theatre and Festivals,* Basingstoke: Palgrave Macmillan.

NOTES

1. I am using both the Hungarian and Romanian (and the German, where applicable) denomination of the cities in accordance with the European Union's minority policies, the European Charter for Regional or Minority Languages (ECRML) created in 1992.

2. Other plays written as part of this UTE project include: *The Dragonslayers* by Milena Marković (2015), *God Waits at the Station* by Maya Arad (2014), *We Chew on the Bones of Time* by Jonas Corell Petersen (2015) and *La Baraque* by Aiat Fayez (2015).

The Economic Communities of the Edinburgh August Festivals: An Exclusive 'Global Sense of Place' and an Inclusive 'Local Sense of Space'

Evi Stamatiou

This chapter proposes to use a cultural materialist analysis and draws upon Doreen Massey's writings (1991, 1994, 2007, 2012) on place, community and the 'sense of place' in order to explore the imagined theatrical communities of Edinburgh's August Festivals (EAFs). 'EAFs' is used as an umbrella term for the four festivals that take place during that time: the Edinburgh International Festival (EIF), the Edinburgh Festival Fringe (EFF), the Free Festival and the Edinburgh International Book Festival. Being an academic and theatre-maker, this essay is informed by my own empirical experience as a theatre-maker performing at the EAFs in 2013. During this experience I negotiated my belonging and otherness in relation to theatrical communities that were defined not by geography or social relations but by the economy of the EAFs. The four main communal identities of the EAFs were: commodities (e.g. artists), consumers (e.g. audiences), direct profit-makers (e.g. promoters, producers, venue owners) and indirect profit-makers (e.g. local businesses).

I created the solo show *Caryatid Unplugged* especially for EFF in August 2013 and I aimed to explore my sense of belonging and otherness in relation to the imagined communities of 'Greekness', European and cosmopolitan. The main themes of the show were informed by my growing fear that, as a result of my uncertain Greek citizenship status after the economic crisis, I would be deported from the United Kingdom, and my nostalgia for the Greek Parthenon marbles, which are kept in the British Museum. In the performance, Rita – a Greek woman – and the Caryatid – the feminized marble column from the British museum – meet in a border office in an airport in London where Rita faces deportation because she is a Greek citizen and the Caryatid is not allowed to leave the country because she belongs to the British Museum. I have written elsewhere (Stamatiou 2017) about how the dramaturgy of the piece and my interaction with the audience allowed me to negotiate my multiple identities: my 'Greekness', rooted in my Greek citizenship, my linguistic habitus as a Greek native speaker and my closeness to the Ancient Greek heritage; my Europeanness, rooted in Greece's membership in the European Economic Area, in my linguistic habitus as a fluent speaker of English, Italian and French and in my sharing of European cultural identities during the EAFs; and finally, my cosmopolitanism, rooted in intercultural consumption, in the idea of an imagined universal community and in the idea of a cosmopolitan democracy, in which each culture has equal symbolic power (see Gilbert and Lo 2007). However, this cultural negotiation, which allowed for the specific power-relations of the festival to emerge, did not take place in a vacuum but within the economic negotiations of the EAFs. These economic negotiations allowed for the specific experience of the theatre-maker to negotiate belonging and otherness within the hybrid economic communities of the EAFs.

Caryatid Unplugged addressed the issue of the show's material conditions in a self-aware and self-reflective way. It critically reflected on my naivety about the festival before the show went into production. My ensuing disappointment drove me to examine my naivety. The show's solo format is a primary example of how the material realities of the EAFs determined the performance. Early in the show, John, the puppet immigration officer, says:

> If you could afford any more actors, you would have cast a whole bloody Greek chorus. But you can't! Because you are Greek! This is the new Greek theatre austerity form; Solo performance ahahahaha Where is the bloody chorus, love? Where is the god from the machine, love? You couldn't even afford some proper lighting for your show!
>
> (Stamatiou 2013: 2)

Throughout the performance, I lampooned the material inadequacies of the show to enact my identity of the less economically powerful artist. This highlighted a contradiction of the show: I was negotiating my belonging and otherness with the same audience that was consuming me, the artist, as cultural commodity, but only in case they could afford the ticket.

The analysis offers insights into the commodification and otherness of the less powerful participants of the EAFs and poses questions about the commodification of Fringe art. It challenges Massey's idea of a 'global sense of place' (Massey 1994: 147) by showing that, during the EAFs, Edinburgh's attempt to reach out to the global is primarily aimed towards the more powerful individuals of the globe, and that the EAF communities are, therefore, exclusive global communities. Consequently, the 'global sense of place' is itself a privilege determined primarily by economic relations and secondarily by space and time. However, I conclude with a positive insight: because my perspective was that of a less powerful artist/participant, in terms of economic, social and cultural capital, for the duration of the festival the EAF communities offered me a spatial and temporal membership to an imagined community defined by the everyday economic interactions, leaving me with a 'local sense of place'. Having said that, I need to clarify that even though artists' power often relates to theatre dichotomies as mainstream vs fringe, commercial vs non-commercial, entertainment vs avant-garde, I consider that the artists themselves do not operate within binaries but rather, they operate within an intersecting gamut with mainstream or commercial or entertainment at one end and fringe or non-commercial or avant-garde at the other end of the same intersecting spectrum; and there are as many variations of artists' power in between those ends as the number of participating artists at the EAFs.

Place, Community and Communal Identities at the EAFs

Massey writes that 'place and community have only rarely been coterminous', and that, to understand a place, one needs to consider the other parts of the world that are connected with it (Massey 1994: 147). This relates to the well-known concept of a 'global sense of place'. Edinburgh is not determined by a homogeneous and coherent imagined community; rather, it needs to be considered relationally as a product of its interactions with the rest of the world. Massey writes that interpreting a 'sense of place' as a homogeneous and coherent community can provide 'stability and a source of unproblematical identity', and is 'a form of escapism from the real business of the world' (Massey 1994: 151). The communal identities in Edinburgh are multiple and are constructed through the interactions of individuals who are negotiating their belonging and otherness. The economic interactions of individuals at the EAFs create hybrid economic communities.

Four broad communal identities are created through the individuals' economic interactions during the EAFs: commodities (e.g. the artists who are portrayed in posters around the city as products ready for sale), consumers (e.g. audience members who not only consume the events of the festival but are also tourists in the city who consume food, book accommodation and participate in tourist activities), direct profit-makers (e.g. promoters, producers, venue owners, who profit directly from the EAFs) and indirect profit-makers (e.g. local business people who do not profit directly from the EAFs, but whose profits are maximized by the influx of artists and audiences).[1] An individual can fluidly move between two or more of these identities. For example, when I was at the EAFs in August 2013, I identified as a commodity (as an artist), a consumer (as an audience member for other shows, a restaurant customer etc.) and a profit-maker (an entrepreneur who was producing her own show), depending on my particular economic interactions.

Drawing from Benedict Anderson's analysis of the nation as 'an imagined political community' (Anderson 2006: 5), I invite the reader to consider the economic communities of the EAFs as also imagined and not real communities. Anderson suggests that 'all communities larger than primordial villages of face-to-face contact (and perhaps even these) are imagined. Communities are to be distinguished, not by their falsity/genuineness, but by the style in which they are imagined' (Anderson 2006: 6). Anderson does not imply that the communities that are not face-to-face do not exist, but he suggests that there are different ways in which they are established in the individual's imagination. For example, in 2013, I imagined that there was a community of artists in Edinburgh during the EAFs, to which I wished to belong. The artists were thousands in numbers, and therefore they formed a limited community, and regardless how little or how much power they held, I had a feeling that I would experience in this imagined community what Anderson describes 'a deep, horizontal comradeship' (Anderson 2006: 7). This imagined community felt political because it had its own interests and values that differed to the ones of other imagined communities during the EAFs. For example, I imagined that there would be a shared deep sense of inclusion and respect for all artists and also a shared artistic identity, and this imagined dynamism was compensating for my material inadequacies.

Although I sometimes identified with other members of the imagined economic community of artists, members of a community do not all share the same experiences. Massey suggests that to identify a place with a community is a 'misidentification' (Massey 1994: 153). Communities can exist without their members being in the same geographical place, and they rarely comprise coherent social groups. Even though individuals belong to the same community and one would expect that they would experience a shared 'sense of place', due to their individual characteristics, like race and gender, they experience a different 'sense of place' (Massey 1994: 147). Similarly, the 'sense of place' of commodities, consumers and profit-makers is conditioned by their individual economic interactions. For example, some do well in the EAFs but others do not. When members of the EAFs communities say, 'I did well in Edinburgh',[2] rather than, 'I did well in the EAFs', they are understood, because the city is identified with the economic interactions that take place during the EAFs.

Massey's idea that members of the same community in the same place can have a different 'sense of place' invites an analysis of the power relations within communities and the different communal identities in a single place. Massey's concept of power geometry enables us to question the idea that capitalism and its developments are sufficient to determine our 'sense of place'. She identifies that individuals' experience is also influenced by their ethnicity, gender and other multiple identities. Power geometry indicates that some people have more power and more control over global flows and movements than others. The fact that my show was about what it means to be a Greek woman in the United Kingdom and Europe after the Greek economic crisis worked with and against the material reality of 'not doing well in Edinburgh'. My 'sense of place' immediately related to my perspective of an artist who holds little economic and non-economic capital and I assume that this experience was probably as similar and as different as in the case of all other members of the artists' community.

The power geometry of the ephemeral material community, which is defined by the spatial dimensions of Edinburgh in August, does not grant all of its members the same 'sense of place'. The community also includes local residents, but even their 'sense of place' during the EAFs is changing and is related to power deriving from economic interactions. For example, a restaurant can be a hot-spot one year because it is located across the road from a crowded pop-up venue and therefore attracts indirect profits from the EAFs, but not the next year because the pop-up venue might not appear. In the materialist analysis of *Caryatid Unplugged*, I aim to show how I fluidly moved between different communal identities during the EAFs while having little power over the interactions that took place and shaped my identities.

The Fantasy of Edinburgh in August

In order to explain to the reader how I developed my specific view of the EAFs' hybrid economic communities, I will use my material experience in relation to the ideological evolution of the EAFs. The EIF was launched after World War II. Its purpose was to be an 'enactment of a European communion' (Steiner in Harvie 2003: 14). I chose to perform *Caryatid Unplugged* at the EAFs not merely to showcase my work but because of EIF's original mission, Edinburgh seemed to be the ideal place to negotiate the Greek/European crisis and the EAFs' relation to the imagined community of Europe. Edinburgh in August was imagined to be a *place-time*[3] where an international artist like me would enact their belonging to an international artistic community. For *Caryatid Unplugged*, Edinburgh functioned as an imaginary symbolic place where I could enact my membership in a European imaginary community from the perspective of the culturally less powerful. The choice of the city was of major importance for such a symbolism. For example, in Athens or London, the political question of 'Greekness' and the status of the Parthenon marbles would likely have been overpowered by the importance of the 'Europeanness' and, by extension, the focus would have been distracted from belonging and otherness of the theatre-maker to the one of a cultural agent.

Edinburgh in August becomes, as Massey describes London in *World City*, 'the whole world in one city', a 'meeting place', 'open rather than bounded', 'hospitable rather than exclusive and excluding' and 'ever changing rather than eternal' (2007: 4). Although there are indications that the EAFs have turned Edinburgh to an international city all year round, the festivals' intensity and the influx of great numbers of audiences and artists[4] cause very distinctive hybrid spatial-temporal communities to emerge: the EAFs' communities. For eleven months, Edinburgh's flows and connections spread around the world. Commodities, consumers, direct and indirect profit-makers prepare for the EAFs by making shows, business plans, travel plans and other economic arrangements. During August, these flows and connections gather in Edinburgh. A great number of people come to the city and a large number of economic interactions take place. However, the neo-liberal community that allows conditional freedom and tolerance for every newcomer or 'other' artist did not fulfil my fantasy of finding a city that was 'hospitable rather than exclusive and excluding' (Massey 2007: 4).

The specific part of the EAFs that has been traditionally accessible to independent artists like myself is the EFF. The EFF arose in response to the EIF's exclusivity, in terms of both artists and audiences. In her analysis of the aims and objectives of the EIF, Harvie observes that 'the Festival reproduces this elitism, reinforcing and propagating its imbalances of cultural power and its anti-democratic effects' (2003: 13), and suggests that, although the elitism may not have 'produced' the EFF, it certainly 'provoked' it (Harvie 2003: 14). No matter how romantic the motivation behind the creation of the EFF was, by 2013 it seemed to have become integral to the assertion and spread of neo-liberalism. I experienced this through my participation as an artist/entrepreneur, who produced her own show and was allowed to participate in the competition of attracting audiences with the aim to achieve economic viability at the EAFs. However inclusive this participation was envisaged at the beginning, the difficulty to compete within a market where established artists and producers had been operating for decades triggered a feeling of intensified economic and cultural powerlessness. My intensified cultural commodification as the 'other artist' was my only and necessary 'selling point'. Interestingly, this commodified 'otherness' seemed to hold a positive value because my cultural offer was expected and welcome. However, because I identified as a Greek, a woman, a newcomer and a low-budget performer, I had less of a cultural power within the economic hybrid community of the artists.

The EFF's slogan, 'Defying the norm since 1947', is indicative of its mission and vision and suggests that the festival is not dependent on the neo-liberal market tendencies that became the norm after the 1970s. From my own material experience in 2013, I would argue that the EFF does not reflect freedom and tolerance for newcomer artists/entrepreneurs but rather leaves them vulnerable to be commodified by the direct profit-makers who have established specific power circuits. Analysing cultural power from a materialist perspective enabled me to identify how material conditions amplified my risk and vulnerability and defined my belonging and otherness in relation to the EAFs community. As Harvie writes, 'a cultural materialist analysis concerns itself with material detail to understand not merely what theatre is but more important, what theatre's political effects are, as well as how they might be changed' (Harvie 2009: 6). I cannot claim that my material conditions are the same as those of all Fringe artists, but they raise questions about the commodification and power geometry of Fringe art. In *World City*, Massey refers to Ken Livingstone's commitment to 'diversity and hospitality' (Massey 2007: 4) in making London a world city. In Edinburgh during the EAFs, diversity and hospitality are highly dependent on the material conditions of the artist.

I performed *Caryatid Unplugged* at the Hill Street Theatre in Edinburgh's new town. It was far from the crowded high street but close to the Book Festival. The theatre is a pop-up venue that does not function as a theatre throughout the rest of the year. Consequently, it did not have an established audience, so it aimed to attract the temporary audiences that visited the EAFs. The venue's location made it hard for last-minute audiences to find the theatre space. Edinburgh is a crowded city in August, but the Hill Street Solo Theatre Festival took place in a very quiet alley. Even local audiences were not aware of its location.

Although I belonged to the imaginary community of the cultural commodities that are offered for consumption during EFF, the remote pop-up venue and the solo nature of the festival emphasized my 'otherness'. In this manner, the Hill Street Theatre supported the political nature of *Caryatid Unplugged* as 'theatre of the margins, [which] continues to signify illegitimacy, a signification many fringe theatres cultivate to create associations of outsider identity and radicalism' (Harvie 2009: 26). If Edinburgh is a global city, then *Caryatid Unplugged* contributed to the city's political responsibility. Massey writes that a place needs to ask, and try to answer the question, '[w]hat does this place stand for?' (2007: 10). Massey considers that this question is urgent and necessary for world cities because they have more 'responsibility in the sense of the magnitude of their effects' (2007: 10). Although politics did not seem to be a priority in the 2013 EAFs, *Caryatid Unplugged* was still included in the festival and I was allowed to present the politics of an outsider identity. Massey continues that a place's political responsibility to address the above question is not only for the local state, but also for all those who 'take part of their identity from the fact that they are here'

(Massey 2007: 10). As an individual who desired to be a member of the Edin-
burgh Fringe artistic community, my exploration of European politics in *Caryatid
Unplugged* seemed to be reflective of a political responsibility that the Edinburgh
Fringe had little interest in at the time. By presenting a piece of work that posed
both direct and indirect political questions, I was asking the Edinburgh Fringe:
'What does Fringe art stand for?'

My intensified feeling of exclusion made the question 'what does Fringe art
stand for?' more urgent and I wondered whether more Fringe artists had similar experiences. Jane Wills, in reflecting on Massey's understanding of the politics of place, suggests that, notwithstanding the significance of global flows and
connections in constituting places such as Edinburgh, it is important to acknowledge the 'locally rooted traditions that may provide valuable political and democratic resources' that can 'allow collective mobilisation around common interests'
(Wills 2013: 133–45). The creation of the Free Festival, which I will discuss in
the next section, derives from a tradition rooted within the EAFs' communities –
an imaginary place within the city of Edinburgh – to resist exclusion of all kinds,
such as taste or financial power.

The Economic Interactions of Caryatid Unplugged

Belonging to the EAFs' community places particular profit-making expectations
on the Fringe artist. Hill Street charged relatively high rent, which affected the
price of the tickets. A ticket for *Caryatid Unplugged,* a play by an unknown artist,
cost £12, whereas a ticket for Steven Berkoff's *An Actor's Lament* cost £20. *Caryatid Unplugged's* high ticket price excluded many people from the performance –
especially young audiences, who otherwise seemed enthusiastic about the show.[5]
Harvie writes that class stratification pervades theatre economies, due to ticket
prices and other forms of capital (2009: 37). The ticket price determined the audiences with which I negotiated my identities. This exclusivity made me a cultural
commodity only for those who could afford it.

I later discovered that there was a part of the EAFs that aimed for audiences who
could afford only certain ticket prices. The Free Festival gives people the opportunity to pay nothing, or as much as they can afford, to see shows. It was started in
2004 in response to the fact that Festival Fringe promoters and venue owners, taking
advantage of the popularity of the festival, had raised their prices. The problem is
such that a performer can sell all the tickets for all the nights at his or her venue and
still make a loss, with the biggest complaint by Fringe-goers being the high price of
tickets. Fringe-goers have blamed artists for the high ticket prices, but it is usually
the venue that sets the prices, often against the wishes of performers.[6]

The management of the Hill Street Theatre was aware of the Free Festival's economic activity and tried to compete with it at the expense of the artists. We were asked to provide special offers and two-for-one tickets one hour before the show, which meant that I had to pay someone £7 per hour to try to sell cheap tickets to last-minute audiences. If any were sold, I would get £6, rather than £12, per ticket. At this price, I was making a loss because of the high rent. According to the Free Festival's website, £6 is a reasonable price for my show:

> The more a show costs, the less people are willing to take a chance on it. If a show featuring an unknown artist costs less than £5, you may take a chance on it. If the same show costs over £10, you probably won't. A Fringe needs to be cheap so it is accessible, or else people will merely see the performers who are already famous – and they don't need a Fringe! The only shows that put money in the pockets of the artists are usually the shows of the already famous.
>
> (The Free Festival 2016)

My position as a Fringe artist seemed less powerful than that of a Free Festival artist, because I was operating within the EAFs' market, which is materially challenging for the artists. My romanticism about the Fringe Festival indicated that I was still functioning within a pre-neo-liberal rationale, which derived from the time when the Edinburgh Fringe was the 'financially radical choice' and its shows took place outside the economic interactions of the dominant EIF. The post-1970s neo-liberal values that determined EFF's exclusive economy led to the creation of the Free Festival, which sought to find ways of functioning outside the neo-liberal economic framework. The Free Festival was created in reaction to the power dynamics of the Edinburgh Fringe, just as the Fringe was created in reaction to the power dynamics of the EIF. The trigger in both cases was the exclusivity of the larger festival, which caused the liberal community to look for ways to restructure the EAFs outside the profit-driven economic market.

This liberal community that functions within the EAFs seems to have supported my function and determination within the EAFs. As stated in the introduction, when I realized that negotiating my belonging from the perspective of a 'less powerful' member of the EAFs community was another determinant political factor that highlighted my 'otherness', I decided to make it integral to *Caryatid Unplugged*, in which I was already expressing my politics of the 'other'. Alison Oddey writes that it is important 'for the deviser to create work that expresses her beliefs and politics and addresses her own needs' (2013: 11). *Caryatid Unplugged* originally aimed to express my politics as experienced outside the EAFs but when I faced the challenging material realities of the EAFs the play resulted to be about the inside politics of the EAFs as well.

The play itself was difficult to create, due to my limited budget and problems with my collaborators, but my need to communicate made me determined to complete the project. I did so despite the material resistance. I embedded my determination to finish the project in the script and performance. I had limited time to rehearse in the theatre space before the opening night and the first preview was the second time during which I was rehearsing with the set and props. The first preview was instrumental to how the script would change as a result of incorporating all the extra-theatrical hardships of the show's creation.

After five minutes in the first preview, the paper-lips of the puppet Rita, which also had a mop-body and CDs-eyes, fell off. In an attempt to keep the audiences focused despite the props' failure, I broke off character and within a mixture of worry and auto-sarcasm, I improvised saying: 'oops, Rita needs a makeover after the show'. The audience laughed and their laughter was encouraging. Five minutes later and ten minutes in the show, there was a flashback song, a parody of Pulp's 1995 song 'Common People' (Stamatiou 2013: 5). During the song, I had to transform the 'puppet theatre stage' into a 'shadow theatre curtain', behind which I would perform Rita's flashback story, and then change the 'shadow theatre curtain' back to the 'puppet theatre stage'. The change proved to be impossible and the poorly made set fell apart. I was singing while struggling with the set and the audience was laughing and this laughter encouraged me to use my failure and transform it into a clown 'slapstick' scene that celebrated failure. During the musical bridge of the song, I managed to concentrate and fix the set. I improvised and addressed the audience: 'Low-budget stories. This is where Greek austerity theatre is heading to'. Similar lines were used later in the show, for example when the lipstick I would use to write on my body would break or when I could not find specific parts of the costume. The material realities of the show added an extra layer where I would negotiate with the audience my identity as the artist who lacked economic capital and was challenged by the EAFs' economies and could not foresee how the sharing of culture in the EAFs can be undermining and humiliating for artists of specific capital.

During the 23 shows' run at the EAFs, I got used to the dysfunctional set and costumes but I incorporated the humiliating impact of my material inadequacies within the script of the show. During the musical bridge of 'Common People', I added the patter:

> Now there is a long musical bridge. Usually, we have some Greek people late-comers joining us. Or the set just falls apart. Low-budget stories. Lately, I am managing the set better and Greek people cannot afford the ticket anyway. So we still have some time for choreography.
>
> (Stamatiou 2013: 6)

I would finish the musical bridge with a clumsy choreography with the puppets. As Nick Awde observed in his review: 'Gleefully blaming her low-budget show on Greece's economy, Stamatiou flips in and out of physical and clown-style roles, occasionally bursting into song, and creates extra characters from mops – Rita and John' (Awde 2013). I embraced the material conditions of the show to highlight how the material conditions of the EAFs further intensified my feeling of powerlessness and for comic effect. Awde continued: 'It's a little rough and ready, but Stamatiou turns this to her advantage plot-wise, while her infectious delivery wins over the audience' (Awde 2013). Even though the script was already self-aware about how the extra-theatrical economic aspect of the show affected its form and dramaturgy, the theatrical struggle with the poorly made set and costumes was constantly holding a mirror in front of me where I could see the reflection of my minimalist capital. This added to the self-awareness of the show and challenged my own confidence and control over the material that I had created and was performing. The material inadequacies seemed to be challenging on the levels of my own social capital as an artist, my reputation, and made me consider that my choice to perform comedy, which often welcomes failure as a device for comic effect, was coincidentally extremely useful.

The performance was under-rehearsed because some collaborations failed at the last minute and because I had little space. My accommodation was provided through the support of Greek residents of the city. Edinburgh is so crowded in August that I had to rehearse the show in some unexpected places, such as the bathroom of the house in which I was staying. Conscious that I had just rehearsed my *grand oeuvre* in a bathroom, I observed that I was enacting the communal identity of the powerless who surrenders to the economy of the EAFs in a bathroom both inside and outside the performance space.

Someone with prior experience of the EAFs might wonder why I expected otherwise, but as a romantic newcomer I was unaware of the EAFs' material reality. It was only during the show's production that I realized that EFF shows are considered successful if they manage to recuperate the money invested into the production. The great influx of people to Edinburgh during the EAFs raises rents, and securing funding seems impossible. When I approached a charity for funding I was told that it would not fund anything political, and through crowdfunding I made barely enough money for the poorly made set and costumes.

It is very difficult to make a profit at the EAFs. Artists usually focus on getting good reviews and meeting producers, so they can take their shows to other venues, festivals and tours. Members of the EAFs' communities therefore not only come from around the world, but aim to spread globally in every possible direction. Artists come to the EAFs to promote their work globally. Their economic interactions in Edinburgh are an investment in their global appeal and future profitability.

I do not assume that all artists think as such, but the EAFs' communities seem distinctively outward-looking and, at times, vain.

The Exclusive 'Global Sense of Space' and the Inclusive 'Local Sense of Space'

Nevertheless, even from the perspective of the 'less powerful', I was still able to participate in the EAFs, interact economically and negotiate my communal identities, which is not possible for someone less powerful than the EAFs' 'less powerful'. The fact that the EAFs exclude not only particular artists but particular audiences is at odds with the romanticized idea of the EAFs as somewhere to share culture, and suggests that they are 'overweening, grotesquely outsized and highly commercialized' (Michael Billington in Harvie 2003: 25) and have turned the city of Edinburgh into a 'cultural desert' and a 'shortbread Disneyland' (Irvine Welsh in Harvie 2003: 25). Edinburgh during the festivals offers an amplified 'global sense of space', but only to those who can afford to participate in its economic activities.

The extent to which an artist would afford to participate in the EAFs is immediately linked to their cultural capital, which Pierre Bourdieu has described as the symbolic goods that an individual has accumulated, which can turn into economic capital (Bourdieu 2003: 64). The international community of artists at the EAFs did not seem to be homogenous as I had imagined it but seemed to be operating within a classification system that is linked to both material and symbolic goods. Both the material and symbolic capital linked to how much exposure in posters, promotional material and theatre reviews the artists would get and this was amplified and determined by the profit-makers of the EAFs. Established artists would use their social capital from previous exposure whereas newcomers would focus on their 'edgy', 'provocative' and 'innovative' work that seemed to be the 'legitimate' symbolic capital for a newcomer artist. Both established and newcomers would use their capital with the aim to attract audiences and further invest in their symbolic capital – reputation – and ultimately transform the symbolic capital into economic capital. In the meantime, they would also participate in the EAFs as consumers, choosing to consume what could be called 'legitimate' culture that would further amplify their own symbolic capital.

The distribution of the artists' and festival organizers' capital was functioning simultaneously locally in the city of Edinburgh and globally. Harvie observes that:

> our city is local when we act locally, when we share experiences with our neigh-
> bours in the streets or in the theatre. It is global when we recognize how it is
> linked beyond its borders: our neighbours may be immigrants, as we ourselves

might be; we hear many languages on its streets; we buy things here from far away – including tickets to international theatre events. In a 1991 article, geographer Doreen Massey has famously called this sense of the global in the local 'a global sense of place'.

(Harvie 2009: 74)

During the EAFs, Edinburgh transforms into the 'city of the festivals', characterized by pop-up venues and pop-up 'others' and identities. It is expected that the pop-up 'others' will be in Edinburgh, and they are appreciated for their presence – maybe more because they are cultural commodities that support the city's economy and less because they share culture. They are allowed for the month to have a sense of belonging in the imaginary EAFs' communities. Such 'other' identities are not obscured by a minority or an inferior status, but function within the 'neo-liberal equality', which allows them to represent their 'otherness' and do their 'other thing' for the duration of the EAFs. Their 'artist/commodity' communal identity also puts them into the vulnerable position of trading within the established economic circuit of the profit-makers, whereas their 'consumer' identity makes them most welcome for both direct and indirect profit-makers.

This kind of membership allows for a temporary and conditional locality. People become neighbours, friends and co-workers for the month, and this locality slowly unravels as the days pass. Each day feels longer because of its intensity. This extends the duration of a person's locality to the duration of an intense month, which is different to the sense of time outside the festivals. The locals of the 'festival city' include Edinburgh residents and national and international artists and audiences. They might identify themselves as locals, nationals, internationals, immigrants or foreigners, but within the fluidity and multiplicity of their identities there is a resonance with a cosmopolitan identity that allows them to become members of an exclusive 'universal community'. Edinburgh in August becomes a city where one can have an intense experience of participating in an exclusive international and diverse community.

This community reframes the city in opposition to what Massey and Harvie describe as 'the sense of the global in the local "a global sense of space"' (Harvie 2009: 74). Edinburgh in August offers a sense of the local in the global. I would call it 'a local membership sense of space'. This sense of 'local membership' worked with and against the cultural commodification of *Caryatid Unplugged,* and allowed me to negotiate my belonging and otherness in relation to the EAFs' economic communities. It relates not to the durational local that the city of Edinburgh offers but the temporal local that the EAFs' communities construct.

Caryatid Unplugged offered its otherness for consumption and contributed to Edinburgh's local economy both directly and indirectly. From my position as an

145

entrepreneur and consumer of both culture at the EAFs and also products and services during my everyday interactions, I not only contributed to the local economy but I also economically contributed to the EAFs and the culture of the city. Due to my consumption in Edinburgh, I was granted temporal locality. From a global perspective, *Caryatid Unplugged* offered an identity representation of a participant with a lower symbolic value and capital. In a certain form, it served universal cosmopolitan values of intercultural sharing but it also invited EAFs' hybrid economic communities to reflect on the ways neo-liberal power geometries are established and economic interactions commodify Fringe art.

REFERENCES

Anderson, Benedict (2006), *Imagined Communities: Reflections on the Origin and Spread of Nationalism*, London and New York: Verso.

Anon. (2015), 'What the Fringe?! After 50,459 performances of 3,314 shows, the 2015 Edinburgh Festival Fringe draws to a close', The Edinburgh Festival Fringe Official Website, 31 August, https://www.edfringe.com/learn/news-and-events/what-the-fringe-after-50-459-performances-of-3-314-shows-the-2015-edinburgh-festival-fringe-draws-to-a-close. Accessed 5 May 2019.

Awde, Nick (2013), '*Caryatid Unplugged*', review, Theatreguide.London, http://www.theatreguidelondon.co.uk/reviews/edinburgh2013-1.htm. Accessed 18 October 2017.

Bourdieu, Pierre (2003), 'Social reproduction', *Culture: Critical Concepts in Sociology*, 3, p. 62.

Featherstone, David and Painter, Joe (2012), 'Introduction', in D. Featherstone and J. Painter (eds), *Spatial Politics: Essays for Doreen Massey*, Oxford: John Wiley & Sons, pp. 1–18.

Gilbert, Helen and Lo, Jacqueline (2007), *Performance and Cosmopolitics: Cross-Cultural Transactions in Australasia*, London: Palgrave Macmillan.

Harvey, David (2005), *A Brief History of Neoliberalism*, Oxford: Oxford University Press.

Harvie, Jen (2003), 'Cultural effects of the Edinburgh International Festival: Elitism, identities, industries', *Contemporary Theatre Review*, 13:4, pp. 12–26.

—— (2009), *Theatre & the City*, London: Palgrave Macmillan.

Marx, Karl (1976), *Capital* (trans. Ben Fowkes), vol. 1, Harmondsworth: Penguin Books.

—— (1986), *Capital: A Critique of Political Economy – The Process of Production of Capital*, vol. 1, Moscow: Progress.

Massey, Doreen (1991), 'The political place of locality studies', *Environment and Planning, A*, 23:2, pp. 267–81.

—— (1994), 'A global sense of place', in *Space, Place and Gender*, Cambridge: Polity Press, pp. 146–55.

—— (2007), *World City*, Cambridge: Polity Press.

—— (2012), 'Power geometry and a progressive sense of place', in J. Bird, B. Curtis, T. Putman and L. Ticker (eds), *Mapping the Futures: Local Cultures, Global Change*, London: Routledge, pp. 59–69.

Oddey, Alison (2013), *Devising Theatre: A Practical and Theoretical Handbook*, London and New York: Routledge.

Pulp (1995), 'Common People', *Different Class,* CD, London: Island Records, http://www.lyricsmode.com/lyrics/p/pulp/*common*_people.html. Accessed 16 February 2016.

Stamatiou, Evi (2013), *Caryatid Unplugged,* unpublished play.

—— (2017), '*Caryatid Unplugged*: A cabaret on performing belonging and otherness in exile', in J. Rudakoff (ed.), *Performing Exile: Foreign Bodies*, Bristol: Intellect, pp. 195–216, http://www.oapen.org/search?identifier=645370;keyword=performing%20exile. Accessed 21 March 2019.

The Edinburgh Festival Fringe (2016), 'About the Edinburgh Festival Fringe', www.edfringe.com, https://www.edfringe.com/about-us. Accessed 29 March 2016.

The Free Festival (2016), 'About the Free Festival', freefestival.co.uk, http://www.freefestival.co.uk/aboutus.asp. Accessed 2 July 2017.

Wills, Jane (2013), 'Place and politics', in D. Featherstone and J. Painter (eds), *Spatial Politics: Essays for Doreen Massey*, Oxford: John Wiley & Sons, pp. 133–45.

Editors' Note

For an interesting account on the EAFs' social aspects see Waterfield (2015). Recently, an important study dealt directly with the EAFs' brand and its relation to Edinburgh as festival city, within the area of tourism studies. See Todd (2014).

Further reading

Todd, Louise (2014), 'Developing brand relationship theory for festivals: A study of the Edinburgh Festival Fringe', in I. Yeoman, M. Robertson, U. McMahon–Beattie, E. Backer and K. Smith (eds), *The Future of Events and Festivals: Advances in Event Research Series,* Abingdon: Routledge, pp. 157–76.

Waterfield, Carran (2015), 'Social theatre at the Edinburgh Festival: A report from a theatre-maker', *Research in Drama Education: The Journal of Applied Theatre and Performance*, 20:2, pp. 237–41.

NOTES

1. Marx would call these communal identities 'personifications of economics relations' (Marx 1976: 179n3, 1019–20).
2. The name of the city is used as shorthand for the festivals – especially for the Fringe, rather than the official festival.

3. The concepts of space and place are problematic. It is unnecessary in this essay to clarify their distinctions and slippages. In *Space, Place and Gender,* Massey attempts to formulate concepts of space and place in terms of social relations (1994: 2). In this essay, place and space are primarily considered in terms of the temporal economic community in Edinburgh during the EAFs in 2013.
4. In the 2015 Edinburgh Festival Fringe, there were 50,459 performances of 3314 shows in 313 venues across the city (Anon 2015: n.pag.).
5. A group of students from Taiwan and two young Italian residents of a hostel voluntarily assisted with promoting the show after watching a performance.
6. You can see more information about The Free Festival at their official website at: http://www.freefestival.co.uk/aboutus.asp. Accessed 6 March 2019.

Strategies of Empowerment: Postmigrant Theatre at the Ballhaus Naunynstraße

Hasibe Kalkan

The history of Turkish theatre in the Federal Republic of Germany is as old as the country's history of Turkish migrant workers. The theatre first appeared back in 1961, but for various reasons the German public was scarcely aware of its existence. From the beginning, there were numerous Turkish amateur companies, many of which were self-financed. A Turkish theatre ensemble directed by Peter Stein performed at the Schaubühne from 1980 to 1984. This was later followed by the establishment of the independent Turkish theatre Tiyatrom. The point of reference for these projects was theatre life in Turkey; the staging language was Turkish, which was why these kinds of theatres were seen mainly as places of cultural isolation.

In 2008 a theatre, whose intentions differ from those of traditional Turkish theatres in Germany, was founded. The Ballhaus Naunynstraße, located in an ethnically mixed quarter called Kreuzberg, defines itself as postmigrant, being at the same time intercultural and transcultural. This small theatre is housed in the backyard of a former ballroom in Kreuzberg, which is one of the so-called problem areas of Berlin, because half of the population has an immigrant background and most of them are Turks and Arabs. Approximately 40 per cent of the young people living there do not have a college degree and the unemployment rate is very high, reaching 23 per cent (Mannitz 2006: 187). Kreuzberg often appears in the media and in public in pictures of crime, drug trafficking and poverty, which are usually associated with migration. It is also one of the neighbourhoods of Berlin, where a so-called parallel world is established on Islamic values and lifestyles. For the majority of the Berlin population with German roots, this parallel world is inferior. In her book *Die Himmelsreise: Mein Kampf mit den Wächtern des Islams (Sky Travel)*, the sociologist Necla Kelek, who is celebrated in many circles in Germany as an offensive critic of Islam, claims that Islam has never arrived at

149

modernity: 'Because Islam does not make a distinction between tradition, religion and law, it has turned into a core culture with its own value system [...] leading to a behaviour unusual in German society' (Kelek 2007: 11).

Necla Kelek's description of the life of the Turkish community in Germany creates a controversial picture, which consists of two mutually incompatible core cultures, the Islamic and the enlightened Christian. For the majority of Germans, a reconciliation of the two cultures is only possible with the absolute adaptation of the minority to the dominant culture. The little subsidized theatre that has arisen under these polarized conditions declared war on the dominant German core culture and has redefined its community totally. Shermin Langhoff, the artistic director of the Ballhaus Naunynstraße, has brought it into life primarily using the power of language, which is expressed by the philosophy of language of John L. Austin. According to his conception, the performative character of language does not only reflect social reality but also creates reality (Fischer-Lichte 2008: 24). Shermin Langhoff has created a new linguistic repertoire and formulated clear objectives for the Ballhaus. These objectives were:

1. To bring together the network of existing artists with migrant parents and new artists without academic background and to give them the opportunity to develop and try new concepts and forms.
2. To raise public awareness for the problems of migrants from their own perspective.
3. To change the structures of the subsidized municipal theatre, which are still, according to the formulation of Rene Pollesch, 'male, white, heterosexual'. Nevertheless, it does not appeal to the reality of the existing society. The Ballhaus should serve as a stepping stone for artists with migrant background in public institutions.

The key concept under which Shermin Langhoff and her team wanted to achieve these goals was taken from postcolonial literary and cultural theory. They called the Ballhaus and their work 'Postmigrant Theatre' (Stewart 2017: 56).

Postmigrant Theatre

For Langhoff and Kulaoğlu the postmigrant concept means the space of métissage, the third space. It is about the cultural practices of the people with foreign roots but who have not experienced the trauma of migration. It is a reflection from a new German perspective. This new German perspective means that the confrontation of the affected second and third generation of adolescents, who have to develop an appropriate behaviour towards the society in which they live because of the origin of their parents and societal attributions. For a long time in Germany many felt that the children of guest workers live between two cultures; they feel that they belong neither to the country of their parents nor to the country in which they live. In this context, 'postmigrant' refers to a 'border space', a space that was described by Homi Bhabha with the term 'hybridity' or by Edouard Glissant as 'métissage' (Yildiz 2015: 20). This refers to cultural encounters and new realities that do not simply result in a product that is composed of two different cultures, but create a new, so-called 'third space'. From this third space, the protagonists are able to define themselves differently than it was possible through the conventional migration discourse that was prevailing in the public space. This is similar to colonialism. Just as colonialism refers to the ongoing decolonization of global power relations and the objectification of those affected, the subjects, the migrants, are de-personalized in the discourse; they lose their personality, are reduced to objects and thus lose their freedom of action. The Other is constructed to define himself, problems are projected upon him, he becomes an 'incurable' other and 'retarded' (Randeria and Römhild 2003: 21). The Ballhaus makes this practice visible and deconstructs it in its productions; it is an empowerment strategy. Those who have the power of definition are replaced by the 'affected' to wield this power themselves.

Here, too, the theatre largely resorts to the discourse on postcolonialism in order to provide those affected with means to exercise this power of definition, by becoming aware, in Stuart Hall's words, that:

> cultural identity is not a fixed essence, that it is always constructed through memory, fantasy, narrative, myth. Cultural identities are the points of identification, the unstable points of identification or suture, which are made, within the discourse of history and culture.
>
> (1994: 226)

The term 'postmigrant' thus stands for stories of the second and third generation, since it is in the context of migration, but of people who themselves have not moved any longer and want to actively position themselves in the dominant society instead of being positioned by it. The Ballhaus is in this context a place where 'the transnationalism that exists in Kreuzberg, the stories of migration, the struggles of migration, a part of German history which is often not told, can be expressed in this theatre' (Florino 2012).

At the beginning of her theatrical career, Shermin Langhoff largely relied on her experience in the film industry, because in the cinema the process of self-empowerment took place much more earlier than in the theatre. Before Shermin Langhoff came to the Ballhaus Theater, she had worked in film and was the assistant of Fatih Akin on the movie *Gegen die Wand* (*Against the Wall*) (2004). Meanwhile, there was a new concept developed at the international arena called '*cinéma du métissage*'. The concept evolved from the French *cinéma beur* and translates roughly to 'cinema between cultures'. As Hülya Özsarı argues,

> The international phenomenon of cinema 'du métissage' describes a hybrid form and depicts the authentic life within and between two or more different cultural identities. The filmmakers, who were born or grew up mostly in Germany, speak two languages and live in two cultures and their films are in the context of migration.
>
> (Özsarı 2010: 52)

The Ballhaus Naunynstraße

The theoretical foundation of the theatre, which has been strongly based on the postcolonial theory as described above, was developed by Shermin Langhoff, especially in her work at the Hebbeltheater am Ufer (HAU), where she curated the festival Beyond Belonging from 2006 to 2008, before she started working for the Ballhaus. Her main aim at this festival was to combine the existing artistic forces in a widely ramified network and to give them a space in which they could experiment with ways of dealing with migrant artistic contents. Since the largest proportion of people with foreign roots in Germany originated from Turkey, most of the artists had a Turkish background. But because the resources here were quite scarce in their homeland, many of the directors and actors who were active in the Ballhaus, such as Neco Çelik or Ayşe Polat, came from the film industry. Furthermore, importance was also given to the latest developments in dance, film, music and literature. The plays that were produced at the Ballhaus Naunynstraße were quite varied, in both form and content. For instance, documentary pieces based upon the life-story of the first, second and third generation emerged from the perspective of the self-taught. Productions such as *Lö Bal Almanya* or *The Swans from the Slaughterhouse*, both by Tunçay Kulaoğlu and Nurkan Erpulat (2010), reworked the migration history of Turkish guest workers and their life in Germany. Also popular are novel adaptations, such as *Snow* by Hakan Savaş Mican (2010), originally by the Turkish Nobel Prize winner Orhan Pamuk.

In this chapter my focus is on documentary pieces based upon the life-story of the first, second and third generation emerged from the perspective of the self-taught. Especially through the Academy of Autodidacts, which she started at the HAU, Shermin Langhoff created an important resource for artists. The Academy of Autodidacts is a conceptual work approach to provide young gifted migrant artists with different artistic skills such as dance, music and acting – many of them self-taught, without academic training – access to cultural production, in particular to the theatre. The Academy also created a direct link to life in the neighbourhood and offered access to theatre to these young people. Arun Florino quotes Shermin Langhoff:

> Often we enter into discussion with people who try 'to bring culture' among teenagers or among the 'poor migrants' for themselves without even knowing what culture is or having the concept of culture ever defined. That is just the reason why many young people can do nothing with culture. We try to make it clear to young people and adults that culture is everything. That no borders are open. We try to work with young people so that we give them the space where they can develop themselves. There is only one culture and no subdivisions in high culture and the other.
>
> (Langhoff in Florino 2012)

Shermin Langhoff transcends and deconstructs the boundaries between high and popular culture as defined by Bourdieu. Langhoff states that young people should be motivated, regardless of their origin and status, to have access to cultural and democratic ownership in order to make it possible for them to foster their intellectual and social skills. From Bourdieu's perspective:

> The science of taste and of cultural consumption begins with a transgression that is in no way aesthetic: it has to abolish the sacred frontier which makes legitimate culture a separate universe, in order to discover the intelligible relations.
>
> (1984: 6)

Apart from the theatre courses, which are open to everybody and to the collaboration with some schools, another important project of the Ballhaus in this context is the so-called monthly neighbourhood show.

The Kiez Monatsschau

The main objective of the Kiez Monatsschau is to produce a film documentary of approximately 60 minutes every two months with different groups of migrant youths. Everyday topics such as 'the elections', or questions like 'what does it mean to be a postmigrant?', 'what does freedom mean?' and politically explosive events in the neighbourhood, by which young people are directly affected, are discussed and implemented in film clips. In dealing with the personal experiences of the participants, they become familiar with artistic issues and more conscious about the media. In addition to a small permanent team, which consists of an artist as a project manager and camera/sound/editing technicians, there are changing

153

leaders from the fields of film, theatre, and journalism who work with these young people. The workshops take place continuously and a one-hour Kiez Monatsschau is shown in the great hall of Ballhaus Naunynstraße and subsequently discussed with young people and the public. Klaus Hoffman asserts that: 'Studies have shown that culturally active young people define the confrontation with foreign cultures as enriching for their own cultural development. As such they get in touch with different perceptions and interpretations of reality' (Hoffman 2007: 1–2).

For Hoffmann 'this may enable young people to reflect on their own culture and their own location and thereby develop openness and dialogue capability' (Hoffman 2007: 1–2).

The paper will dwell upon *Holiday Camp, The 3rd Generation* (2009), another example of the theatrical work of the Academy of Autodidacts.

Holiday Camp, The 3rd Generation

In *Holiday Camp, The 3rd Generation*, the self-taught artists who stand on the stage are young Turkish people, born in Berlin Kreuzberg and taking a look at their own lives. (They do not really play themselves, but the texts are documents of their own lives.) In a large room are eight iron beds in which five girls and three boys sleep. Accompanied by emotional music, two angels, one with white, the other with black wings enter the room. The audience is informed of these sleeping young children through the conversations of the angels. A footballer, an unemployed young man, a faithful servant, a housewife, all drift towards a life of hopelessness. They gradually wake up and one after another, begin to talk about their lives. In doing so, they reflect their personalities in different scenes.

One of the boys cannot stand the ringing of a mobile phone any longer, stands up, takes it and throws it against the wall. He immediately regrets the impulsive action and tries to patch up the phone again. He obtained his first cell phone when he was only 13. However, until now, no one has called him. He goes on to tell of his tendency towards violence. Then he starts dancing until he collapses. The following sentences of Tamer, this young boy, will illustrate his state of mind clearly:

> TAMER : ... The doorman of Dante, the old geezer ... Says: foreigners do not come in here! And I say: you're a foreigner! - He is Russian. - At once he slammed. You little chickenshit!, he says to me ... but I have that behind me now. I mean, I was also drunk, but ... Because that has really excited me, really ... ! Standing there in front and see us in the back of the queue ... and he says: My three there, you cannot get in! You can already get out from the queue and get off... You can go! And that tells me a Russian! ... There are thousands, so

I'm exaggerating, Asians and blacks come in without problems. But as soon as one looks like a kind of a southerner ...

(Collective 2009: 8)

The hopelessness of young people about not being accepted by society leads to a sense of aggression when it comes to dealing with each other and their environment. According to social scientist Klaus Wahl 'form and intensity of aggression are created, activated or inhibited by the genetic makeup of the individual, his socialization and social circumstances' (Wahl 2009: 67).

Mad Blood

Another example shows how the director Nurkan Erpulat mixed autodidacts with professional actors. This play, entitled *Mad Blood* (2010), with its energy and its depiction of current issues, became one of the most successful and most discussed productions of the Ballhaus Naunynstraße. This Ballhaus production was so successful that it was invited to the Berlin Theatre Meeting in 2011, as well as to international festivals.

Mad Blood is inspired by the 2008 French film *La Journée de la jupe* (*Today I'm Wearing a Skirt*) featuring Isabelle Adjani as a teacher who tries to teach her almost feral students Molière's plays. The dramaturg of *Mad Blood*, Jens Hillje, not only transported the plot to Berlin, but also changed the entire context of the production. The name of the play is a translation of the Turkish word *Delikanli*, which alludes to boys going through puberty. This means a period when the blood of the youngsters boils and they act out of control.

The stage gives the impression of a boxing-ring. Its smooth surface seems to be a projection screen. After putting on their costumes in front of the audience, the young actors adopt poses displaying all kinds of common clichés. The director determines the frame of the play with the first scene: the deconstruction of existing clichés concerning teenagers with a 'migration background'; teachers working with these teens; and finally the attempt to find a solution to all these problems by means of traditional education.

Then Sesede Terziyan, the teacher, enters the classroom. She wants to read texts by Schiller with the students, while struggling to impose her authority upon them. In the rush, she gets hold of a weapon one of the kids has brought with him to school and, holding the weapon in her hand, she forces her students to play scenes from *The Robbers* (1781) and *Cabal and Love* (1784). 'Only when man plays, he is in the fullest sense of the word a human being' (Erpulat and Hillje 2010: 42), she cites madly from Schiller and this situation is acted exactly at all levels.

The pistol symbolizes violence as well as helplessness; fear and weakness dominate the entire play. The one who holds it is always the one who gets a position of power. The pistol comes to signify the desperate fight for recognition in a compartmenting society that robs people of their vital human needs. According to Charles Taylor, misrecognition or underestimation of people:

> shows not just a lack of due respect. It can inflict a grievous wound, saddling its victims with a crippling self-hatred. [...] Nonrecognition or misrecognition can inflict harm, can be a form of oppression, imprisoning someone in a false, distorted, and reduced mode of being.
>
> (1994: 25, 42)

The boxing ring where the characters are acting stands for the scene of human beings incarcerated in such a distorted life.

As the play progresses, the handsome Ferit begins to understand why Karl has to be a rebel; and the shy Hasan can finally remove the 'sad fate' of his Kurdishness. At the end he no longer wants to slip out of his role as Franz, since he feels strong in that role.

Despite their initial protest and fear of their uncontrollable teacher who shoots again and again in the air, these adolescents begin to identify with their roles. Their German pronunciation starts improving; the relationships between the students, in particular, between the male and the female classmates become friendlier. The teacher comes to an awareness that aesthetic education works. The success of the teacher on stage is accentuated, as the students do not want to let her out of her role as a leader and even Maryam, one of the students, voluntarily takes off her headscarf slowly at the end. In doing so, she becomes liberated in a country where women with headscarves are not believed to be free. The sarcastic ending of the play demonstrates a tableau of the women who are free; the students grow into responsible individuals who are even able to forgive the outrages of their classmates. In the end, the teacher gives up playing and the play-within-the-play eventually comes to an end.

Contrasts and fractures that create an ironic stage language that is not only the tone of this production are an integral part of the aesthetic language of the Ballhaus Naunynstraße and these are easily seen in many of their productions. The instrument of irony has a complex function in the productions of the Ballhaus. In the first place, it provides the artists with Turkish roots with a kind of self-protection, because irony creates an emotional distance to the contents described here and also to themselves. Irony paves the way to the world of freedom, because with the help of irony they succeed in overcoming all the prejudices imposed upon them. The ironic exaggerations and the clash of differences also serve similar functions as the visualization of social stereotypes in the cabaret. For example, in spite of the fact she acknowledges and tries to teach her students Schiller's freedom of thoughts and emotions, the teacher transforms the classroom into a prison, in which students are held with violence, because she believes that if she does not hold the gun, her students will not be able to understand anything.

As already mentioned above, the small Kreuzberg theatre reached a wide range of people from the German population with *Mad Blood*, although this part of Berlin was actually rather strange. That the play was received so well in wide circles of the German middle classes was a surprise to all who were involved in the production. Initially the success of the play was attributed to the publication of Sarrazin's highly controversial book *Germany Abolishes Itself* (2010) at the same time of the play's production. But after a while it became apparent that the ironic level of *Mad Blood* was not fully appreciated by a part of the audience. Shermin Langhoff, the artistic director of the Ballhaus, justifies this failed reception as follows:

> It seems important to me that the dominant cultural chauvinism has been ingrained so strongly in some part of the audience that they cannot perceive artistic examination precisely and they take the critical stance of the play as a triumphant confirmation for their beliefs.
>
> (Langhoff 2011)

Thus the reception among the German middle classes in some cases failed. *Mad Blood* clearly shows that the Ballhaus has attracted a great deal of attention of a German middle class that lives away from the transnational reality of Kreuzberg, yet it has barely changed its perception about it.

Conclusion

Due to the great attention that some productions aroused in the general public, in conclusion it can be argued that Shermin Langhoff managed to turn the small backyard theatre in Kreuzerg Berlin into a site that on the one hand represents a strong reference point for the adolescents for their identity and on the other hand a curious middle class far away from the Kreuzberg reality to be lured into the theatre. Also the Ballhaus largely succeeded in realizing the above-mentioned objectives and setting up enthusiastic discussions about a part of society that appears to be reflected as deficient in the media. The possibility of offering a special platform to the marginalized to render themselves visible to the society is established by the Ballhaus. This argument is espoused by Miriam Soufi Siavash who states in an article that you should 'talk about yourself to shape your perception' (Siavash 2011: 85). Langhoff also succeeded in redefining the theatre community with her word at the Ballhaus, in that the theatre, which has an almost 100 per cent capacity utilization, managed to appeal to a diverse crowd of viewers, similar to the city's population. According to Shermin Langhoff, 30 per cent of the visitors come from the neighbourhood. And it is estimated that about a third of them are theatre-distant audiences who come for specific political or educational interests (Langhoff 2012).

But I believe that the greatest impetus for a more nuanced perception of post-migrants came from the director Shermin Langhoff. She received various awards, because with the concept she created in the Ballhaus, she managed to draw the attention of the public and the media to migrant culture and to counteract prejudices. In addition to numerous newspaper articles, reports and television programmes, the subject of the postmigrant theatre has been discussed in a variety of scientific papers. According to Sabine Schiffer '[t]he choice of a certain sign in the media – word or image – decides to which part of reality attention is directed – and which part remains unseen' (Schiffer 2005: 1). Shermin Langhoff has introduced a new linguistic repertoire, with which she seized every opportunity in a very profound way, in speech and in written form, formulated her social criticism, as well as the programme of the theatre. Accordingly, more than its aesthetic success, Langhoff has managed to stimulate a renewed interest in the Ballhaus by creating a new linguistic repertoire. And in doing so, she has made it possible for both the Ballhaus theatre and the subjects depicted to remain so popular.

Acknowledgements

Research funded by Bilimsel Araştirma Projeleri Birimi, Istanbul Üniversitesi (56440).

REFERENCES

Bourdieu, Pierre (1984), *Distinction: A Social Critique of the Judgement of Taste*, Cambridge, MA: Harvard University Press.

Collective (2009), *Holiday Camp, The 3rd Generation*, Berlin: Ballhaus Naunynstraße.

Erpulat, Nurkan and Hillje, Jens (2010), *Verrücktes Blut*, Berlin: Ballhaus Naunynstraße.

Fischer-Lichte, Erika (2008), *The Transformative Power of Performance: A New Aesthetics*, Abingdon: Routledge.

Florino, Arun (2012), 'Postmigrantische Gesellschaft behaupten, eine neue Perspektive auf die Szene Europa', in *Andere Europas,* Berlin: Humboldt-Universität zu Berlin, https://www.euro-ethno.hu-berlin.de/de/archiv/studienprojekte/other_europes/forschung/Postmigrantische%20Gesellschaft%20im%20Ballhaus%20Naunynstrasse. Accessed 26 November 2017.

Haakh, Nora (2011), 'Islamisierte Körper auf der Bühne, identitätspolitische Positionierung zur deutschen Islam-Debatte in Arbeiten des postmigrantischen Theaters Ballhaus Naunynstraße Berlin', unpublished master's thesis, Berlin: Freie Universitaet Berlin.

Hall, Stuart (1994), 'Alte und neue Identitäten, alte und neue Ethnizitäten', in S. Hall (ed.), *Rassismus und kulturelle Identität*, Hamburg: Argument Verlag, pp. 66–88.

Hoffmann, Klaus (2007), 'Theater heute und die Interkulturalität', *kultur-kompetenz-bildung: Konzeption kulturelle Bildung*, July–August, pp. 1–2, http://www.kulturrat.de/dokumente/kkb/kkb-11.pdf. Accessed 11 March 2015.

Kalkan, Hasibe (2011), 'Searching for identity', *Glimpse*, 13, pp. 79–83, https://www.pdcnet.org/glimpse/content/glimpse_2011_0013_0079_0083. Accessed 11 March 2019.

Kelek, Necla (2007), *Die Himmelsreise: Mein Kampf mit den Wächtern des Islams*, Köln: Kiepenhauer und Witsch.

Langhoff, Shermin (2011), *Aufklärung und Rassismus, oder die komplizierte Sache mit dem verrücktem Blut*, Berlin: Der Theaterverlag.

—— (2012), 'Wozu postmigrantisches Theater?', *Frankfurter Allgemeine*, 15 January, http://www.faz.net/aktuell/feuilleton/buehne-und-konzert/gespraech-mit-shermin-langhoff-wozu-postmigrantisches-theater-11605050-p2.html. Accessed 25 April 2017.

Liebig, Manuel (2015), 'Das Postmigrantische: Ein neues Kozept für eine kritische Migrationsforschung?', unpublished essay, Berlin: Humboldt-Universitaet zu Berlin, Institut für Europaeische Ethnologie.

Mannitz, Sabine (2006), *Die verkannte Integration: Eine Langzeitstudie unter Heranwachsenden aus Immigrantenfamilien*, Bielefeld: Transcript Verlag.

Özsarı, Hülya (2010), *Der Türke: Die Konstruktion des Fremden in den Medien*, Berlin: Universitätsverlag der Technischen Universität.

Pieter, Verstraete (2013), 'Turkish "postmigrant" opera in Europe: A social-historical perspective on aurality', in *The Legacy of Opera: Reading Music Theatre as Experience and Performance*, Amsterdam: Brill Rodopi, pp. 185–207.

Randeria, Shalini and Römhild, Regina (2003), 'Das postkoloniale Europa: Verflochtene Genealogien der Gegenwart – Einleitung zur erweiterten Neuauflage', in S. Conrad, S. Randeria and R. Römhild (eds), *Jenseits des Eurozentrismus*, Frankfurt: Campus Verlag, pp. 9–31.

Romhild, Regina and Bergmann, Sven (2003), *Global Heimat: Ethnographische Recherchen im Transnationalen*, Frankfurt am Main: Institut für Kulturanthropologie und Europäische Ethnologie.

Schiffer, Sabine (2005), 'Der Islam in deutschen Medien', Bundeszentrale für politische Bildung, 10 May, http://www.bpb.de/apuz/29060/der-islam-in-deutschen-medien?p=1. Accessed 24 January 2014.

Schneider, Wolfgang (ed.) (2011), *Theater und Migration: Herausforderungen für Kulturpolitik und Theaterpraxis*, Bielefeld: Transcript Verlag.

Sharifi, Azadeh (2012), *Theater für alle? Partizipation von Postmigranten am Beispiel der Bühnen der Stadt Köln*, Frankfurt am Main: Peter Lang Verlag.

Siavash, Miriam Soufi (2011), 'Wer ist Wir? Theaterarbeit in der interkulturellen Gesellschaft', in W. Schneider (ed.), *Theater und Migration: Herausforderungen für Kulturpolitik und Theaterpraxis*, Bielefeld: Transcript Verlag, pp. 83–90.

Stewart, Lizzie (2017), 'Postmigrant theatre: The Ballhaus Naunynstraße takes on sexual nationalism', *Journal of Aesthetics and Culture*, 9: 2, pp. 56–68.

Taylor, Charles (1994), *Multiculturalism: Examining the Politics of Recognition*, Princeton, NJ: Princeton University Press.

Wahl, Klaus (2009), *Aggression und Gewalt: Ein biologischer, psychologischer und sozialwissenschaftlicher Überblick*, Heidelberg: Spectrum Akademischer Verlag.

Yildiz, Erol (2015), 'Postmigrantische Perspektiven: Aufbruch in eine neue Geschichtlichkeit', in M. Hill and E. Yildiz (eds), *Nach der Migration: Postmigrantische Perspektiven jenseits der Parallelgesellschaft*, Bielefeld: Transcript, pp. 19–48.

Editors' Note

The Ballhaus Naunynstraße is currently co-led by Wagner Carvalho, founder of the Brazilian dance festival Move Berlim, and dramaturg Tunçay Kulaoğlu. Shermin Langhoff became artistic director of Berlin's Maxim Gorki Theatre from the 2013–14 theatre season. Migrant theatre and refugee performance is a fast emerging area of theatre research and recent monographs as well as special journal issues deal directly with theatre and migration in a contemporary context. Stephen Wilmer's most recent monograph *Performing Statelessness in Europe* (2018) gives an extensive analysis on how European theatre addresses current migration. Emma Cox and Caroline Wake's special journal issue deals with 'Envisioning Asylum/ Engendering Crisis' (2018) and the special issue of *Modern Drama* edited by Meerzon et al. gives an important account on 'Migration and Multilingualism' (2018). Furthermore, Azadeh Sharifi's book chapter 'Theatre and migration documentation, influences and perspectives in European Theatre' (Sharifi 2017) is an indispensable study into migrant theatre across Europe.

Further reading

Cox, Emma and Wake, Caroline (eds) (2018), *Research in Drama Education: The Journal of Applied Theatre and Performance*, special issue, 'Envisioning Asylum/Engendering Crisis', 23:2.

Meerzon, Yana, Pewny, Katharina and Martens, Gunther (eds.) (2018), *Modern Drama,* special issue, 'Migration and Multilingualism', 61:3.

Sharifi, Azadeh (2017), 'Theatre and migration documentation, influences and perspectives in European Theatre', in M. Brauneck (ed.), *Independent Theatre in Contemporary Europe*, Bielefeld: Transcript Verlag, 321–415, https://www.oapen.org/download?type=document&docid=627657. Accessed 21 March 2019.

Wilmer, Stephen (2018), *Performing Statelessness in Europe*, Basingstoke: Palgrave Macmillan.

PART IV

Creative Encounters:
Changing Ecologies

While the previous part discussed theatre communities in 'globalized' artistic environments and amidst migrant theatre initiatives, this part of the volume aims to give voice to theatre-makers and artistic directors in order to reflect on actual creative practices and artistic philosophies in contemporary theatre-making. Understandably, besides the aesthetic approaches, politics remains at the core of the debate among contributors of this section. In fact, politics is at the centre of Part IV of this book, a section that is comprised of interviews and conversations from the United Kingdom, Greece and Romania. Vicky Featherstone, while describing the work of the Royal Court Theatre in reaching out to the wider community that would not otherwise have visited the theatre, notes that the Royal Court is actively working to perform, in English, works that were originally written in other languages. All this is contextualized within the changing UK politics with regards to the European Union. The dissonance between the prestigious theatre district of London and the contiguous under-privileged Tottenham area that Vicky Featherstone's work at the Royal Court Theatre tries to highlight and bridge is echoed in George Sachinis' reflections on the UrbanDig Project. Working in communities with an attractive facade aimed at attracting visitors but which also hide a reality of residents being pushed out or marginalized, UrbanDig focuses on communal activities through which residents create knowledge about the spaces they inhabit and about their lives. David Schwartz challenges the concept of community as used by neo-liberal politics to group people together for political expediency rather than to create any advantages to the individuals banded together as a community. Likewise, he is very critical of community theatre that does not have a clear political agenda and that does not problematize the relationship between artists and collaborators. Although he acknowledges the usefulness of his own theatre practice, he is sceptical of being able to reach any political objectives through it, unless it can lead to a different political order.

Community and Ownership: Uncovering New Voices at the Royal Court Theatre

Mark O'Thomas in conversation with Vicky Featherstone

Vicky Featherstone became the Royal Court Theatre's first female artistic director in 2013. The Royal Court is the home of British new writing for the stage and has a 60-year history of producing groundbreaking work that challenges the status quo. In addition to promoting playwriting around the world through its International Department, the Court has also attempted to reach new audiences in London through its Theatre Local strand and its more recent partnering with Joe Murphy and Joe Robertson's Good Chance Theatre project in Calais' Jungle refugee camp. Featherstone has brought a plethora of new ideas and fresh insights to an organization that undoubtedly now forms part of the UK theatrical establishment where the future continues to offer challenges for artists interested in working towards a better world through their collective enterprise and struggle.

The original interview took place on 22 August 2016 with a follow-up session on 7 November 2017.

MARK O'THOMAS (MO): Talking to you about this idea of 'redefining theatre communities' feels both timely and quite strange. We are now in a post-Brexit referendum era and it feels to me like that one event, that referendum decision, has completely reshaped how I think about everything. I can remember talking to Dominic[1] about some of these issues long before the referendum had even been conceived. He told me that one of his great concerns about the Royal Court, and coming in as the new artistic director, was that you sit in this area of immense privilege in central London, where real estate prices are some of the highest in the world, and what do you do? How do you respond to that? Theatre Local[2] was certainly one way in which he tried to tackle it and I guess to begin thinking about how a theatre such as this relates to communities might be to start off by thinking about that idea of the local and what that means for the theatre community. This inevitably goes back to the post-Brexit thing. This idea that we are all living in a liberal bubble and we didn't see what was there in front of our eyes – that we all felt it was all OK.

VICKY FEATHERSTONE (VF): I didn't. I'm not in a bubble.

MO: Oh?

VF: No. I've been here for two-and-a-half years, and before that I was in Scotland which had its own referendum, although they did vote 'stay'. But one of the big things for me about coming to this job was feeling really nervous about what the context was in which I would be making decisions at the Royal Court. The job that I'd done before at the National Theatre of Scotland was one where the context was entirely clear all of the time. It was one where I was making theatre for and about Scotland which had to reach the widest possible audience. It has to have a national conversation with its communities as a kind of internal conversation and then for Scotland to have an external conversation with the rest of the world about itself and the global community. So that was really very clear, and actionable at the outset. And then you come to the Royal Court to do a job that everyone aspires to, especially if you are obsessed with playwrights and new writing, and you sit here and you start to feel a huge discomfort, rather than pride at what you're doing. So I really share the same thing as Dominic and I had to ask a lot of questions about why I'd come. Not fundamentally about *why* I'd come but in terms of that sense of the moral compass as to how I made decisions, which is about our sense of theatre, our sense of place in the world and our relationship with community. And one of the questions that I really thought about was – what had it been like when the Royal Court began? So, of course, in 1956, when the Royal Court started, this was a very different place. This was bohemian, it was weird, complex. You can understand what a sense of place was and of course now it's quite different. So I think what I did, and Dominic had already started with Theatre Local, was I thought a lot about them. One of the traditional aims of audience development has been to try and get as wide an audience as possible into the theatre. Obviously, you take that as a no-brainer now. But having worked for the National Theatre of Scotland with direct experience of engaging in this issue, I realized that

164

architecture is often an issue for people. I am referring here to what the community feels in terms of its relationship with certain architecture and art. This is most definitely a theatre which is extraordinary but it can be intimidating – it's designed to have that kind of really intimidating architecture from the inside. So my big thing was that we have to try and take the work to people and build things with people. What Theatre Local did which was very interesting: it took work which you could have seen at the Royal Court to another place. I think that was sort of stage one for me of the Royal Court's relationship outside of the Royal Court building. What I wanted to do was to tour more anyway so to be more regularly taking a work outside the Royal Court. Consequently, it felt to me that Theatre Local really was a sort of lesser version of touring – that you're only going to one place. So the relationship with community at the Royal Court has been a sort of amalgamation of things that I've learned over the years with the National Theatre of Scotland alongside the purity of the Royal Court. This gets me to a point where we ask: how do we immerse ourselves in a community without taking products to them and asking how they should engage? How do we enable them to know about what we are and then to start creating themselves and to start finding a voice for themselves and to start feeling an ownership of the work? I really believe that a relationship with the community outside of the conventional theatregoer or someone who might think, 'oh, I'm going to buy a ticket!' is about ownership, and it's about them believing that what we're looking for is *voice*. Now that can be interpreted in lots of different ways and we will nurture that and take it very seriously.

MO: Is there a difficulty, then, with the Royal Court brand? I mean just the word 'royal'.

VF: You see, it's interesting. I would have thought there would have been so my immediate position is 'yes'. But when I think about the projects in Tottenham we've been doing over the last three years, it's interesting to reflect on how things have turned out differently. I think it's a sort of middle-class snobbishness that thinks there's a problem with the Royal Court brand whereas to say that there is this amazing theatre in Sloane Square but we are based in Tottenham offers something new, something that is surprising and can unlock something.

MO: There is also a snobbishness within the theatrical world when words such as 'community' and 'theatre' come together.

VF: Yes, that's hugely important. For me, it's never ever been about making separate work. It always has to be about centre. So it's about whether the decision-making for projects is bad, who listens to the work that comes out of it, and how to really engage with those communities. That work can be successful if it's coming right from the centre I feel.

MO: The writers that you used in Theatre Local seemed to have a direct link with those communities – Bola Agbaje, for example.

VF: Yes, and they became really good ambassadors. But not only for their actual work but also around the issue of trust. But I think the work that we're now doing beyond the Court is much deeper than that. It's still about finding those voices and taking them back to those communities. And it's about trying to make a more fundamental shift than just buying a ticket at 7.30 and seeing a show.

MO: Can you say something about where the work in Tottenham is now?

VF: Well, we're at the end of our second year. This summer, we bought a shipping container and placed it down in the car park. We worked at the Bernie Grant Arts Centre, we worked with the Hasidic Jewish community, and engaged in very different communities. We created a series of short films that young filmmakers from Tottenham made and then staged a sort of grime theatre event called Platform Tottenham. It then came to the Royal Court for the first time, and there were 40 grime artists from Tottenham who had spent two years working with us and had never been to the Royal Court. When they turned up, they were like, 'oh yes, the Royal Court.' And that was really interesting. There was no sense of them feeling intimidated by a big theatre. It felt as if they had been naturally waiting for this moment. So now we're going to the third year of that project in Tottenham and it's now about those artists, those young voices making a piece of theatre themselves which will be a big event. But the other project that we've been working on is with one of our closest communities in Pimlico where there are two big council estates that have a very complex relationship with each other. So the other beyond the Court work has been in those estates trying to say that we're actually their neighbourhood theatre. It's very interesting that when we behave like we're a neighbourhood theatre and recognize that we have a community, it's good for us and it really challenges us.

MO: Those are good examples of working with local London communities, what about the Royal Court's work with refugee communities or migrant communities?

VF: Through the International Department, the Royal Court has been working and thinking about the nation's refugees for a long time now, as you know. Our work here has been connecting with misplaced people in countries that are threatened. In some cases, they are misplaced politically, where they haven't yet become refugees but philosophically they remain refugees from their countries in terms of what their belief systems are or what the stories are that they need to tell of the history of their country. More literally, we have the work that Elyse (Dodgson, director of the International Department) has been doing in refugee camps in Lebanon, her work in Palestine, which has been going on for some time. Again, it's quite profound, long-term meaningful work that has developed and encouraged writers' and directors' voices so much so that a lot of those artists would really attribute a lot of their international success to the confidence in voice that they built through Elyse and her department. So that's been going for a long time before the word 'refugee' became so prevalent in our society. But more recently we've had a very close relationship with the Good Chance Theatre in Calais, which was set up in a way that was not so dissimilar to how we have been working in Tottenham. This is using theatre as a space to communicate, to talk, to be, to create, but not necessarily as a space for structured performance. Some of our people here were instrumental in setting it up and supporting it. Interestingly, I think what worked less well, and I would never have done it, is taking readymade bits of theatre over there. I don't find that particularly interesting. I'm much more interested in what theatre is in terms of its community, not us having to be rigid about what our theatre looks like. It's about being much more flexible in looking at the interface of this conversation and what comes out of it. So that's really what our relationship was with Calais and that's really where we got to with Theatre Local as well. It's not about taking a piece of theatre that represents what we think theatre should look like, but working with the community and questioning the interface. That's what makes it a completely new thing that none of us could have imagined and it really excites me when that happens.

MO: Is there ever a struggle, then, when you are forced to disentangle some of the expectations that is aroused in those communities?

VF: Yes, and of course what happens then is that you start a conversation with those different communities in different ways so that they are then able to trust the relationship. They might then come to you to see the work that you do at its best in that environment that you're in control of. So you have this two-way thing happening where you are not expecting one thing to be everything.

MO: While we are talking about the Royal Court and its different configurations of communities, it strikes me that another kind of community that the Royal Court sits in is its European community of fellow artistic directors and their associated buildings. And again in the past there have been very fruitful relationships – with Schaubühne in Berlin, for example. Post-Brexit is that likely to change?

VF: We have had some fantastic co-production with the Schaubühne such as *Ophelias Zimmer* (2016), which Katie Mitchell directed. I think that post-Brexit, our individual ideologies will still match but more partnership will be needed and I think there has been a sort of reaching out to each other around that. The danger though is – and this is a terrible generalization – that ultimately the European opinion formers and people with power will tire of my upset about the decision that the rest of the country has made and my lack of power to be able to meet them equally in a financial sense on a European stage. So currently it feels like we're still understanding the grief stage we're in, but once we're out of that, we will be left high and dry and they will be carrying on as normal. We haven't had to face that yet. At the moment, we still feel like we're still in solidarity but once we are unable to make equal offers to them financially, things might change.

MO: It's how the isolationism becomes legitimized by institutional entities that we have no control of.

VF: Yes, that's exactly right.

MO: On a more optimistic note, can you tell me something about the coming collaboration with the Black Cultural Archives?

VF: We have two amazing plays coming up and we've got another play which we're about to announce with debbie tucker green next year. Suzan-Lori Parks' play *Father Comes Home from the Wars* (2016) is extraordinary from its beginning with the American Civil War, the history of slavery and what it means to be a free man. It's interesting because it is often a part of history that we don't really connect with in this country. I think what's so extraordinary about it for me is that in a very different way from *12 Years a Slave* (McQueen, 2013), it has a much more playful, celebratory form. There's a kind of dissonance within it, which I really like, between a hellish truth of the politics and a fundamental celebration of humanity. So the dissonance within it about where we sit in all of that really excites me. And then with *Torn* (2016), Nat Martello-White has written a play about his family – his granny is Irish and he was brought up in Brixton. When you look at the stage, it looks like the most multicultural play that you've ever seen. Seen in the context of *Father Comes Home from the Wars*, it's really beginning to show that we don't need to stage plays about a black agenda. So I think that what's really important with our relationship with the Black Cultural Archives is that it helps us get to a new place. Of course, it's really important still to talk about history because that hasn't been given enough of a platform, but we need to talk about history in a way that is formally different – inventive and creative. Eventually, we want to get to a place where we are able to put stories on stage where you won't necessarily have to deal with the issues that we attribute to that community. That, for me, is the big breakthrough. We have to do more of that and debbie's play is very much part of that onward movement.

MO: I guess class is also part of this debate and the Royal Court has had a long relationship with class, hasn't it? Its history of attempting to put the working-class voice on the stage, for example, which, I guess, it has done with varying degrees of success.

VF: I think the Royal Court's relationship with class is so important because one of the originating facts behind the formation of the Royal Court was putting a different voice on stage and this was at the height of a West End of Noel Coward and Terence Rattigan. And so it was *Look Back in Anger* (1956), John Osborne, Joe Orton, John Arden – all those people were those voices who put two fingers up to the class-ridden elitism of the West End at that time. The Royal Court has always been that alternative. I think what the Royal Court has also done has offered a mix of plays about class and plays about ideas. Sometimes those two things separate out. Sometimes they can be quite intellectual and quite academic and then other times, the work that we do can be much more about putting lives on stage that we don't see very often. I think what the Royal Court does at its best is uncover new voices and give those voices a platform. Now sometimes the voices that we uncover are upper middle class, with writers from a certain kind of upbringing who write things in a certain way – Cordelia Lynn who wrote *Lela & Co* (2015) for us or Laura Wade who wrote *Posh* (2010) are examples of women who wanted to explode something. But on the other hand, you're always hungry for the voice that we might have missed out on, who didn't get that space to create. I see less and less of this happening in new writing in the rest of London, because it costs so much to put it on. A lot of the fringe work that is being put on looks like it's about class, but it's about class from a *Guardian* point of view. Whereas what the Royal Court has been able to do is to genuinely give people the opportunity to write the plays that they would never have been able to write before.

Afterword: January 2018

MO: It's now almost eighteen months since we last sat down and discussed the idea of 'community' and theatre and so much has happened since then. I know we even began to wonder about the validity of what was said at that time. Reading back over our discussion, we covered such a range of issues from Brexit and its potential impact, working with London communities, working with marginalized groups outside of the United Kingdom, and of course that wider constituency of theatre and its own theatrical community, which has itself been very much in the spotlight recently. If we go back to where we started from, then, are your fears the same – around Brexit, and how we continue to operate in the international space as part of that community as an equal player?

VF: My fears are no longer irrational musings but the actual realization that we are heading for an era of splendid isolation where funding and routes for collaboration and the cross-fertilization of stories are being radically compromised. The withdrawal of the European City of Culture funding was a shock and a wake-up call as to what lies ahead. Our mission at the Royal Court is always to be seeking out the most vital and urgent voices and for those stories to be told and we have always been at our best when we have an open source to the influences and movements outside our immediate domain. My concern is also that so much of our work will deal with this in subject matter that we will have to strive more than ever for a diversity of idea. Artists are finding it hard to respond to Brexit as it is still such an unknown and the predominant voice around it is a parochial and inward-looking one that does not bear much analysis or creativity. We will strive to remain open-minded, encourage artists from Europe and beyond to work with us and to ask the questions of our times – this is needed more than ever, but I am left with the deep frustration that were we given another opportunity to reflect on the question, we might now make a very different choice.

REFERENCE

Aston, Elaine and O'Thomas, Mark (2015), *Royal Court: International*, London: Palgrave Macmillan.

Editors' Note

Aleks Sierz's 'Dark times: British theatre after Brexit' (2017) discusses British theatre-makers' reaction to Brexit, focusing on plays that have been written since the referendum and are perceived as commenting on the political situation brought about by the referendum. A year later he posted an update on the situation in an article for the same journal (Sierz 2018), referring to Vicky Featherstone's work at the Royal Court Theatre. Dan Rebellato's 'Nation and negation (terrible rage)' in the *Journal of Contemporary Drama in English* (2018) locates the almost universal convergence of British theatre-makers in the Remain camp in the different conceptions of citizenship and belonging vis-à-vis the nationalistic vision championed by Brexiteers.

Further reading

Rebellato, Dan (2018), 'Nation and negation (terrible rage)', *Journal of Contemporary Drama in English*, 6:1, pp. 15–39.
Sierz, Aleks (2017), 'Dark times: British theatre after Brexit', *PAJ: A Journal of Performance and Art*, 39:1, pp. 3–11.
—— (2018), 'British theatre after Brexit: One year on', *PAJ: A Journal of Performance and Art*, 40:3, pp. 60–70.

NOTES

1. Dominic Cooke was artistic director of the Royal Court 2006–13. See Aston and O'Thomas (2015).
2. An initiative to move the work of the Royal Court outside to other areas, such as Peckham, South London.

UrbanDig Project: Theatre for Neighbourhoods

Zoe Zontou in conversation with George Sachinis

In Greece, theatre has always had a central role in educating and raising audiences' awareness on social and political issues. For example, in Ancient Greece, theatre was strongly situated in the cultural and civil life of the Athenians (Barker 2014). In the modern history of Greece, theatre was used as a platform for expressing resistance and/or promoting social cohesion and unity. This was evident in politically complicated historical periods, such as the Nazi occupation (1940–44), the Civil War (1946–49) and the dictatorship (1967–74). For example, during World War II, the guerrilla soldiers of the resistance theatre in the mountains staged plays from the classical repertoire. Additionally, on the Greek Prison Islands during the Civil War, the exiles staged plays such as *Antigone* (ca 441 BCE) and *Philocretes* (409 BCE) by Sophocles and *Prometheus Bound* (ca 430 BCE) by Aeschylus (Grivas 2004; Van Steen 2010). In recent years, the relationship between theatre, citizenship and activism has become prominent in the context of the current economic and political situation in Greece. The economic crisis and austerity measures have eviscerated the country's social welfare programmes and curbed access to cultural and educational opportunities. In addition, the financial crisis has led to an alarming increase in mental health problems, homelessness, drug addiction and suicides (Kentikelenis et al. 2014; Serraos et al. 2016). In the same vein, the cuts into the public sector had a detrimental impact on artistic productions. Under this climate of acute economic, social and humanitarian instability, one would expect that theatre, and arts at large, would be under threat. Nevertheless, this has not been the case. On the contrary, a number of authors (Tsiara 2015; Zisis 2014; Euronews 2013; Zervou 2017) stress that there is a boom in the art and creative scene in Greece despite the economic crisis. Artists have become more productive, proactive and even more provocative in the ways they express themselves. Since the beginning of the economic crisis in 2010, there has been a growing interest in socially engaged theatre with a greater emphasis on audience participation. Chris Zisis makes reference to, a burgeoning and increased number of self-managed theatrical teams in Greece with some common elements: a so called *do-it-yourself* spirit, a sense of collaboration, interactivity with the audience and urge for active participation, performances outside the determined theater venues, from abandoned factories, military camps, empty villas and houses to the very public space and streets, alternative practices against the norms of classical theater institutions or the established ways of funding theater in Greece.

(2014: 44)

This multitude of theatrical groups and arts organizations have been widely documented by Omikron Project (2016). For the purpose of this introductory section, it is worth mentioning a few of these collectives such as the Mavili Collective, Moving Theatre Unit of Neos Kosmos Theatre, Theatre of the Oppressed-Greece and Tsiritsantzoules, among others. In addition, a number of festivals, such as the Fast Forward Festival, and the Anti-Fascist Festival of Performative Arts, among other initiatives, introduced Greek audiences to new theatrical forms that are characterized by an emphasis on audience engagement: forum theatre, documentary theatre, site-specific theatre and so forth. As Natalie Zervou (2017) maintains, the lack of financial support encouraged a collaborative approach to art making, which placed a particular emphasis on the performativity of the pedestrian and collective action such as sit-ins and strikes. In addition to this, it vitalized the use of abandoned buildings and other sites as venues. Artists became more imaginative in finding ways to counter austerity by making effective use of their surroundings and the social structure. She moves on to suggest that artists found new ways of dealing with the challenges presented to them because of the austerity measures by turning them into an opportunity for reconfiguration. This resulted in the formation of new modes of collaboration, spatial practice, bodily presence and audience participation. In turn, this inspired a new form of aesthetic that Zervou refers to as a 'precarious aesthetic' (2017: 105). She argues that 'the precarity of everyday life shapes the conditions for artistic production, which are inextricably linked with the methodological approaches chosen and the aesthetic of frugality that has also emerged as a common trope' (2017: 105). The notion of the precarity of the everyday life as a form of aesthetic offers itself as an opportunity to promote alternative methods of social engagement through the arts.

This chapter aims to offer an exemplar of social engagement through the arts practice in Greece since the beginning of the economic crisis. In doing so, it will explore the work of UrbanDig Project.

UrbanDig places an emphasis on enhancing the participants' *social imaginary* (Taylor 2003) and by doing so facilitating the re-imagining of their city. UrbanDig's work echoes Jill Dolan when she puts forward the idea of performance as a space in which affirmation, warmth and love should be experienced and expressed 'regularly and effectively' (Dolan 2005: 14). She makes the case that performances have the potential to unite the audience to such a degree that they are 'rallied to hope for the possibility of realizing improved social relations' (Dolan 2005: 14). By taking Dolan's views into consideration, this chapter sets up to explore the company's innovative model of social engagement. Using conversation analysis as a mode of enquiry, Zoe Zontou has conducted a series of interviews with George Sachinis about his experiences of designing and delivering the UrbanDig Project. This chapter is composed of four themed sections: project rationale, theatre and social engagement, creative process and impact. In each of these sections Sachinis offers a detailed account of the project's ethos and methodology.

ZOE ZONTOU (ZZ): What is the UrbanDig Project? Can you conceptualize it in reference to the situation in post-2010 Greece?

GEORGE SACHINIS (GS): UrbanDig Project is a platform of artistic and community activities that the Ohi Pezoume, a non-profit performing arts company, applies yearly to a different urban neighbourhood. The platform creates a voluntary multidisciplinary network of scientists, artists, researchers, students, people working in institutions, local professionals and residents, all of who are interested in researching and mapping the neighbourhood through collective processes and public events. This 'UrbanDig community' of all ages and various backgrounds, nationalities and interests collects material about the past, the present, the aspirations and challenges of the neighbourhood, based on a given research question or the growing interests of the community itself. Participation is on a voluntary basis and is realized through public events such as mapping walks, interactive festivals, games, artistic workshops involving collection and curation of oral history, collective installations etc. The design, the programming and the production of each UrbanDig Project is realized through step-by-step partnerships between this growing community formed by the project and Ohi Pezoume's ten core-members with backgrounds from the arts, sciences, cultural management, architecture and city planning. Apart from creating a local archive with a community around it, each UrbanDig Project results in a varying number of artistic, educational and place-making deliverables. Artistic works and curated presentations of the material collected, academic papers, school projects, digital tour apps, contributions to municipal urban-planning processes are examples of these deliverables, many of them produced through partnership of very different stakeholders (residents, local informal community and artistic groups, academics, digital experts, schools, cultural institutions, the municipality) taking part in the project that wouldn't have met otherwise.

Before moving on to the next neighbourhood, Ohi Pezoume always concludes the project with a site-specific performance in streets and buildings of the neighbourhood inspired by the people and the findings of the process. This final artistic event is what drives the company to create each UrbanDig Project. The extent at which the programming, the community, the archive and the deliverables created through the project continues to exist in the neighbourhood after the departure of the company is a local decision connected to the quality of relationships and partnerships formed during the project. The stronger these relationships and partnerships, the most inspirational the project both for Ohi Pezoume's final performance and for the local neighbourhood to continue what the project started there.

Making time to build a collaborative project in order to deepen citizen participation and allow for the creation of substantial partnerships between those participating in the project is not an easy task, in terms of the production requirements, in post-2010 Greece. However, we see some good examples around us in Athens; there are people to share stories with, in order to strengthen this part of our ethos. UrbanDig Project contributes to a neighbourhood's 'place-making' throughout its process, as most of it happens in public space through locally designed and collaboratively created events that at the same time 'dig' for local stories and present them to passers-by and audiences. It is crucial for us that the local community is involved not merely as participants but as partners in this 'place-making' and that there is local ownership of the process and its deliverables. We hope that we are contributing to the existing culture for participatory processes in urban planning and decision making in Athens, coming primarily from citizen initiatives but also appearing at various depths in a growing number of institutional processes.

As most of UrbanDig activities are literally on the streets, it is unavoidable and therefore an integrant part of our process to get to know and collaborate with people from all walks of life. In co-designing the public activities of the research phase of the project, Ohi Pezoume and the growing local 'UrbanDig' community make sure to address and invite people of all ages, backgrounds and interests (academic, cultural, commercial, tourism, civil society etc.). We believe that bridging different worlds, establishing common goals and language and building trust between different 'islets' of background, interest and specialism need to be central to decision making in 'post-2010' Greece. UrbanDig works in the setting of urban neighbour-hoods as an epicentre of a wider community. In that respect, we seem to follow current international trends of using the city as the ground or vehicle for testing and developing sustainable processes in many fields from arts and sciences to governance.

Our urge to dig into the secrets of the neighbourhood and our fun way of 'digging' become the ice-breaker for very different stakeholders to meet and work together. Curiosity about the place, interest in digging up stories, discovering its potential or simply communicating with each other about life in the neighbourhood are some of the reasons why different people get involved in the project and end up on the same table as collaborators, unlocking possibilities for synergies. Having fun, being creative, express-ing oneself are also important reasons for joining our project. UrbanDig's 'research' activities are open, entertaining, playful, often performative and interactive which has proven to be a good ground for this 'un-locking' to happen between people, even if they come from conflicting sides (e.g. polit-ically). The artistic tools and the different voices heard in our processes also help unlock empathy, perception and imagination. The artistic objective of the company, our humble mission to make a site-specific performance, and the intensity and time of our engagement with the people of the neighbour-hood help establish the trust needed for people to take their initial involve-ment to a next level. Our role and function as an artistic company in all this help us break through from the entrenching artistic clichés that still domi-nate some of Greece's artistic landscape. We train ourselves in employing our artistic tools and vocabulary to introduce a community-in-the-making to each other, to inspire trust, to un-lock empathy, perception, imagination about a neighbourhood.

Given the difficulty of funding and initiating art productions in Greece with the crisis, UrbanDig does not rely on the pre-production process. Our approach is organic and depends largely on what UrbanDig's ever-grow-ing community of researchers and stakeholders will bring to the table. In a sense, we strive to draw special attention to the contemporary Greek performing arts, taking it outside of the theatre. In Greece, theatre produc-tions continue to be dominated by the ancient Greek tradition, and are driven by a fascination with Ancient Greek history and its connection to the present. We are interested in illuminating contemporary performance practices that are conceptual, have many dimensions and are hidden in the stories of people who reside in marginalized and forgotten neigh-bourhoods of the city. Our vision is to forge opportunities for creativity, communication and trust.

ZZ: Can you give us one example of your work?

GS: *Dourgouti Island Hotel* (2015–16) was a two-year UrbanDig Project in Dourgouti, partly supported by an EU Culture project entitled '*Hotel Obscura*' (2013–16) in which we were the Greek partners. Dourgouti is a historical yet generally neglected neighbourhood bordering Syngrou avenue, an avenue in the process of becoming a new museum-mile for Athens. Dourgouti is a neighbourhood full of unknown stories of migration and resistance. Refugees from Smyrna and Armenia developed it in 1922 and ever since it has been a destination of all waves of migration that arrived in Athens, contributing much to the Greek resistance in World War II. The local cultural capital had not been systematically researched or managed prior to *Dourgouti Island Hotel* project. On the contrary, both the municipality and many owners of the old housing blocks have systematically neglected it, which has resulted in many complaints from its residents.

The striking contrast between the massive buildings of five star hotels, banks and cultural institutions on the 'shore' of Dourgouti towards Syngrou avenue and the housing block neighbourhood inwards, with its old, mostly neglected buildings and nice squares where you hear only birds sing, was the main source of inspiration for us. Being one of the most recent immigrant neighbourhoods of Athens that transformed from huts to housing blocks in the 1960s, Dourgouti was the right place for attracting people with strong memories of its ghosts to share their stories as a starting point of our UrbanDig there. The programme evolved into almost 100 days of activities, exploring all sides of Dourgouti's history and cultural capital of the past and its current condition including challenges and aspirations. 68 groups, institutions and companies ranging from the local home for the elderly and a student band to three Greek universities (Panteion, Charokopeion and Pireaus) and a UK university (Leicester) actively collaborated in our events. 632 people in total have collaborated (either through these groups or as individuals) including international artists, scientists, community activists, students and many residents that formed four research and activity sub-groups. In addition, more than 3000 spectators have participated in our events.

We made it a point that residents and people whose workplace was around the area constituted more than half of the formed UrbanDig community. We were not interested in creating external gentrification effects in Dourgouti that would create the danger of reducing its residential character. On the contrary, we wanted to increase awareness of its cultural wealth as a way of creating a wide cross-sectoral community of 'Dourgouti

FIGURE 8: UrbanDig 2015. Photo credit: Irene Fosgeraou.

neighbourhood supporters' supporting the historical residential status of the community and strengthening local processes of cultural management and place-making. Dourgouti's cultural heritage if discovered and then managed at neighbourhood level could become a platform for collaboration between the neighbourhood and the municipal as well as other local cultural, touristic and academic institutions, especially now that Syngrou avenue is becoming a 'museum-mile' in Athens.

Following the completion of the project, Onassis Cultural Centre, a nearby institution and an important stakeholder contributing to the development of Syngrou's identity, collaborated with members of Dourgouti's UrbanDig community for adopting some of the local stories into libretti for a concert, for an exhibition and for a free open-air dance piece. The municipality is considering creating a yearly cultural festival in the area with the collaboration of the neighbourhood. An international festival in Naples invited a Dourgouti high-school cultural team for an artistic project after they saw what the pupils produced in the *Dourgouti Island Hotel* project. These are three examples out of a few showing us that things continue towards the direction we envisioned when we delivered the *Dourgouti Island Hotel* project to make the area's cultural wealth and capacity more visible to the world, involving the neighbourhood in this new place-making.

ZZ: How do you facilitate audience engagement?

GS: As the neighbourhoods that we visit become theatrical stages for us, we strive to be as active as possible in our role as artists and audiences. Urban-Dig travels to urban areas in order to excavate the hidden cultural and social capital collectively with residents and a wide range of local or relative stakeholders. We develop cross-sectoral horizontal partnerships within the neighbourhood and between the neighbourhood and the world of the arts, culture, technology and education, even outside city/country borders. With site-specific performance being our main output, we also support the initiatives of the partnerships formed (e.g. festivals, walks, touring apps, website). We are motivated by the idea that we and all local and international partners, collaborators, participants and audience members of our activities,[1] co-develop into active audiences of the neighbourhood's stories; active not only in collecting but in interpreting these stories and co-creating new visions of their city.

Our audience development strategy refers to expanding in numbers and quality the active-audiences of the city, i.e. the excavators and/or carriers of new narratives about our urban reality. The tools we develop for doing that are tools for community engagement and active citizenship through our artistic lens as a core-team. The majority of the programme's activities are a mixture of community action, field research and participatory creative activities, all of which serve the purpose of generating material for a site-specific performance. The performance is additional to the other project outcomes, which are: digital touring tools, conferences, publications, documentaries and walks. Our core-team uses a synthesis of tools from visual arts, performance and improvisation. Our participatory activities focus on trust, creativity, imagination, fun and storytelling. Hence, the mapping and presentation of the neighbourhood's stories are often happening simultaneously. They become an integral part of the collective creative process. The participants offering or collecting stories are participants-spectators in the process. They do not just witness the stories of others; they are responsible for curating or directing how they wish to deliver these stories to the research groups. This process as well as the types of activities outlined earlier consists of our audience development plan. Our aim is not only to develop an active audience, but most importantly to create ways of seeing, that the city is the 'stage'.

ZZ: Can you describe your structures and processes by using an example?

GS: UrbanDig programme of activities comprises of a research/community mapping phase and then a performance and other curated outputs' production phase. In both phases, the 'stage' is the city, especially its less visible layers. There are four stages of audience engagement:

1. Our core team that sets the strategy and facilitates the project.
2. Members of the sub-groups, those who organize the community-mapping phase as well as get involved in the artistic phase of the project.
3. Participants of the open mapping activities, the various research workshops and the audience of our usually interactive promenade performance.
4. Members of the general public who have expressed an interest in our project, and wish to interact with the stories, and the vision of the city as it has been produced through events like presentations, workshops etc. or through social media.

For all the aforementioned stages, our audience development strategy has a twofold goal:

• Capacity development: To acquire skills and experience of becoming an active audience of the city as stage, of the stories, the narratives and visions that it contains. By participating in the project, members are automatically involved in excavating, synthesizing and articulating their own narratives.
• Expansion: To involve as many people from different backgrounds as possible into becoming an active audience of the specific urban area's stories, narratives and visions. 'Active' is understood as a synonym of simultaneously acting as excavators/curators and observers.

Our aim as a team is to involve as many people as possible. We make sure that at each project, each member of our team takes on different roles at different points of the project in order to better understand the project in its totality and build relationships with the residence-participants e.g. as a member of a community mapping group and as a participant in some mapping activities and finally through performing. This is necessary for the development not only of the project but also for our personal ability to interpret the city in multiple ways from the participants' viewpoints. At the other end of the spectrum, our aim for the community mapping groups is to ensure that these groups are as inter-disciplinary as possible. This in turn will generate partnerships that otherwise would have seemed improbable.

Creative Process

The first stage of our programme at each neighbourhood involves organizing a range of activities aiming to generate interest for the project. These activities

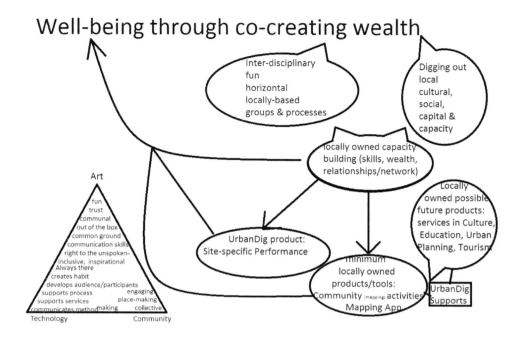

FIGURE 9: UrbanDig creative process.

happen at very different settings in order to attract a wide range of participants/ perspective group members. From interactive historical tours and festivals in the neighbourhood's square to presentations at the local university, to sensory mapping walks involving local schools, to site-specific art workshops in culture/ art/community centres in the vicinity.

These activities formulate the basis of the project. It is during this phase that we concentrate most on audience development both in numbers and in terms of capacity development. At this stage, we fully implement our strategy in order to successfully transform the neighbourhood's residents and associates into an active audience of their city. *Dourgouti Island Hotel*, as mentioned before, involved 632 people, about half of them locally based, coming from a total of 68 institutions and informal groups or individuals. About a third of those were associated with public institutions (municipality and primary, secondary and university education), a quarter had an individual interest in the project, and the remaining cohort was related to private institutions, informal groups, associations in the fields of culture, education, science (from cultural management to history, geography, dramaturgy, urban architecture), active citizenship, tourism, church, technology and sports.

The open research and mapping activities aim to attract people from a wide range of ages, backgrounds and regions. These activities also serve the role of

FIGURE 10: UrbanDig 2015. Photo credit: Irene Fosgeraou.

presenting the neighbourhood to their participants. They are fun, interactive activities that often take place outdoors. The majority of our activities were designed to involve a wide range of participants. For instance, some activities involve mapping based on the research project 'Glossopoly' by M. Phillips (University of Leicester n.d.). The age range of participants in our activities spanned from 12 to 80 year olds. Many of our activities are designed to reach audiences from places and institutions that are 'distant' from that specific neighbourhood (e.g. local authorities, international artistic scene or academia, hospitality industry). With most of our activities happening within the limits of the neighbourhood, our project creates in-flows of unfamiliar audiences to that part of the city, thus creating new relationships and new ways of experiencing and imagining the city.

Digital social interaction tools, such as social media and our webpage, are used as a platform to document and disseminate the project outcomes. The digital archives are curated by the community groups and uploaded to the Internet or to free digital tour apps such as www.dourgouti.gr and cliomuseapp. Invitations to present our work into mainstream media are re-shaped usually by us into opportunities for the community to voice themselves. Creating awareness of the project's activities for us means creating more links between people and the community (real or digital). It often demands from community members to work on communication and presentation skills – oral or written – and on ways to publicize their research and mapping results to a wider audience. This methodology expands the numbers of (live or digital) audiences of the city and deepens the ways of viewing, relating and interpreting their own neighbourhood.

ZZ: What is the impact of the project?

GS: Meeting with each other and working together in collaboration as artists, scientists, students, researchers or simply citizens helps to create awareness about multiple sectors and forms of action. The following selection of case studies evidence *Dourgouti Island Hotel*'s impact:

- Two local cultural/community groups working with children, despite the proximity of their local offices (200 m) were unaware of each other. The project brought them together for the first time.
- A geographer, expert in digital mapping, continues his collaboration with a local community group, after their partnership in a research group within the project.
- The project became mostly popular with people in the age range around 20s (university students), 40s and 70s, stimulating intergenerational conversations and collaborations.
- The involvement of students from four universities resulted in about 300 course projects including a number of master's and doctoral theses. During a local conference curated by UrbanDig, a number of these research findings were presented to the neighbourhood's residents who, for the first time, had a direct dialogue with academics about issues of their concern.
- Eight local high-school students were invited to AltoFest, an art festival in Naples, after generating the interest from the festival programmers who visited Dourgouti activities. Local primary and secondary school students presented their Dourgouti work in conferences, impressing delegates with their presentation skills.
- Residents of all ages expressed their views in interviews and co-authored articles about the neighbourhood.
- Residents of all ages worked with international scholars and artists during open workshops of the *Dourgouti Island Hotel* process (e.g. geographer Dr Martin Phillips from Leicester University, artistic groups GK from France and Triage from Australia).

FIGURE 11: UrbanDig 2015. Photo credit: Anna Kanta.

- The activities of the programme took place both in public spaces rarely visited and in local cultural/sport organizations in need of more visibility, which, through these partnerships, were achieved.
- The local Oral History Research Group and a local community group dealing with current neighbourhood issues were both initiated as a result of the neighbourhood's reactivation initiative during the *Dourgouti Island Hotel* project.
- The neighbourhood's cultural richness and current cultural activity were disseminated in at least twelve cities worldwide either via conferences presentations, workshops or through partners abroad. It was showcased as a good example of the dynamism that emerges at neighbourhood level in Athens of crisis.
- The municipality is considering creating a yearly site-specific festival in collaboration with the community at Dourgouti.
- Onassis cultural foundation collaborated with local members of our research community to curate local stories into musical libretti.

The most important impact of this UrbanDig Project was our relationships with some people in the neighbourhood and in the UrbanDig community formed during the project. We believe in the power of artistic projects to be transformative agents, certainly to be catalysts for truthful relationships and the starting point of unexpected synergies even with people from very different walks of life.

REFERENCES

Barker, Derek Wai Ming (2014), *Tragedy and Citizenship: Conflict, Reconciliation, and Democracy from Haemon to Hegel*, Albany: State University of New York Press.

Dolan, Jill (2005), *Utopian Performatives: Finding Hope in Theatre*, Ann Arbor, MI: University of Michigan Press.

Euronews (2013), 'Ελλάδα: Η τέχνη σε καιρούς κρίσης' ('Crisis Art in Greece'), 13 December, http://gr.euronews.com/2013/12/13/crisis-inspires-a-surge-of-creativity-in-greek-art/. Accessed 2 July 2016.

Grivas, Kleanthis (2004), *Αντίσταση στην Εποχή του Τίποτα*, Thessaloniki: Ianos.

Kentikelenis, Alexander, Karanikolos, Marina, Reeves, Aaron, Martin, McKee and Stuckler, David (2014), 'Austerity and health in Greece: Authors' reply', *The Lancet*, 383:9928, pp. 1544–45.

Omikron Project (2016), *Map of Grassroots Groups in Greece,* 2nd ed., Athens: Omikron Project, http://omikronproject.gr/grassroots#Art_and_Culture. Accessed 2 July 2016.

Serraos, Konstantinos, Greve, Thomas, Evangelos, Asprogerakas, Balampanidis, Dimitrios and Chani, Anastasia (2016), 'Athens, a capital in crisis: Tracing the spatial impacts', in J. Knieling and F. Othengrafen (eds), *Cities in Crisis: Socio-Spatial Impacts of the Economic Crisis in Southern European Cities*, London: Routledge, pp. 116–38.

Taylor, Charles (2003), *Modern Social Imaginaries*, 4th ed., Durham, NC: Duke University Press.

Tsiara, Syrago (2015), 'Contemporary Greek art in times of crisis: Cuts and changes', *Journal of Visual Culture*, 14:2, pp. 176–81.

University of Leicester (n.d.), 'Glossopoly', University of Leicester Official Website, https://www2.le.ac.uk/departments/geography/redundant-content/research/old-research-folder/projects/ConCom/glossopoly. Accessed 5 May 2019.

Van Steen, Gonda (2010), *Theatre of the Condemned: Classical Tragedy on Greek Prison Islands*, Oxford: Oxford University Press.

Zervou, Natalie (2017), 'Rethinking fragile landscapes during the Greek crisis: Precarious aesthetics and methodologies in Athenian dance performances', *Research in Drama Education: The Journal of Applied Theatre and Performance*, 22:1, pp. 104–15.

Zisis, Chris (2014), 'Political/socially-engaged/interfering art in Greece during the years of the economic crisis: Tendencies in cinema, theater and public art', *Kulturrevolution: Zeitschrift für angewandte Diskurstheorie*, 66/67, pp. 39–50.

Editors' Note

A recent article provides an important analysis of the UrbanDig Project, see Chatziefstathiou et al.'s article 'UrbanDig Project: Sport practices and artistic interventions for co-creating urban space' (2018). Of particular interest is the discussion of space in these projects. For emerging approaches in the area of performance and public spaces, please see Pais (2017).

Further reading

Chatziefstathiou, Dikaia, Iliopoulou, Eirini and Magkou, Matina (2018), 'UrbanDig Project: Sport practices and artistic interventions for co-creating urban space', *Sport in Society*, February, pp. 1–14, https://www-tandfonline-com.ejournals.um.edu.mt/doi/abs/10.1080/17430437.2018.1430485. Accessed 6 March 2019.

Pais, Ana (ed.) (2017), *Performance in the Public Sphere,* Lisbon: Black Orpheus.

NOTE

1. Such mapping activities include sensory mapping walks, interactive festival receiving/presenting neighbourhood secrets, collective mapping fests, oral history workshops etc. For a full list of activities please refer to http://www.urbandigproject.org. Accessed 5 June 2019.

Community Theatre as Political Theatre: Towards a New Political Theatre Practice

Marius Bogdan Tudor and Ionuț Sociu in conversation with David Schwartz

In order to understand the context in which community theatre has emerged in Romania in the past decades, one has to look at this phenomenon from a broader perspective. The way in which contemporary theatre deals with politics is intimately connected to the way in which one looks back at the past. In post-revolutionary Romania, the debate about the past was (and still is to a certain extent) dominated by a twofold line of discourse, monopolized by right-wing intellectuals: a scathing criticism of the communist period, combined with a nostalgic and glorifying representation that aims to re-create the interwar period reconstructing an idyllic image of those times.

Through this idealization of the interwar years, one refuses to see the extremism, intolerance, poverty and violence that pervade that period, which in turn enables the dissimulation of the fascist chapter of Romania's past. This phenomenon was visible not only in the Romanian theatrical community, but also in the neighbouring countries. In his essay 'History and politics: The Polish theater fights for imagination', the critic Witold Mrozek states:

> Indeed, it may be that, when we lose our ability to create utopias, when we stop imagining the future, the whole energy of the society's fantasy concentrates upon the past? But historical fantasies have a very real equivalent in the political actions of today. This is well known to the Polish right, which bases its actions on historical politics. Thus, to cut it short, the absolute delegitimization of the Communist-Socialist period discredits any political emancipation; even the unemployment benefits begin to look like shameful totalitarianism. History transfigured into fairytale – the interwar Poland, authoritarian in its peak years, is transformed into the lost garden of Eden, where we return after half a century.
>
> (quoted in Popovici 2014: 180)

It comes then as no surprise that the 1990s are associated with a more apolitical stance in terms of theatrical practice. But the end of the decade and the beginning of the third millennium mark the beginning of a 'romantic phase', a dynamic period, that stimulates the formation of groups, the launching of new directions and the founding of platforms dedicated to local realities (see Popovici 2008). A first important step was made by Alina Nelega and the Dramafest Foundation (established in 1997), followed, after 2000, by programmes such as DramAcum (DramaNow), Dramaturgia Cotidianului (The Dramaturgy of the Everyday) or tangaProject. These projects launched dramaturgy contests, emphasized the collaboration between directors and playwrights, equated the dramatic text with a script (as a flexible working material) and paid close attention to the immediate reality, thus generating a change of paradigm in Romanian contemporary theatre.

In the mid-2000s, another phase appeared: an attempt to get closer to various communities and a shift from *centre* to *margin*, from big cities to smaller areas. The intention was to understand what was going on in rural areas and in poverty-stricken regions and, to quote from *Underground: Valea Jiului after 1989*[1] (a performance created by David Schwartz and Mihaela Michailov in 2012), 'to salvage the social life of the people, the community traditions, their hopes and expectations'. In this period, the theatrical themes became particular, the focus moved from macro-stories to local stories and personal histories, approached by the artists by means of different forms, from community theatre to documentary theatre. Simultaneously, this strong interest in present-day realities was linked to a need of confronting the past through theatrical means.

Regarding the social and artistic climate of this period, *The Calvert Journal* reports:

> As Romania's urban centres continue to grow and change, the experience of urban life shifts as well. For some, it means less access to public spaces for gathering, for others it means fear of forced eviction in gentrifying neighborhoods like the Rahova-Uranus neighborhood in Bucharest. Ten years ago, its proximity to the city center marked it as a site for development, and the neighborhood's low-income residents began to be forcibly removed from their homes without options for alternative housing. As a collective started by Maria Drăghici, Bogdan Georgescu, and Irina Gâdiuță, Ofensiva Generozității facilitated projects in which artists and local residents collaborated to lead art workshops, stage plays in the neighborhood and organise performances. The contributions by local residents and other artists provided new ways to embolden the community's political engagement. Eventually, the collective established a community center, LaBomba, in a former discotheque that was partially being used as a sewing shop. After its forced closure in 2011, Scoală în Stradă

(School on the Street) turned streets and pavements into free spaces for learning. Through a process of collective creative engagement, a community which 'once had no voice in the future of its neighborhood configured spaces of its own to convene, learn, debate and empower itself.

(Harsanyi 2016: n.pag.)

Some of the artists belonging to this generation have formed an association called O2G, which develops projects of social and cultural intervention, educational projects, community theatre, theatre and documentary film. The objectives of this association are: the recovery of the social and political role of art, facilitating access to culture and education for everyone, developing the concept of community theatre, documenting and archiving contemporary realities. During many years of activity, the association implemented several projects for active art and community theatre including: *Build your Community!* (2007), *Touring the Countryside* (2009), *4th Age* (2009–present), *The House of the People* (2011), *Physical History* (2012); documentary theatre projects such as *Heated Minds 13th-15th June 1990* (2010) and documentary films including *Flexible 1* (2008) and *Flexible 2* (2010), *Unwritten Theatre Group from Şanţ Village* (2011). The association also coordinated several educational workshops in the fields of anti-racism, development of community art projects, active art involving the Roma and Jewish minorities, Arab migrants and sexual minorities. The projects of the association also focus on facilitating access to culture for communities and social groups that are economically and geographically disadvantaged via conducting community art projects in marginalized communities (Rahova-Uranus in Bucharest, Moses Rosen Retirement Home, Craiova Penitentiary) and touring in geographical areas with limited access to culture (cities in Valea Jiului and Baia Mare, a northern Romanian mining region, but also across villages in the country).

David Schwartz (born 1985) is one of the theatre artists who has been very active within this group. As a theatre practitioner and theoretician, he is interested in counter-hegemonic perspectives towards local and global history; the social and human impact of the post-socialist transition. He is the co-founder of the arts and politics magazine and website *Gazeta de Artă Politică* (*Journal of Political Arts*),[2] co-initiator of the Political Theatre Platform[3] and member of the self-organized artists' and workers' collective MACAZ – Bar Theatre Cooperative. In 2016, he finished a Ph.D. at Babeş-Bolyai University, Cluj, researching the political and ethical aspects of the interactions between artists and subaltern groups (including migrants, elderly people, people evicted from their homes or threatened with eviction and working-class families). Since 2009, David Schwartz has been involved in several community theatre performances within the *4th Age* project, a community arts programme developed together with the residents of the Moses Rosen Retirement Home in Bucharest.

Regarding this project, David recalls: 'We've been working together for seven years, during which we made seven very different performances, which became more and more complex'. Indeed, one can notice how this project has evolved and gained more public attention. In a performance like *Post-Scriptum* (2013), the residents of Moses Rosen Retirement Home talk about who they wrote their first letters to, how the writing ritual unfolded, who they wrote love letters to (and thus the performance represents the performing of a vanishing social ritual), while in *Closer than Close* (2014), some of the residents of Moses Rosen Retirement Home and some of the staff members, who are with the residents on a daily basis, came together on stage to reconstruct everyday rituals, dance, reminisce about their lives together and tell stories about the connections between them, about what keeps them together and what they have learnt from each other. *Closer than Close* depicts the history of everyday life in a retirement home.

In the following conversation, we attempt to present David Schwartz's perspective on his own work, but equally, we wish to reflect on the social and political context that has shaped Romanian contemporary political theatre in the past decade.

MARIUS-BOGDAN TUDOR (MBT): I suggest we start by questioning the term 'community'. Let us not forget that this term is a hallmark of neo-liberal discourse. What I find interesting in this is that the discourse on community harbours a conformist direction under the umbrella of diversity. Each community is allotted its own square, without any regard for the multiple distinctions of class, gender or different attitudes within those communities themselves.

DAVID SCHWARTZ (DS): That is right. There is a fine line between the discourse focusing on the community and the idea of the community *as an issue* 'which needs to be solved'. This is how the whole debate about the 'integration' of the communities and 'building community spirit' started. In a neo-liberal sense, the term has slowly begun to replace the idea of the social. We stop talking about society and social principles, which would represent a common basis for everyone, and we start talking about separate communities. Which can also be okay, but at a certain point it starts obscuring class specifics and differences.

IONUȚ SOCIU (IS): How does it obscure them?

DS: We stop talking about class interests and instead we bring up communities with different interests. This is how people who are on the same side, part of the same class, end up being separated and often start perceiving

190

themselves as having opposing interests. But why would they be treated differently? The root of their problems is the same, they are part of the same oppressive capitalist system which functions in a very diverse way: for instance, some are poorly paid contractual workers, others are paid under the counter at even lower rates, and others are simply slave labourers. These are different instances of the same system of production and property relations.

IS: If we enter a bit into your history, when and how did your encounter with community theatre start to take place?

DS: The term started being used in Romania in the mid-2000s. Bogdan Georgescu, a colleague from my generation, was the one who initiated the first community theatre projects after coming back from the USA. Whether we like it or not, we were looking towards the West, nobody can deny it. However, what is important to mention is that he did not engage with this direction from a desire to imitate, but merely suggested using tools from the West to tackle specific local issues and the dissatisfaction many of us felt regarding the role of the artist in Romania. That is why I do not agree with the idea that everything borrowed from the west is mere self-colonizing, especially since this is an idea that disregards syncretism; elements from other cultural spaces can be borrowed, reused and re-signified in a way that is useful and necessary for that particular space. In a context where the local educational system did not provide any original bypasses of the dominant aestheticizing bourgeois paradigm, even some of my professors turned to western models to escape this model. Of course, there is more to talk about here and there is also the question: why relate to western models and not Latin American or African ones, which are at least as rich and interesting as their western counterparts. To answer this, we have to return to the power dynamics and post-Cold War spheres of influence which positioned Romania and all of Eastern Europe in the Western European/North American backyard.

IS: Why do you believe there were no 'original escapes' from the dominant model?

DS: Left-wing theatre, as well as workers' and peasants' theatre, has not been very developed in Romania, and popular tradition has been lost. It has not been documented in due time and already in the interwar period it had become virtually unknown, and was to be later rejected by socialism.

Workers' theatre was poorly developed, with only a handful of attempts in the interwar period. Nobody knows what happened during 45 years of popular socialist theatre between 1945 and 1989. We are only told there were a bunch of idiots in artistic brigades shouting, 'long live Ceausescu!' Personal histories and testimonies tell us that there was much more than that. But nobody bothered to look into what really happened, let alone share the knowledge publicly. So basically we cannot truly relate to a history of Romanian political theatre which works with oppressed groups and communities. Researchers are primarily at fault here; after 1990, socialism was seen as a void in history, which led many to believe the period did not require any research. Only the crimes of the regime were worth studying. But there are several inlets which are worth pursuing.

IS: Could you give us some examples of such inlets?

DS: One important marker would be Șanț theatre in Bistrița. A peasants' theatre, it was the subject of research of the team of sociologist Dimitrie Gusti. It was established at the end of the nineteenth century in a village in Bistrița. It was a form of spoken theatre, there were scripts devised by peasants on issues of social and political satire. Bogdan Georgescu tried to recover the tradition of the Șanț theatre by making a documentary film[4] about it. As he was saying in an interview, 'I had to go to the US to uncover what was a mere 100 km away from the place I was born in' (Bortun 2015: n.pag.). And they were doing that 100 years ago! There are other interesting things. From our experiences in the Jiu Valley, from the talks we had with miners who had been part of the artistic brigades during socialism and with the residents and staff of the Moses Rosen Retirement Home in Bucharest (where we have been working for many years), we found out about the fundamental role these brigades played in bringing the community together.

Sometimes they even fostered acts of disobedience towards the socialist regime. For instance, several miners in the Jiu Valley were talking about how they were singing carols in the brigades, which was completely forbidden by the socialist authorities. Sure, we can discuss to what extent singing carols is an emancipatory act, but in relation to an oppressive regime that did not allow the free practice of one's faith, it was an act of rebellion.

IS: I understand that you are now sceptical about certain ethical aspects pertaining to the practice of community theatre. How was it at the beginning?

FIGURE 12: Domiciliu Instabil (Instable Residence), 2016. Photo credit: Vârsta4. Featuring Margareta Eschenasy and Mihaela Bârlegi.

DS: At first I was very enthusiastic, I found the whole community theatre thing fascinating. The first projects, the interaction with the people from Rahova Uranus (a neighbourhood in downtown Bucharest), meeting people threatened with eviction, all this had a strong impact on me and represented a sort of political school, which changed some of us. It changed me, at least. It changed my worldview and my perspective on the reality of the transition from socialism. However, in a very arrogant way, our first project there was called *Build your Community* – we were starting from the idea that we were helping to build their community, when we could barely build our own artistic community. As a matter of fact, we did have some misunderstandings later on. So, we started out from a kind of arrogant standpoint, in a way, but we were also very curious. If we had not been open about things, we would not have remained friends with the people in the neighbourhood for years. Indeed, the project in Rahova-Uranus evolved from an artistic project with social goals to a more radical political project, with the people in the neighbourhood taking responsibility and being in charge of all the artistic and political activities. So, on the long term, I would say it has been quite successful in terms of the self-organization of the 'community'. But I have to admit that in the past ten or eleven years, I've come to be wary of terms that are overused. The moment a certain term is taken over and integrated in the liberal mainstream, it's a sign that there's something wrong with it.

IS: What other terms or phrases are you wary of?

DS: There are many other terms, for instance the newest are 'the voiceless' or 'the invisibles'. We hear it increasingly often: 'let us give voice to those on the margins'. But in fact we see how this discourse of making the invisible visible is used by the *very visible* to earn cultural and financial capital. That is why you constantly have to rethink and rearrange your political discourse in order to push the boundaries and see where the lines which people refuse to cross are. In a way, there are always limits, for example with the use of the term 'political'. People do not venture to use it very often. If you look at the local context, you see that there is talk of social theatre, community theatre, documentary theatre, but there is rather little mention of political theatre in an explicit way. Every context has its own taboos regarding radical discourse. We are currently in a relatively primitive phase of political thought, a phase in which the term 'political' itself is very radical. I don't mean it is primitive in relation to Western Europe or any other region, but in relation to an elaborate system of political thought.

IS: To what extent did contact with those communities shape your performances and your aesthetics?

DS: This was the outstanding thing about those experiences. Meeting and working with the people shaped our performances, at least in the first couple of years. On the one hand, it mattered that we were performing in the neighbourhood, there were people around all the time and we got a direct and immediate reaction from them. We knew straight away when people understood or did not understand what we were doing, when they were having fun and when they were not, when they agreed or did not agree, and this could have a big impact on the performance. The rehearsals in the neighbourhoods were awesome. On the other hand, this kind of experience really challenges you. For instance, a person tells you things about his or her life. How much of what they say can you use and in what way? To what extent is it ethical to change that material and mix it with other people's stories? Is it ethical to construct theatrical situations based on their life stories? For a long time I believed everything was at the fringes of ethics – and I still do. When someone confesses his or her experience to you, but does not take part in the creative process, the only way to reproduce that story is to transmit its essence, keeping what that person wishes to convey as accurately as possible and not jumbling up perspectives. I mean, you can do whatever you like, but when that person comes to see the performance, they not only have to recognize themselves, but also feel that their perspectives have been transmitted accurately.

IS: Maybe from this point of view, the experience at Moses Rosen Retirement Home is a good example, since the residents take part in the performances themselves.

DS: Indeed, that is the ideal model. The experience is different at the home, they actively take part there. But the question is to what extent does that work every time? For *Nu ne-am născut în locul potrivit* (*Born in the Wrong Place*) (2012),[5] for instance, we were confronted with this issue. People do not want to expose themselves. And it is not just that, but they are taking huge risks, especially when it comes to refugees. That is why our responsibility as project initiators is very big. Depending on the case, each topic, each performance and each initiative has its own ethical and political solutions which generate particular aesthetic solutions.

IS: After seven years of working there, how would you describe the experience at Moses Rosen Retirement Home? How did your relationship develop, both in the performance realm and the personal one?

DS: It has been a very powerful experience. It was a long-term project, even longer than Rahova-Uranus. We see each other weekly, and when that happens, you develop friendships and a feeling of belonging to that community. You become part of the life of that home. And there is also a mutual learning process. Some of them learned to use the computer and create blogs, but I also learned a lot about history and things I would not have thought about, relating to my family history. They helped me see those things in a different light, and I gained a lot personally. From a theatrical perspective, such an experience creates all sorts of pressures. We are talking about 80-90-year-old people who want to perform, want to expose themselves, to be in the foreground.

It's not just an exciting experience; it also creates meaning in their lives. Especially since a retirement home is generally considered as an end-point, 'the place where you go to die'. This forces you to use the resources that are available. When you are working with an actor, you have certain

FIGURE 13: Domiciliu Instabil (Instable Residence), 2016. Photo credit: Vârsta4. Featuring Pompiliu Sterian and Ioseph Cotnăreanu.

demands, but here you always have to see what the right choice is: do I use a microphone or not, do I use dialogue or not, do I learn a certain text or not? These are things pertaining to the resources and the condition of those people. On the other hand, there are a lot of pluses. You come across people who are great singers, or great writers, or have an extremely rich life experience. All these determine and shape the performance. The performance is being built together with them.

IS: Regarding these performances, I think it is very important that they also offer a perspective on recent history.

DS: It is obviously a process of recovering recent history and complex, paradoxical perspectives which you don't really learn about in school. It is one of the most valuable aspects of the project.

MBT: There is this idea that artists come to 'enlighten' the communities, to teach them things. I'm curious about the exchange of knowledge between the artist and the people in the communities.

DS: I see what you mean, there is an issue with those who go to teach people 'what it's all about'. At the same time, there is the opposite trap, which is very visible with anthropologists and somewhat visible with artists, namely that you are going into a community and they will serve you with the absolute truth. You see the middle class looking for revelations in the slums and in encounters with these 'decent paupers who tell us the truth about the world'. And I believe both are serious issues.

IS: Maybe symmetrical anthropology is the solution.

DS: Exactly. As mundane as it might sound, the truth is somewhere in the middle. You understand that it is actually an exchange: these people have knowledge you lack, but you also have knowledge that they lack. But you do not have to know or understand everything. What has been really important in all the projects I worked on is that I never started out thinking I will get something out of that project. I always started with the idea that there might not be anything there (I am referring to talking with the communities). If you start off thinking you will get your big break, there is more chance you might screw up. Compatibility is important. If I go to work with a group where we disagree fundamentally, that will not change, and then there is no point in continuing. At the same time, I am becoming increasingly sceptical about the idea of going to a certain community. I think it works in certain cases, like the Moses Rosen Retirement Home, which is a fixed location and where the peoples' needs are obvious. But I think you have to be very careful about going to other oppressed groups or communities. When, how and why are you going there? I was recently talking to several Colombian artists who are engaged in a form of community theatre, but they originally came from the impoverished communities they are now working with. They went to school, they studied theatre and then went back to do theatre in the same area they had left. This is very important, because they had a completely different relationship and communication issues, as well as a different level of understanding. And on the other hand, I think these initiatives are relevant as long as they are accompanied by serious public policies, not just art. As interesting as it may sound, to teach kids and involve them in all sorts of activities – see the creative and horizontal education – it is better to help them not fail math. Some will say that is not true, that school is stupid and they will teach themselves more without school, but the objective reality – and many people in poverty will confirm this – is that lack of the education is clearly limiting their access to resources and a decent life. It is that simple.

MBT: This would be something you have been directly confronted with.

DS: Yes, and it gradually became visible, especially after this idea of holding school in the street appeared, with artists running creative workshops for kids: generating ideas, drawing etc. As the people from the community started to understand how our world functions, they began reacting. The women said, 'first we need to tutor them in Romanian and math, then we need to tutor ourselves, so we can finish high-school and find a better job'. And here of course I am contradicting myself slightly, because those people might never have had the same capacity of organization and autonomy if it had not been for the experience we took part in for years. So it is a bit more complicated.

IS: You mentioned there were tensions between the group of artists. What did not work out?

DS: I think there were several issues. First of all, we were all very young and searching for something, but were not sure which direction to take. Secondly, non-hierarchical organizing is a noble goal, but it is very hard to practice. There are always two risks – that one individual might become authoritarian – and the second is that some people will not make any effort. How do you balance these issues which pertain to the specifics of non-hierarchical organizing? Everyone has faced them at least once.

IS: If you were to look back, what role did school play in you artistic and political development? And what other influences shaped you?

DS: I attended theatre school by chance, I wanted to study film. Initially I was fascinated by the novelty of things, but I didn't understand much in the first two years of school. It did matter, however, that I studied Brecht in my second year. Reading Brecht, I was introduced to a different perspective. Back then, I had little political conscience, I was just another young man with a rudimentary right-wing education – anti-communist clichés from the 1990s – received from my family. Then came my professors, Nicolae Mandea and Cristian Hadji-Culea, and on top of this came all the other experiences. All of this challenged me to search for a discourse on the world, on all the paradoxes I could not grasp anymore. Something did not add up; if we were living in the best of possible worlds, how come so many people are oppressed in so many ways? And if socialism was so terrible, how come some of these people were better off then? These questions make you hit the books. Besides this, there were the personal experiences stemming from the objective historical conditions of the economic crisis of 2008, which marked a point of de-mythicizing capitalism. All this left an indelible mark on us, we were the generation who were 21–22 when Romania was admitted to the EU (in 2007) and we thought it would become a land of plenty. But then the austerity measures came along, the funding for cultural projects started being cut and you could not really get into any state theatre and things like that. The years 2009–11 were the toughest. For the performance *Capete înfierbântate* (*Heated Minds*) (2010),[6] made with Mihaela Michailov and Alexandru Potocean, we used our own money, my father paid for props. Fees were out of discussion. And it is not just about me, an entire generation became more heavily politicized during that time.

MBT: At the same time, it can be said that this was a turning point for the middle class as well, since living became more precarious under a continuous crisis.

DS: Yes, of course, their lives were also made worse during the crisis and the austerity measures that followed.

MBT: After all these years, what are your thoughts on the impact and the aftermath of these performances on those communities?

DS: It varies from one to the other. The Rahova community became more politicized, more autonomous, they built their own organization and created cultural events, which signalled the issues with evictions and the visibility of those issues is far greater now. The Common Front for Housing Rights (FCDL) was established and housing became a regular item on the agenda of many NGOs, politicians and even for some right-wing liberal groups. Things have visibly changed and we played a part in this change, of course. Ten to fifteen years ago nobody was talking about evictions, even though there were ten times more of them happening then than there are now. There is a positive political impact, while the impact on the actual people is almost non-existent. The state has not built any social housing, evictions keep occurring, and the level of gentrification has sky-rocketed. What truly put a damper on gentrification was not the artistic or political projects, but the economic crisis.

At the Moses Rosen Home, things are different. You can see the progress, you can see people coming from just reading a bit of text in a performance to acting, learning lines, dancing and singing. You can see how the people have changed and the group got bigger. We have been working together for seven years, during which we made seven very different performances which became more and more complex. This is also the project which caught a lot of media attention, it went from the national television all the way to the BBC.

IS: Maybe that is because the Moses Rosen Retirement Home performances are more emotionally charged and generate more empathy.

DS: Yes, that is true. But the political content is also there, but not that explicit, which is why they are more easily promoted, unfortunately. Regarding the performances documenting life in the Jiu Valley, there has been visible progress here as well. You are not hearing anymore the discourse that reduced all miners to mindless brutes and communist idiots in contrast with the young intellectuals, at least not as much as seven or eight years ago. But we still need long-term political projects in places like the Jiu Valley. It would be significant if people who work in those areas, like teachers or cultural managers, could specialize in political art practices.

MBT: Many of these theatre projects draw attention to issues of public interest. To what extent have the authorities reacted to your message and tackled those issues?

DS: They have not. And we are naïve to keep using this bourgeois rationale – thinking that if we point out the issues of the people to the state authorities, the state will take action just because we ask them to. Our practical experience shows that this is profoundly wrong and stupid. The state knows the bad conditions people are living in better than we do because it interacts with them on a daily basis. The only thing that will change that is a project for a revolutionary state. We can discuss about a revolution without a state, but I'm sceptical about that. Our mission is to lay down the foundation, to plant the first seeds of such a change. I know what we are doing might somehow appear insignificant, but as we are aware from so many other situations, feeling the historical moment and being aware of your role and position is the starting point of political action.

REFERENCES

Bortun, Andreea (2015), 'Regizorul Bogdan Georgescu: "Am descoperit teatrul comunitar in Los Angeles, cand puteam sa-l descopar acasa, langa Bistrița"', Pro TV, 19 June, http://stirileprotv. ro/manifestul-tinerei-generatii/regizorul-bogdan-georgescu-am-descoperit-teatrul-comunitar-in-los-angeles-cand-puteam-sa-l-descopar-acasa-langa-bistrița.html/. Accessed 16 May 2017.

Harsanyi, Anna (2016), 'Creative action: How a new generation of Romanian artists is tack-ling societal problems head on', *The Calvert Journal*, 11 January, http://www.calvertjour-nal.com/articles/show/5251/romanian-activist-art-theatre-civic-community/. Accessed 7 August 2017.

Iacob, Oana, Mocanu, Gina and Novac, Rodica (2015), *Obținerea Rezidenței pe Termen Lung și a Cetățeniei Române: Material pentru Pregătirea Specifică în Vederea Obținerii Cetățeniei Române* (*Obtaining Long-Term Residency and Romanian Citizenship: Specific Preparation Materials for Obtaining Romanian Citizenship*), Bucharest: ADO SAH ROM.

Popovici, Iulia (2008), *A Theatre on the Side of the Road*, Bucharest: Cartea Românească.

——— (ed.) (2014), *New Performing Arts Practices in Eastern Europe*, Chișinău: Cartier and Sibiu International Theatre Festival.

Schwartz, David (dir.) (2013), *Valea Jiului after 1989*, Michaela Michailov, Sub Rahova and elsewhere, 8–18 June.

Editors' Note

Ileana Alexandra Orlich's *Subversive Stages* (2017) can serve as a good introduction to contemporary theatre's relationship with the political past in Eastern Europe. For an in-depth cultural analysis on post-communist aesthetics, please see Anca Pusca's recent monograph entitled *Post-Communist Aesthetics: Revolutions, Capitalism, Violence* (2016). The young generation of Romanian theatre-makers is the focus of Cristina Modreanu's article 'Elements of ethics and aesthetics in New Romanian Theatre' (2013) with a special focus on the productions of David Schwartz.

Further reading

Modreanu, Cristina (2013), 'Elements of ethics and aesthetics in New Romanian Theatre', *New Theatre Quarterly*, 29:4, pp. 385–93.

Orlich, Ileana Alexandra (2017), *Subversive Stages,* Budapest: CEU Press.

Pusca, Anca (2016), *Post-Communist Aesthetics: Revolutions, Capitalism, Violence,* London and New York: Routledge.

NOTES

1. *Underground: The Jiu Valley after 1989* aims to document the economic situation, life and work of the miners during post-socialism. Theatre Underground is a project of performative reconstruction of the document-stories that set the foundation for the history of the communities in the Jiu Valley, communities that find themselves somewhere between survival, migration, disappearance and possible reconstruction. The performance aims to

re-evaluate the stories, the issues and the culture of those social categories often ignored in post-socialist Romanian theatre, especially working-class communities.

2. *Gazeta de Artă Politică* (*GAP*) is an independent magazine created by Mihaela Michailov, David Schwartz, Ionuț Sociu and Marius Bogdan Tudor. *GAP* is a publication of both critical reflection and action that focuses on the performing arts and adopts an egalitarian and horizontal perspective on sociopolitical art: www.artapolitica.ro/en. Accessed 5 June 2019.

3. The Political Theatre Platform 2015 is a drama and education project that aims to archive, document and debate, through theatre performances and workshops, histories that are often marginalized within mainstream systems that manufacture their own legitimizing narratives in order to justify their alliance with a 'convenient history'.

4. *The Unwritten Theatre from Șanț: A First Type of Community Theatre in Romania* (2011) made by Bogdan Georgescu (Ofensiva Generozității), Tania Cucoreanu and Andrei Ioniță (Veioza Arte).

5. The performance *Born in the Wrong Place* (by David Schwartz and Alice Monica Marinescu) intertwines the life stories of five people who have gone through the experience of seeking asylum with fragments from *Obtaining Long-Term Residency and Romanian Citizenship: Specific Preparation Materials for Obtaining Romanian Citizenship* (Iacob et al. 2015). The performance aims to problematize and discuss, in the public sphere, issues that are of crucial importance in the current global context, issues such as the institutional fight against migration taking place at the same time as the need for migrants in the development of the capitalist economy grows, the need for asylum, the right to travel as the fundamental right of every individual and the instrumentalization of 'the foreigner' as a scapegoat for social and economic issues.

6. The performance *Heated Minds* retrieves a slice of living history from the perspectives of the social actors involved in the events and reactivates it in the public conscience. The truth about these events is represented by the sum of mostly contradictory viewpoints, and therefore impossible to limit to one single perspective. The project is built on a documenting process involving several methods: interviews with witnesses, newspaper accounts, reports filed by different organizations and institutions, discussions, public debates, workshops etc., focused on the events that took place in Bucharest during 13–15 June 1990.

PART V

Emerging Practices: Connecting through
the Digital and the Verbatim

This closing section of the book looks at emerging practices that attempt to re-form theatre communities on and off-stage. Digital media have changed the way we communicate, inform and entertain ourselves. They have become a part of most human activities, and theatre is certainly not excluded. While most theatre tries to keep live performance and digital media separate, formally asking spectators to switch off their mobile phones before settling to watch a performance, some theatre-makers have embraced the possibilities created by digital media not only to create different performances but also to allow their spectators to interact more actively with the performance and actually replace many of the functions of traditional performers. Ágnes Bakk discusses various ways how digital media and theatre arts interact, and in doing so brings up ethical issues that remain unresolved. While traditional theatre spectators felt relatively safe in their seats, the use of digital tools conceals dangers that theatregoers do not usually encounter. However, these technological innovations also create new possibilities for creating new communities of spectators, as the relationship between them and with the performance is very different from those in a traditional performance setting. Naďa Satková discusses a further example of the gamification of performance in *Remote X* by Rimini Protokoll (2013–present). The writing focuses on the shift that takes place in this particular performance in the role of the spectator who becomes an active participant. Here too a community is created, formed of individuals who are brought together by their interest in experiencing the performance. As hinted at by Satková, the existence of this community is more obvious to the passers-by who experience the participants as a highly visible group rather than to the participants who have limited contact with other participants. In contrast, the performance discussed by Bettina Auerswald, described as 'communal verbatim theatre' creates and dissects relationships in ways that technology in theatre has until now not managed to do. Communal verbatim is produced by going into the local community to reconstruct an often-traumatizing story and then giving the reconstructive narrative back to the community. In spite of some of Auerswald's misgivings about verbatim theatre as a form, one feels that her example brought about a level of engagement within the community that would be difficult to envisage with the use of more technologically determined forms of performance.

The emerging practices discussed in the final section of the book question traditional modes of kinship in theatre and performance and point towards temporary and/or micro-communities gathered around singular theatre events either online or offline. With the emergence of new forms of spectatorship, new communities are being created. These communities not only participate in the overall reception of theatre productions via their spectatorial gaze, but actively shape the performance event and foster new aesthetics.

New Technologies for a New Audience? Using Transmedia Storytelling towards a New Experience Design Form

Ágnes Bakk

New technologies, especially Internet technologies, have become more and more prevalent in our habits of cultural consumption. We get news on our mobile devices, we look for further details on Facebook and we buy tickets online. Progressively advanced technological devices are transforming our everyday lives. These devices are not only reshaping the society's communication strategies on the individual level, but are also offering new types of cultural consumption habits and these new types of goods have their own respective audiences. The new types of audiences, especially younger people who make up what is called Generation Y, have to feature more prominently in current debates on theatre and emerging communities. Moreover, based on their common consumption, they form new types of communities. Lately, cultural institutions and performing art companies have been putting more emphasis on developing social media channels, trying to reach out to as many new types of audiences as possible. Museums have come a long way in this process. They began to use online technologies in a dialogical way in order to engage with a wider audience base and to understand both the audience's needs and wishes.[1] Performing arts institutions and companies (including the venues, creators and the companies/ensembles themselves) on the other hand continuously present live art productions every night, creating a traditional, altogether different type of interaction between performers and audiences. Due to their interactive nature, at each performance there is a unique set of circumstances that influence and shape the audience's 'autopoietic feedback loop', a term introduced by Erika Fischer-Lichte (2008: 38–39) to define the audience's reflexive reaction to the performance, that is, the audience's reaction that in turn shapes the audience's further reaction itself in a loop.

When museums store and exhibit artworks, the aesthetic effect of the art does not depend on performers. In the case of museums, their online presence has already become controversial, many art professionals thinking that making parts of the collection accessible online, or introducing new gamified techniques to attract new visitors to websites, will cause the public to refrain from visiting museums. However, these predictions have proved to be wrong in the case of the most frequented museums.[2] Performing arts institutions and companies are behind the curve in providing a similarly abundant online presence. In fact, they could potentially go further in using such techniques, by involving narrative design and other key tools such as game design in their working methodologies. However, the use of complex, live and tailor-made strategies for audience engagement requires very meticulous planning even when the potential audience, especially infrequent theatregoers, might never actually engage with such content (see Walmsey 2016).

In this chapter I aim to draw attention to the importance of the inclusion of new technological tools and game design elements into performance productions in a reflective way (not only as add-ons), as well as presenting topical productions that take place online. The relatively small number of such tools and elements is due not only to lack of funding, but also a lack of experimentation time that could serve as a learning period and would be especially helpful in the discovery of the kind of design thinking that would naturally incorporate the use of digital/new technological tools in theatre-making. Although many creators already use these techniques, in many cases this is mostly due to the expectations of the funding bodies for each project that imposes specific requirements on the usage of new technologies in their grant guidelines. The usage of new technologies as an obligation to receive funding, rather than as a tool in itself to enrich the possibilities of performance, may not only result in the superficial deployment of these technologies, but carries the risk of alienating theatre communities from these otherwise fruitful new experimental methods. In order to understand the mechanics of these tools we need to learn more about their working methodology, including an understanding of current video gaming and VR trends. According to Evert Hoogendoorn, one of the founders of the Design for Virtual Theatre & Games Department at the HKU School of Theatre in Utrecht, Netherlands:

> If you look at the bigger picture, development of the media, storytelling in general, this is the way that everyone is following, only in theatre there will be a niche that will be missing. [...] If we don't make an effort to step on this wagon, then it could be that this will be more and more a niche. And we have seen it in game design where the X-box was the big industry, but there was an independent small change: the smartphone came and now X-box is the niche.

It might happen the same in theatre development. Suddenly our mainstream now in theatre will be niche, and there will be no new big thing behind it to fill up the mainstream, and the new mainstream will be the Disney world.

(Bakk 2016b: n.pag.)

According to Hoogendoorn, the most urgent issue is providing live art creators new ways of expressing their art in a manner that has the potential to captivate not only an existing audience base, but also attracting new audiences.

To highlight the importance of the use of novel technological tools, I will provide a short insight into the beginnings of the performances and productions that solely required online presence from their users. My aim is to present these performances as examples of productions that use new technologies, including Internet technologies, in a comprehensive way, combining artistic practice (i.e. non-commercial product) alongside adequate technologies, used in a reflective way with new technological tools in both aesthetically and conceptually coherent forms in performance. I will attempt to define the specificities that make these performances comprehensive, and how new technological and transmedia storytelling tools can be used for further artistic and marketing activities. These activities can then create wider transmedia events out of the unique performance events taking place not only in physical venues, but online, including social media platforms.

Making a performance accessible online does not affect the physical attendance of the conventional theatre-going audience since most of this audience would likely attend a show in real-time, live. However, the act of participating in a performance event involves new forms, as technological tools that enhance the ludification side of the performing arts continuously develop. As Irwin argues:

The presentation and performance of self through the creation and 'up-loading' into the virtual theatre of a personal website, and the interaction of a performance website, have created significant alternatives to existing narrative modes, forms of representation, dramaturgies and within these architectures of performance, the virtual actor, the avatar may be brought into existence and may walk upon an entirely new space and within a completely new re-visioned scenography of performance.

(2011: 148)

The online presence and networks that can be formed by performance visualizations can help in captivating new audiences, but better-defined strategies to this effect are still needed and are still under construction.

A Short Introduction to Online Performances

The earliest forms of cyber-performance can be traced back to the first part of the 1990s. The history of cyber-performances begins as early as the first half of the 1990s, where we can see such performances in their early forms. The first 'interactive' *Hamlet,* or as it was called, *Hamnet,* was created in 1993 in the Silicon Valley, California by Stuart Harris, a former actor and computer professional. It involved a MIRC-channel where audiences could enter a chatroom called *Hamnet* and 'watch' online, or follow a fixed number of players as well as the rest of the audience. There was little interaction. The 'performers' were 'playing' in character and the text was adapted to a newly developed chat language and signs such as:

```
**<< Action >>** : _Enter Hamlet [9]
**<< Action >>** : _Enter Ghost [10]
<Hamlet> re, Ghost. Zup? [11]
<Ghost> Yr uncle's fucking yr mum. I'm counting on u to /KICK the bastard. [12]
======== GHOST /MODE * +o Hamlet [13]
```

(The Hamnet Players 1993)

Later, Harris founded his company Hamnet Players, and actors joined the company, unfortunately with high turnover in terms of personnel. Harris went on creating two other performances after *Hamnet*: *PC Beth* (1995) and an *IRC channel named Desire* (1995) (see Sant 2013). After Harris' attempt to create an interactive online performance, Herbert Fritsch, a German actor and director looking for innovative ways to develop performances, created the first, truly interactive online *Hamlet* computer game. From 2000 to 2004, Fritsch created the website Hamlet X. Within this framework he filmed 111 short films with young actors, including well-known performers, as well as creating a website where the audience could access three computer games about *Hamlet*. After *Hamnet* and other web-based theatre projects mentioned above, many similar artistic creations came to life combining different genres that were also inspired by computer games. While it is clear that these productions were distorting a sense of spectacle, especially from an aesthetic point of view, the question remains: have such cyber-performances really invented new and original aesthetic concepts and methodologies as a result of replacing the live performance act with new technological tools; or can such replacement of 'liveness' only be considered as a side effect of these particular theatre projects?

We have to reconsider what technology is offering us in contrast with physical presence and the sense of spectacle. Christina Papagiannouli argues in her book *Political Cyberperformance* that 'the notion of liveness in cyberperformance is directly connected to the interactive and participative character of the Internet, as without real-time engagement the notion of co-presence is weak and, thus, liveness is meaningless' (2016: 10).

Contrary to Papagiannouli's argument, perhaps we should consider liveness, not as a meaningless category in online productions, but as a performance element modified or replaced with other means. We need to find new concepts to grasp and describe current concepts of liveness of an artistic production, as something that is both built in and actively used in technological terms. Perhaps, separate concepts can be developed to aid thinking about separate forms of liveness that do and do not require physical presence, and also those that do or do not feature interactivity. Fischer-Lichte's concept of an autopoietic feedback loop can also help us to develop further concepts to talk about different types of participation and interaction both in the case of performance and the audience.

In the next part of the chapter I will make an attempt to outline how the interactive technologies used in these productions can offer a platform for audience participation with no (or mixed) real-time action while still enabling the audience to define themselves as a community. I will analyse two artistic productions that took place online and I will present two perspectives that can be constructive in analysing similar productions in the future. I will take a closer look at their online presence and the effect they had on individual participants. The first production I will be focusing on is developed by the UK-based Blast Theory, which created an interactive app entitled *Karen* in cooperation with the National Theatre of Wales in 2015. This app uses narrative design strategies to create interactive situations between the app and its users, although the users never meet and can only learn about each other at a later stage. The second performance I will be analysing is a new experiment by two young Hungarian creatives, Dóra Lakatos and Eszter Zewde who are/were drama teachers at a youth theatre group, as well as students at the Hungarian Theatre and Film Academy (SZFE). Together, they put *Hamlet* on Facebook with a variety of possibilities for transmedia storytelling. While comparing the two productions I will look closely at how their dramaturgy was constructed as well as what kind of strategies were used to engage the audiences. As Ranciére stated in *The Emancipated Spectator*:

> Being a spectator is not some passive condition that we should transform into activity [...] We do not have to transform spectators into actors, and ignoramuses into scholars. We have to recognize the knowledge at work in the ignoramuses and the activity peculiar to the spectator. Every spectator is already an actor in her story; every actor, every man of action, is the spectator of the same story.
>
> (2009: 17)

Both of the performances were using formats that were building on the reactions of the audience, incorporating these reactions in the storyline, but without changing the narrative path. Liveness here means the possibility of the audience for immediate reactions, with the chance of adding new elements to the creation and the promise that our reaction might count in the storyline as well.

Karen *by Blast Theory*

One of the most prominent creators in the field of immersive theatre is the Bristol-based Blast Theory. They deal with many contemporary topics through games, videos and live art forms. The company also works around topics such as: data protection, consumerism, the financial crisis and ethical issues of using undercover police. One of their latest productions, the app *Karen,* brings up the issue of how much we reveal from our own secrets, and to whom we reveal them to. Arguably, revealing or sharing private information on virtual platforms is a serious issue for individuals and raises important data security concerns. As Ulf Otto, a leading researcher of online performances argues:

> Instead of some virtual reality, that some people tried to sell us as offering all these amazing new opportunities, we are experiencing instead a reality that is connected in more and more ways that is full of sensors, where people, cars and fridges are being connected into more and more crisscrossing networks. And there is nothing virtual about this, it is as real as the train tracks that cut through the landscapes of the 19th century. So what counts, maybe the only thing that counts right now, is who is controlling these connections and who owns these connections and the bad news is, they are owned by private institutions whose sole interest is profit.
>
> (2015: n.pag.)

The relevance of Otto's description of this state of affairs will become apparent as we examine *Karen,* for the app, while meant to provoke thinking about sharing information online, is itself entangled with the complex aspects of online information sharing.

Blast Theory's *Karen* is a 'life coach app': the main protagonist being Karen, a rather sensible and often nosy character who gathers a large amount of data about the app users by asking them different, sophisticated questions. After considerable time spent with 'her' and answering all her questions, the app offers a personalized psychological report to the user based on the answers provided and on the comparative analysis between the individual app user's behaviour and that of

211

other users. Two important questions arise already at the very beginning. First, what are the means and the aim for using interactivity and narrative design for enhancing the app's participatory characteristic? Second, how do creators deal with the users' data security?

As Matt Adams, one of *Karen*'s creators explains 'interactivity is used to subtly grade and change the way how Karen talks to you' (see Adams 2015). Blast Theory used several personality tests in developing the game intending to motivate the users to interact. They were testing whether psychological profiling and such personalization can be incorporated as part of the story, and also looking at different ways the outcomes of these tests can be incorporated into the overall story. Here, the creators of the app used the narrative design technique, known from video game dramaturgy, a system where a player/character and one or more non-player characters engage in a simulated conversation. In *Karen*, the users can choose from a limited set of answers and then Karen, the life coach, responds according to the user's chosen set of replies. The users also have the chance to interfere with and influence Karen's personal life by suggesting different ways to behave in various situations. This narrative design tool carries the risk of making some players feel that they have a predefined character along with a predefined storyline or quest. According to user comments on Blast Theory's website, the most common problem was that the players were expecting a unique live-art product. However, after playing for a second or third time, they realized that, in some cases, no matter how they responded to Karen, she always acted in the same way. As Donald Norman questions: 'When we look toward what is known about the nature of interaction, why not turn to those who manage it best – to those from the world of drama, of the stage, of the theatre?' (Norman and Draper 1986: 170). In *Karen*'s case the players did not realize that the interactivity is actually offered by the app's technology itself and is thereby limited by a lack of live programming. In this situation the users were not taking into consideration the video game's own dramaturgy system (the narrative design system). Instead, they expected a traditional theatre feedback loop process. Nonetheless, the users who were willing to play throughout the end, and were ready to pay a small amount for the psychological report, would receive a unique reward. The app is using multiple choice questions and based on the given answers the main protagonist, Karen, continues to raise other questions or make the next move. The multiple-choice questions are pre-determined; however, the user has the feeling that he or she can control and participate in designing the storyline. By using the branching narrative tool, the app is creating an interactive situation that is motivating the user to participate. The level of participation is also increased by the non-objective and surprising attitude of Karen.

Moving on to our second question raised above, I wish to look at the important issue of data protection and security within this case. The users, by answering Karen's questions, were providing a large amount of highly personal data for the creators. Handling this amount of data is challenging, since hard data and soft data are received at the same time and must be stored in a highly secure environment. *Karen* makes the user the protagonist of her own performance, and is not only gathering data about the users' psychological reactions, but also his/her phone number and IP address as well as details about his/her secret desires and needs. Blast Theory had an adequate protocol to keep this information safe, but, in the future, providing this type of data might create a new layer of risk in terms of data protection, and/or for freedom of speech and thought. The audience can be easily identified through the given data, and even in the case of not providing their own opinions, thoughts and desires, the users would have serious concerns about their data security in such virtual productions. Similar productions can also occasionally be considered scientific experiments in their own right, as Wallace puts it 'the participants are themselves also re-performed/lived, as partakers in the scientific experiments' (2015: n.pag.). Such serious concerns might need to be flagged in future productions, especially the ones that rely heavily on personal data. This will not affect the aesthetic framework of such productions, rather it will trigger the audience to be able to create and switch between different virtual personas and avatars. By creating various avatars, the participants will also be able to join different communities as they will be able to afford a more adventurous online behaviour. Meanwhile of course, the single user has to be careful about what personal real data will be used while participating in such a production. Nick Tandavanitj also states that the group had concrete solutions for keeping all data in a safe place:

> For *Karen*, data privacy and security were key issues. In England, we have strict data protection rules, under which anyone who is holding personal data is regarded as a data controller. This requires that we have to set out and comply with a data privacy policy for works such as *Karen* and make sure that we take steps to ensure the security of people's personal data. For *Karen*, any data that personally identifies you, such as e-mail and geo-location, is stored separately from the behavioural and profiling data, and is stored as encrypted and at rest. You can request that your data is deleted at any time or request a copy of it.
>
> (Bakk 2016a: n.pag.)

Karen is based on single, peer-to-peer participation. At the end of the performance all the participants receive a psychological report about their reactions and information about how the other app-users, those who they had not met while playing, behaved throughout the performance. Such productions are important not only for the users but also for artists as they embark on a learning curve by using the means of such platforms in order to create transmedia storytelling or other gamified productions. In order to analyse more closely how a performance that invites mass participation engages its audience to create a community, we now turn to a more popular platform, Facebook.

Hamlet Online

Throughout the past decade, social media has been increasingly influencing human interactions. It has also been modifying our behaviour in regard to how we perceive live events and how we take part in those events. Parallel to these behavioural influences, multimedia storytelling has been on the rise and infiltrating performance art.[3] Such infiltration also occurs during the PR-marketing campaigns leading up to the performance. A notable example in this respect is the Gorki Theatre's (Berlin) 2012 season. The creators started a real online transmedia storytelling campaign for the performance of *Effie Briest 2.0* (2012). The play features a 17-year-old Effi Briest, the daughter of a German aristocrat, who is to be married off to the 38-year-old Baron Geert von Innstetten, who has also courted Effi's mother, Luise. The performance began on Facebook, where the participants could follow Effie Briest's story. The creators opened a social media scene and formed a group where the audience could join and 'like' or comment on the event or pictures.[4] The audience could also help Effie to choose her wedding dress or write a love letter, and post love songs for the characters. This created a whole new community, the main aim being to have audience members actively participate in the storyline. How can we describe the performative event in this case? Do we consider Effie's imaginary wedding, or rather, the offline performance itself taking place after the Facebook campaign as the performative event? After one month of preparation on Facebook, the theatrical performance followed, where the audience could not influence the ending of the story. It was partly used as a promotional measure, but also involved the audience with the performance by having them determine some aspects of the performance itself. This example gives us a relevant insight into different ways Facebook is used for theatre-related interactive actions, through which audiences are engaged right from the outset, theatre-makers asking them to collaborate in framing the performance and defining its aesthetic composition.

In 2016, two young drama instructors, Dóra Lakatos and Eszter Zewde (students at the Hungarian Theatre and Film Academy) 'directed' Shakespeare's *Hamlet,* under the title *Hamlet Online,*[5] the production using Hungarian as its working language. The narrative of the play is well-known in Hungary, *Hamlet* being performed in Hungarian theatres since 1794. The play is also a mandatory reading material in Hungarian schools. However, Hungarian students generally do not have a deep understanding of the play and are estranged from the play partly due to the use of an old Hungarian translation containing archaic language, not readily accessible for young generation of readers. By choosing this play for such an open format, the creators' goal was to display new aspects of the play with the young generation in mind. Although their main goal was to draw young people's attention to the drama, it is very important to highlight and understand this play development as a transmedia storytelling project online.

In the short overview published by Toni Sant and Kim Flintoff, entitled 'The Internet as dramatic medium' (2007), the authors mention educational drama as a separate branch of online performing arts productions whose main purpose is to form 'critical pedagogy'. The creators of *Hamlet Online* first designed the plot for Facebook, and published an open call for 'performers' who would launch and manage the profiles of the main protagonists of the play: Hamlet, Ophelia, Gertrude, Claudius, etc. In the creation of these profiles we can observe a certain type of theatricality in the production. Following the definition of Erika Fischer-Lichte in her work *Semiotik des Theaters*, we can define theatricality as an actor representing or playing a certain role while the spectator is watching, which is common to theatrical situations, and in this case observed online by different actors impersonating characters so that they can perform and express their characters in their own way (see Fischer-Lichte 1983: 16). As the creators stated, although it seems much easier to pre-create content, the personalization of the characters and keeping the characters unique and fresh is possible only through different impersonators. In this case, it is very important to differentiate between two concepts: embodiment and impersonation, the latter applying in our case. Facebook and other social media are giving us multi-layered possibility to enter into someone else's character, and by doing so the 'actors' can re-create the protagonists' avatars. Similarly to conventional theatre productions, the end of the play is pre-determined, but it is up to the impersonators to fill in the details of the character.

Another important matter concerns the platform itself, providing us the opportunity to consider the various behavioural acts and the fact that the 'actor' does not have to put themselves directly on the stage. 'It is not about identification, about being the character or the glance from above, but about the control and possession of the character' (Otto 2013: 189). The feedback loop from the audience's end is much more visible, since the viewers, compared to traditional audiences, have a richer toolkit, visually much more obvious and durable. They can like, dislike, comment, chat and also make their own contribution to the performance. A transmedia characteristic also appears strongly in the performance: different kinds of presences mix with the videos. For example, the audience sent congratulations to the newly crowned king, and received sneak peeks from the coronation party, held in an existing bar in Budapest and documented by pictures, posted online. The creators also planned a live ending, where they would present the last act and finish off with a party; this element of the project however has not taken place (see Bakk 2016c). The question remains, in what respect can we talk about inter-activity or participatory practice in *Hamlet Online*? Henry Jenkins describes the difference between interactivity and participation as follows:

> For me, interactivity is a property often designed and programmed into the tech-nology and thus is much more likely to be under the control of media produc-ers. Participation, on the other hand, is a property of the surrounding culture and is often something communities assert through their shared engagement with technologies, content and producers. An emphasis on interactivity pulls inevitably towards the idea of technology as itself liberatory (or constraining), whereas my own work is primarily focused on cultural practices that emerge around and often reshape the technological infrastructure.
>
> (2014: 296)

In the case of *Hamlet Online* we can draw attention to the technological enabling of a participative culture, which has the potential to be developed with an educa-tional goal in the future. Based on Jenkins' definitions, this would mean that Facebook and other platforms enable an interactive context that would be ready to host such participatory initiatives. But how can these participatory audience communities be built and maintained? In the case of *Hamlet Online*, their page attracted more than 600 likes on Facebook, and from this number almost 100 participants formed an active community.

When discussing online and offline audience engagement, both in the case of *Karen* and *Hamlet Online* we need to consider the fact that both productions had a fixed ending, such as in conventional theatre production. The variable component that could make the participants more active was still missing. Theatre-makers will soon face the challenges of creating performances with open endings, under growing pressure to provide a safe environment for all the participants in terms of data protection. With an ever-growing number of cyber-performances, using growing numbers of transmedia products we will need to rethink our concept of theatricality. Furthermore, the challenge of keep-ing our data safe while interacting with complete strangers online, even in the context of an online production, is raising a series of questions both on indi-vidual and societal levels, questions that developing artistic practices should address. Asked about his vision of theatre in 30 years' time, Blast Theory's Nick Tandavanitj responded:

What seems striking in technology circles at the moment is the amount of interest in virtual headsets and 'immersive' technology. The idea of standing in the middle of your living room with a headset on fills me with no happiness at all. In terms of technology, I hope that in situations where we are constantly surrounded by digital or network connected devices, the technology can be used, in some way, to re-insist on our co-dependence and co-presence. I suppose it's the difference between going to see a film like Transformers IV, where 80% of what you see on screen is CGI; it's the work of very clever people and amazing technology, but everyone has a perfect skin, and it's very efficient. It delivers entertainment. It's the difference between this and something about making things alive, with a sense of humanity. New forms of technology, will hopefully allow people's sense of humour, sense of irony and vulnerability remain present. I don't know what form it will take, but I hope we still feel equally vulnerable and sensitive to each other.

(Bakk 2016a)

Constructive interactions between video games, interactive storytelling and theatre are in the early days of meaningful development slowly forming a distinctive genre. The 'grammar' and modus operandi of such new genre awaits to be formed and understood. As demonstrated in this chapter, using such alternative forms of (theatrical) storytelling can be highly relevant in various educational settings and these forms of usage have implications in further development of gaming technology. Video game mechanics are offering different practices for storytelling and performances to create new ways of engaging with audiences, offering new methods in developing a different sense of community. Although it seems as a solitary type of participation at first sight, by analysing the details of such new theatrical forms, it becomes clear that new virtual communities come to life alongside the discussed productions. Paraphrasing Jacques Ranciére, we can state that the theatre is still the only place where we face a community.

Acknowledgements

This work was supported by a grant from the Ministry of National Education, CNCS – UEFISCDI Romania, project number PN-III-P4-ID-PCE-2016-0418.

REFERENCES

Adams, Matt (2015), 'How *Karen* uses interactivity', Blast Theory, April, http://www.blasttheory. co.uk/matt-adams-explains-how-karen-uses-interactivity/. Accessed 5 June 2019.

Bakk, Ágnes (2016a), 'A mission to maintain a sense of liveness and participation', interview with Nick Tandavanitj, *ZipScene Magazine*, 14 June, https://zip-scene.com/2016/06/14/87/. Accessed 6 March 2019.

—— (2016b), 'Between the niche and Disneyland', interview with Evert Hoogendoorn, *ZipScene Magazine*, 27 July, https://zip-scene.com/2016/07/27/between-the-niche-and-disneyland/. Accessed 6 March 2019.

—— (2016c), 'To like or not to like?', interview with Dóra Mészáros and Eszter Zewde, MaNDA, 31 May, http://mandarchiv.hu/cikk/5786/To_like_or_not_to_like. Accessed 6 March 2019.

Fischer-Lichte, Erika (1983), *Semiotik des Theaters,* Tübingen: Gunter Narr Verlag.

—— (2008), *The Transformative Power of Performance*, Abingdon: Routledge.

Irwin, Kathleen (2011), 'Staging the Internet: Representation (bodies, memories) and digital audience', *Canadian Theatre Review*, 148, pp. 54–60.

Jenkins, Henry (2014), 'Rethinking "rethinking convergence/culture"', *Cultural Studies*, 28:2, pp. 267–97.

Norman, Donald A. and Draper, Stephen W. (1986), *User Centered System Design: New Perspectives on Human Computer Interaction*, Hillsdale, NJ: L. Erlbaum Associates Inc. S, XI.

Otto, Ulf (2013), *Internetauftritte*, Bielefeld: Transcript Verlag.

—— (2015), 'Virtually performing the space', *IETM Budapest Plenary Meeting 2015*, Akvárium Klub, Budapest, 5–8 November.

Papagiannouli, Christina (2016), *Political Cyberperformance*, Basingstoke: Palgrave Macmillan.

Ranciére, Jacques (2009), *The Emancipated Spectator*, London: Verso.

Sant, Toni (2013), 'Theatrical performance on the Internet: How far have we come since *Hamnet*?', *Journal of Performance Art & Digital Media*, 9:2, pp. 247–59.

Sant, Toni and Flintoff, Kim (2007), 'The Internet as dramatic medium', Interactive and Improvisational Drama, 24 July, http://www.interactiveimprov.com/onlinedr.html. Accessed 5 June 2019.

The Hamnet Players (1993), '"Hamnet" ==== Shakespeare's play adapted for irc.', http://www.marmot.org.uk/hamnet/hscript.htm. Accessed 5 June 2019.

Wallace, Jillian (2015), 'Naive comedy in a dangerous virtual world: Expanding theatrical presence with online devices', *Body, Space & Technology*, 14, https://www.bstjournal.com/articles/10.16995/bst.37/. Accessed 5 June 2019.

Walmsley, Ben (2016), 'From arts marketing to audience enrichment: How digital engagement can deepen and democratize artistic exchange with audiences', *Poetics*, 58, pp. 66–78.

Editors' Note

Erin B. Mee's 'The audience is the message: Blast Theory's app-drama *Karen*' (2016) gives a detailed discussion on one of the performances this article examines. For a relevant introduction to the uses of new media in theatre, see Bake (2014) and for an extensive discussion on the histories, practices and trends in new media and performing arts, see Dixon (2015).

Further reading

Bake, Bill (2014), *Theatre and the Digital,* Basingstoke: Palgrave Macmillan.

Dixon, Steve (2015), *Digital Performance: A History of New Media in Theater, Dance, Performance Art, and Installation,* reprint ed., Cambridge, MA: MIT Press.

Mee, Erin B. (2016), 'The audience is the message: Blast Theory's app-drama *Karen*', *TDR: The Drama Review: A Journal of Performance Studies,* 60:3, pp. 165–71.

NOTES

1. This includes using different audience engagement strategies like the Twitter mention @askacurator initiated by Mar Dixon, or the digital art exhibition by British Council *I Dreamed a Dream The Other Night*, where one can a have a virtual walk in the exhibition place. See https://exhibitions.britishcouncil.org.tr/dreamexhibition/EN/Entrance/. Accessed 5 June 2019.

2. Further information at: http://oritgat.com/Global-Audiences-Zero-Visitors-How-to-measure-the-success-of-museums. Accessed 15 June 2017.

3. Examples include the Royal Shakespeare Company's *Such Tweet Sorrow* (2010), the first professional Twitter-based performance based on Shakespeare's work, or *Midsummer Night's Dream* (2016) for which RSC partnered with Google+.

4. Trailer available at: https://www.youtube.com/watch?v=8tuaphWCd0Y. Accessed 28 May 2016.

5. The performance's Facebook page can be accessed at: https://www.facebook.com/hamletonline/?fref=ts. Accessed 5 June 2019.

Manipulation of Reality through an Interactive Game: *Remote X* as an Example of New Modes of Spectatorship

Naďa Satková

This study aims at pointing out specific performances that require a different behaviour on the part of the spectators, who are encouraged to establish a kind of a temporary community, be active and make their own decisions during the performance. The study focuses on changes in modes of spectatorship. Apart from a description and analysis of one particular production, we also suggest that the methods applied by the production being analysed actually remind of techniques and principles characteristic of psychodrama and sociodrama. Identifying important psychological and sociological themes connected with such theatrical approaches, we also discuss social, political, historical and cultural identity.

A series of political, geographical and economic transformations have changed the relationship between theatres and the communities that surround them. Not only theatrical forms but also modes of reception have been transformed.

The study focuses on *Remote X* (2013-present), a project carried out by three artists united under the label Rimini Protokoll. They have worked as a team of authors and directors for more than fifteen years, and they are seen as inventors of a new form of documentary theatre, sometimes referred to as the 'theatre of reality' (Garde and Mumford 2012). Instead of presenting actors playing characters in dramatic texts they present common people, whom they find through elaborate research and casting procedures.

Rimini Protokoll explore a theatre of protagonists who are not professional actors but, rather, specialists in some other field of activity: people who are experts on the life they live. This may include call-centre employees, Vietnam War veterans, policemen, long distance lorry drivers as well as elderly ladies. Rimini Protokoll create the performances through their stories.

They have clearly hit a nerve amongst, somewhat exceptionally, theatre practitioners, critics and audience alike, with a theatre that is documentary – that is, relating directly to the world as we experience it, an experience that often seems to evade our gasp. At the same time, (unlike most television documentaries) they are not crudely affirming a reality but presenting a complex world in which the individual is fundamental and the truth is always narrative.

(Dreysse and Malzacher 2008: 8)

The reality is not dramatized, but it is sometimes combined with fiction and transferred to the stage. Documentary material is confronted with subjective views, the general meets the individual, popular beliefs are challenged by personal opinions and impressions.

Productions that do not use actors, but 'experts', have a significantly higher level of authenticity. Although 'experts' are stage personalities, these personalities are not parts of a fictive world. Florian Malzacher, one of the leading specialists on Rimini Protokoll, remarks: 'Authenticity is fictionalised just as fiction often dragged into reality' (Dreysse and Malzacher 2008: 39).

Most of their performances deal with topical, often unpleasant themes in society. Themes like war, immigration, ageing, death or unemployment are easily applicable in the contemporary situation in the European Union. For example, the production called *100% City* (2008-present) asks questions like: 'What if the population of a city with millions of inhabitants is represented on stage by one hundred people, carefully cast to reflect local demographics? Who exactly are our neighbours?' The production *Home Visit Europe* (2015-present) takes place in private apartments and interweaves personal stories with political mechanisms of today's Europe. Rimini Protokoll focus on topics connected with people tangled up in social phenomena of present life. Thomas Irmer remarks that Rimini Protokoll are playing with experimental aspects of services, which emphasize consequences of globalization (Irmer 2006: 25).

Remote X is quite different from productions like *100% City* or *Home Visit Europe*. The project started in Berlin in 2013 and it has since been hosted in over fifteen cities worldwide (some of them more than once). Rimini Protokoll's work on this project takes several steps. The artists stay in the chosen city for approximately two months, getting acquainted with it and looking for stories that form the 'face' of the city. They always prepare a brand new, city-specific version of the production, named after the city it takes place in (*Remote Berlin*, *Remote Lisboa*, *Remote Paris* etc.). Each production is influenced by the particular place. It does not considerably refer to the history or landmarks of the city, and all stories are fictional. Having developed the dramatic structure of the production, Rimini Protokoll usually put on one performance a day over a period of two or three weeks.

Personal Experience and Observations

This writing will make use of my own experience with one of these performances, *Remote Vilnius* (2015). Personal experience allows me to describe not only objective facts but also certain findings based on my subjective observations. I do not consider this approach academically inadequate; on the contrary, I find it quite necessary for a comprehensive description of such a special type of theatrical event.

I intentionally use the term 'event' here instead of 'theatre performance', because *Remote X* is far from an ordinary performance. Similarly I substitute 'spectator' with 'participant', as the latter term is much more appropriate.

Remote X involves about 50 participants. People who have ventured to attend this event accept to become part of a group, a temporary community of sorts. They are asked to wear headphones and obey instructions given by a synthetic voice. The voice directs the movements of the participants, who as a dispersed group walk through the streets of the city (walking being the most natural activity there), with the voice as their guide. The way one walks through the city is never the same. Each pedestrian is simply affected by the rhythm of the steps of the others. Headphones separate participants from ambient noises and thus induce split of perception: the present surroundings are perceived through sight, while audio track lures participants into the past or fiction.

The real-life city is transformed into an imaginary playing field. It is simultaneously a stage and a scenography. The tour is intentionally guided to places where people have developed irrational behaviours or to places where people co-exist with machines. Rimini Protokoll's piece is a clever reflection of the urban public space as a forum for strolling, meeting, jogging or demonstrations, also reflecting the long tradition of occupying streets for political reasons.

The members of the group are encouraged to participate in this 'game', be active and do simple tasks. For example, they are asked to sit down on the lawn in an old cemetery, close their eyes, listen to the music in their headphones and think about people who are dead. Then the participants are asked to walk down a corridor in an old hospital and reconstruct the local patients' life stories based on visual or auditory clues.

The voice in the headphones guides the participants to many places in the city and controls the attention of their eyes, ears or noses. The tour enables the participants to explore unknown and hidden territories and see the public space from unexpected angles. The group members visit the downtown as well as the suburbs, so they can form their own opinion on the contrast between the trendy, well-kept city centre and neglected, socially unattractive localities. The tour is intentionally guided by its organizers (artists) through different parts of the city. The artists do not address a political agenda through this choice, but they would like to turn participants' attention to everyday problems encountered by the general public.

This approach is certainly attractive for a participant who is visiting the city for the first time. But the tour also caters for participants who know the city well. These are skilfully pushed to explore it from another perspective, and are provided an opportunity to re-think social and political issues or to become aware of issues connected with cultural identity. Aspects of local and global perspectives in theatre-making meet here.

The carefully planned trip keeps the group together for over two hours and about seven kilometres. The walk connects theatre with real life because the spectators-participants naturally interact with the locals, meeting them in the streets or in public transport. The tour naturally attracts attention by group-performing activities like a running race, making Mexican waves as if at a sports stadium, or a mass shoe-tying (spectators-participants were asked for kneeling down and making a pretence of tying their own shoelaces). In the eyes of a passer-by, 50 people with headphones on can look like an alien entity or a sect, especially as the movements of the group are more or less synchronized by the instructions given in the headphones.

Psychodrama, Sociodrama and Community Principles

Remote X is not an ordinary production. It breaks many theatrical conventions, yet acknowledges observation of certain principles of psychodrama and sociodrama.

- First, one person directs the others, coordinates and appeals for repetitions or modifications. Here a voice in the headphones has the power to control, coordinate a group of people, and gradually manipulate them into unusual situations, which can be used for inducing certain emotions.
- Second, the roles of actors and spectators are not constant. The participants move as a team, but at particular moments the group is broken down into smaller units with different tasks. For example, some of the participants are asked to wave their hands, whereas others are told to watch them. Nobody knows what the others hear or are asked to do. The fact that not all participants hear the same instructions results in unexpected situations. The participants become spectators and, at the same time, actors, and these roles are changed several times. They find themselves acting yet watching, synchronized yet independent; sometimes they get by without being noticed, only to induce a weird situation a while later.

- Third, the community principle manifests itself in both activities. Jacob L. Moreno (1889–1974) is credited for founding psychodrama and sociodrama, which utilize theatrical forms as therapeutic means. Psychodrama is a method used in psychotherapy, with clients taking part in spontaneous dramatizations, role-playing or dramatic self-presentations in order to gain insight into their lives. During a typical psychodrama session, clients get together and the leader of the therapy uses specific techniques based on methods known from the theatre, such as mirroring, doubling, soliloquy or role reversal. Psychodrama is 'an opportunity to get into action instead of just talking, to take the role of the important people in our lives to understand them better, to confront them imaginatively in the safety of the therapeutic theater' (Moreno 2014: 50).

While psychodrama focuses on one client within a group unit, sociodrama addresses the group as a whole. It is a method through which grouped individuals select and spontaneously enact a specific social situation common to their experience. The concept underlying this sociological approach is the assumption that everybody is characterized by a certain range of roles dominating his/her behaviour. The aim of this method, which deals with inter-group relations, is to explore social events, collective ideologies and community patterns in order to bring about positive change or transformation within the group dynamic.

Similar psychodramatic and sociodramatic principles are found in *Remote X*, but some of them are shifted or modified. People participating in sociodrama or psychodrama therapy are usually selected in advance according to certain criteria, and they often live together in a community, where they have to obey rules and get to know each other. On the other hand, the group of people taking part in a Rimini Protokoll event is formed artificially and randomly. Becoming a member of this group simply entails buying a ticket – there are no other prerequisites.

Most of the *Remote X* participants have never met before. During the event they not only observe each other but they are also expected to interact and cooperate. People shake off their initial shyness as the event unfolds. Social relationships are created naturally, with pleasure or displeasure. The two hours represent an accelerated process of making relationships within a community. For example, the halo effect can be identified – in which an observer's overall impression of a group influences the observer's feelings and thoughts about that entity's character or properties. This confirms that understanding between group members does not come automatically because each member operates on a different frequency.

The social stratification in this artificially and temporarily created 'community' takes place naturally. The participants are sometimes given possibilities to choose from, and they can decide whether they will go with the crowd or against it. As these decisions are taken individually, after some time everybody can recognize who of the other community members is bound to become a leader, who merely wants to be led, who obeys rules without hesitation and who breaks them out of spite.

The creation of these relationships in the group is predictable, but it differs from reality because of the headphones. The participants cannot hear each other and can only communicate by gestures, facial expressions or eye contact. The similarity with nonverbal contact between actors and spectators in certain types of theatrical performance is apparent. The participants cannot say a word to each other but they share the same experience.

The members of the group may feel that they know each other much better at the end of the event. They can feel like 'conspirators'. The voice in their headphones assures them that together they are strong because they make up a crowd. They are even forced to break the law – cross the street on a red light or travel by bus without a ticket. These shared actions unite the members of the group.

Other methods that deal with an experience as a means of influencing a client (experiential education, therapeutic methods and teambuilding activities) also remind of particular principles used in theatre:

- affinity with game principles
- acceptation of the role (not only a role in theatre, but also a social role in society)
- all activities involve strong emotions
- in all activities people are experiencing acting
- people resolve conflicts, which bear no risk of any impact on their existence
- people are in a fictional world (not only in theatre, but also during the therapeutic or educational 'dry run life')

During the theatrical event *Remote Vilnius* the participants had a sense of belonging. Everybody knew they were just one small part of the crowd but they could perceive its collective strength, especially when a law was broken. The participants also perceived that time did not elapse in the same way as during a common day – it was a time of experience, a festive time. Every participant could make up his/her own storyline of the performance in the mind. The situations they were experiencing encouraged them to think about self-determination, freedom, role-playing, role-taking, face-to-face, personal space, crowd psychology and social, political and cultural identity.

Rimini Protokoll are not the only theatrical formation to deal with theatrical elements of our reality. 'Contemporary theatre is characterised by the search for new forms of theatricality, ones that do not depict reality illusionistically but for all that fundamentally deal with' (Dreysse and Malzacher 2008: 10). The concept of *Remote X* is not new. Other performances, too, have dealt with the specificity of the cities in which they take place. For example, the German company LIGNA has developed a radio ballet called *Walking the City* (2013). It invites the local inhabitants to listen to an audio play that addresses the unconsciousness of walk-ing the city. In a similar vein, the Hungarian community theatre KOMA Bázis and the Czech theatre Divadlo na cucky cooperated on a project called *Thousand and one Olomouc*, which took place in Olomouc in May 2015. They found the city of Olomouc as a big map of stories of its inhabitants as well as of people who are only visiting. During the performance the spectators explored a different face of the city. This city street game project livened up various locations with energetic stories that had once taken place there (see Chovancová 2015).

Manipulation and PC Games

I consider *Remote X* more complex and multi-layered than *Walking the City* or *Thousand and one Olomouc*, because *Remote X* deals with two additional topics compared to the other performances: game and manipulation.

The question of control is topical. Do people allow being manipulated and controlled? Who do they believe in? Who tells them how they should behave? Who gives them advice? In the past people were guided by somebody (a shaman for exam-ple, a privileged and prominent figure present at the most important occasions), and people believed in him. Today we are used to obeying instructions given by an impersonal synthetic voice, as we know it from GPS navigators or airport announce-ments. Getting lost in a city has become practically impossible, thanks to mapping technologies like GPS; gone are the days when we had to stop strangers and ask for directions. We are dependent on technology; machines tell us where to go, what to buy or even what to think. During *Remote X* the group was manipulated by the voice in the headphones, a kind of dictatorship also showing the relationship between people and technology. This could be an indicator of current trends.

The actual name of the performance bears computer connotations. X-Remote is a tool to remotely control a personal computer. The application communicates with our PC and lets us operate it remotely. During the event a participant could feel like being remotely controlled by artificial intelligence and taking part in a computer game. *Remote X* was in effect like a game where the participants acted as human beings who exercised certain rights and options but whose range of functions was somewhat restricted.

The entire performance reminded of multiplayer online role-playing games (MORPGs), in which one player interacts with a large number of other players within a virtual world. The players form a specific, temporary community. They assume roles of characters and take control over many of the characters' actions. A 'quest' in role-playing games is a task that a character – controlled by a player or a group of characters – may complete in order to gain a reward.

In the terminology of online games, *Remote X* is a multiplayer game. The participants of this theatrical event are like characters in PC games: heroes with certain skills. These skills are given and have limitations (or are they actually advantages?), as the participants are human and are theatre spectators rather than immortal heroes with great skills and equipment. Although they do not know each other well, they have to cooperate and perform certain tasks together. On the other hand, they take some decisions individually and build their roles within the group. The game is not a military one: the players do not fight enemies or occupy territories but, rather, learn something. Their reward is not an increase in the character's experience in order to get a treasure or access to new locations, the objective is to further develop mental skills – cognition, self-knowledge or new abilities.

The location is given. The participants should walk through individual places in the right order. At specified points they are expected to perform tasks, solve problems – i.e. do quests. They play in a real world, not a virtual one. The inhabitants of the city are not their enemies but they can complicate things. The playing field is the actual, existing city, yet for the participants it represents an artificial parallel world that influences the real one, and vice versa. The soundtrack and sound effects provide accompaniment to the stories, places and tasks, and are synchronized with the surrounding world.

Remote X is not a completely unique project. It bears a resemblance to other projects of Rimini Protokoll (for example *Call Cutta* [2005], *Outdoors* [2011] or *50 Aktenkilometer* [2011]), which happen outdoors and their spectators use headphones or other technical equipment. All these projects dynamically interact with the city, deform the everyday life into a particular dramaturgical shape, and interrogate the border of proximity between reality and fiction. Their spectators have to make meanings from various layers. They 'become urban explorers, finding themselves in a liminal space which is real but performed at the same time in a constructed and fictional situation' (Cavallini 2013: 52). They make sense of their encounters with competing realities; they have to deal with simultaneously processed feelings of immersion, distance and remembering and forgetting. Many contemporary theatrical formations, not excepting Rimini Protokoll, 'have integrated technological elements within their mobile productions specifically as a way of interrogating place' (Sedgman 2017: 352). In mentioned projects, people, place and technology are hard to separate. Physical and digital memories of place are weaved together; relationships between media and materiality are built.

As Cavallini says, Rimini Protokoll's 'theatre of real' reformulates urban space as a ludic stage where borders between the personal and the public are in constant renegotiation (Cavallini 2013: 52). *Remote X* is different from similar above-mentioned projects in some ways, above all in an amount of playfulness. Ordinary situations are built around playful visions and perceptions of reality and its representations. The relationship between play and urban space is activated; the city hosts playful activities and invites participants to remulate the possibilities of action and the notion of public space. 'Experts of everyday life' nor artists (except for them, who care for technical details) do not visibly appear in this production. The production is about participation. An intensity of pleasure and satisfaction of spectators-participants is directly proportional to how much they cooperate and obey the instructions given by organizers (by voices in participants' headphones). When participants accede to a game (with its rules and risks), they do playful controlled activities with only a little role of a coincidence. Although participants can make their own decisions during the production, there are only few things that are not planned in advance. The game/play is a didactical and explorative device. Everyday life permeates with a play in a participative way, transforming viewers into producers. As spectators-participants are pushed to form a horde, it leads to multiplication of meanings and deepening their feelings, because it needs perceiving of more levels of attention and dealing with more levels of reality ('here and now', fictional reality, constructed one).

New forms of theatre, communication between theatres and communities, as well as changes in the modes of spectatorship and innovative forms of theatre that demand a different behaviour on the part of the audience are not new, and neither are links between theatre and political, sociological or psychological themes. They are, however, becoming increasingly popular and frequently discussed. Thanks to productions like *Remote X*, spectators could become more open to unusual theatrical events, during which they could be conscious of temporary duration of an artificially created spectatorial community with a strong feeling of presence and the manipulation of reality. In my opinion, in such productions, the spectator is confronted not only with the content that he can approach from a disinterested perspective, but also with the whole event he is a part of. We should be aware that these kinds of productions also need their own methodology, which can describe them in their complexity. Further development of new methods to understand the process of participation (for example with cooperation with sociological or psychological tools) is necessary.

REFERENCES

Boenisch, Peter M. (2008), 'Other people live: Rimini Protokoll and their "Theater of Experts"', *Contemporary Theater Review*, 18, pp. 107–13.

Cavallini, Roberto (2013), 'Figurations of the infra-ordinary: Play and urban imaginaries in Rimini Protokoll's documentary theatre practice', *Lo Squaderno*, 27, pp. 51–54, http://www.losquaderno.professionaldreamers.net/wp-content/uploads/2013/03/losquaderno27.pdf. Accessed 3 December 2017.

Chovancová, Barbora (2015), 'Kolik Olomoucí znáš, tolikrát jsi člověkem', *Festivalový zpravodaj Divadelní Flory*, 2, p. 6.

Dreysse, Miriam and Malzacher, Florian (2008), *Experts of the Everyday: The Theatre of Rimini Protokoll*, Berlin: Alexander Verlag.

Garde, Ulrike and Mumford, Meg (2012), 'Rimini Protokoll presents "real" experts', *Kultur: Magazine of the Goethe-Institut in Australia*, 23, September, pp. 16–17, http://issuu.com/goetheaustralia/docs/gi_kultur23_sep12/1. Accessed 1 December 2017.

Haug, Helgard, Kaegi, Stefan and Wetzel, Daniel (2008), *100% City*, Cornelius Puschke and Rimini Protokoll, Berlin, 1 Feb.

Irmer, Thomas (2006), 'A search for new realities: Documentary theatre in Germany', *TDR/ The Drama Revue*, 3, pp. 16–28.

Jiřička, Lukáš (2010), 'Nejsme záchranný team', *A2*, 26, https://www.advojka.cz/archiv/2010/26/nejsme-zachranny-tym. Accessed 19 December 2016.

Moreno, Jonathan D. (2014), *Impromptu Man*, New York: Bellevue Literary Press.

Sedgman, Kirsty (2017), 'Audience experience in Rimini Protokoll's *Outdoors*', *Studies in Theatre and Performance*, 3, pp. 350–64.

Editors' Note

The work of Rimini Protokoll is relatively well discussed in theatre and performance scholarship. For an important discussion on the interplays between performance and the urban environment, see a recent special issue of the journal *Navigationen* edited by Judith Ackermann, Andreas Rauscher and Daniel Stein with the theme of 'Playin' the City: Artistic and Scientific Approaches to Playful Urban Arts' (2016). *The Drama Review*'s Fall 2014 issue provides some very relevant perspectives on performance and the city/public spaces, and the issue opens with a provocation peace by Rimini Protokoll's Stefan Kaegi (2014). For an analysis on immersive and digital practices in performance, please see Panayiota Demetriou's most recent article 'Imagineering mixed reality (MR) immersive experiences in the postdigital revolution: Innovation, collectivity, participation and ethics in staging experiments as performances' (2018).

Further reading

Ackermann, Judith, Rauscher, Andreas and Stein, Daniel (2016), *Navigationen*, special issue, 'Playin' the City: Artistic and Scientific Approaches to Playful Urban Arts', 16:1.

Demetriou, Panayiota (2018), 'Imagineering mixed reality (MR) immersive experiences in the postdigital revolution: Innovation, collectivity, participation and ethics in staging experiments as performances', *International Journal of Performance Arts and Digital Media*, 14:2, pp. 169–86.

Kaegi, Stefan (2014), 'Provoking audience', *TDR/The Drama Review*, 58:3, pp. 2–3.

Feeding Back: Verbatim Theatre and/as Communal Practice

Bettina Auerswald

Redefining Theatre Communities with Verbatim Theatre

Verbatim theatre, a subgenre of documentary theatre, traditionally tells 'ordinary' people's stories (see Paget 1987: 317; Soans 2005a) using their edited, but otherwise unaltered words. This material is usually obtained through face-to-face interviews between the actors and those willing to participate in the project. After performances elsewhere, some verbatim theatre productions return to the place where they originated. Herein lies verbatim theatre's prime innovation: it feeds back its stories into the communities where they had come from 'via performance *in* those communities' (Paget 1987: 317). Through its unique devising process, verbatim theatre dissolves the divide between actor and spectator and enables playwrights and theatre companies to take responsible action in their capacity as artists. Thus, verbatim theatre creates and then brings together three different communities: the artistic community engages with the story-giving community and together they enter into a dialogue with the theatregoing community. In many ways, therefore, verbatim theatre can be said to epitomize communal practices and must be of particular interest when examining theatre's potential to incorporate community involvement in its productions. This chapter looks to re-evaluate how communities are created and portrayed in verbatim theatre and to discuss the limits in the role it can play in the context of communities.

Communal and Political Verbatim Theatre

Over the past twenty years, a significant number of verbatim plays have emerged that are journalistic in origin and tone, and have a radically different outlook than those plays that are rooted in theatrical practice and follow first-generation

230

verbatim practitioners' protocol. I call the former, journalistic strand political verbatim and the latter communal verbatim. This classification is necessary, because it moves away from differentiating verbatim theatre on accounts of its source material – tribunal *vis-à-vis* classic verbatim plays – and appreciates that each subgenre acts out of responsibility, even though this responsibility is understood differently in both strands (see Auerswald 2017: 109–12).

The younger of the two strands, political verbatim, focuses on issues of global importance and on the emancipation of its audience. It shares characteristics and practices with investigative journalism and is therefore often criticized for its manipulative tendencies and sensationalism (cf. Bottoms 2006: 58). Examples for political verbatim plays are Victoria Brittain and Gillian Slovo's *Guantanamo: 'Honor Bound to Defend Freedom': Taken from Spoken Evidence* (2004), which examines the questionable holding of detainees in Guantanamo Bay, and David Hare's *The Power of Yes: A Dramatist Seeks to Understand the Financial Crisis* (2009), which addresses the 2008 global financial crisis. These plays are written by the playwrights without the simultaneous involvement of cast and crew, who receive the finished playtext. Hence, there is no direct contact between interviewees and actors. The interviewees are picked for their topical relevance; not to authentically represent a community. Consequently, there is usually a smaller number of dramatis personæ in political than in communal verbatim plays. In political verbatim, the artist's responsibility is focused on making information publicly available rather than on interpersonal interaction.

In contrast, communal verbatim focuses on exploring the limits and functions of theatre as a genre as well as on the responsibility of artists towards their community – and thus on communal practices. Communities are not only strengthened, but also (re-)created; the artists' focus is to facilitate collaboration between different communities. A central characteristic of communal verbatim is the above-described circular devising process and its ability to feed back the stories to where they had come from in the first place (cf. Paget 1987: 317; Kaufman and Tectonic Theatre Project members 2001: vii). Thus, communal verbatim establishes the building of communities as a responsible process on various levels: it dissolves hardened fronts by contrasting diverse voices, thereby promoting empathy. Based on the resulting, new communal self-image, further responsible action can be taken. Examples for communal verbatim plays are Kaufman's *The Laramie Project* (2000), which deals with the brutal, homophobically motivated murder of Matthew Shepard in Laramie, Wyoming, in 1998, and *Counted? A Documentary-Play about British Democracy* (2010) by Look Left Look Right, which enquires into people's disengagement with political participation ahead of the 2010 General Elections. Communal verbatim's main objective is to enable communal interaction: a direct connection between the artists and the story-giving community is established by which art and life enter into a reciprocal exchange.

The Reciprocity of Community and Culture between
Farness and Nearness

This chapter examines communal verbatim theatre as a form of redefined theatre community. I am drawing on Jan and Aleida Assmann's concept of cultural memory, because it is well suited to illustrate central elements of communal verbatim practice (Assmann 1988).[1] It would be equally productive to interrogate the notion of community with one of the leading critical theorists in the field such as Zygmunt Bauman. In *Community: Seeking Safety in an Insecure World* (2001) Bauman presupposes the existence of a singular, all-encompassing, holistic community, which consequently bears totalitarian and, as I would argue, 'monotheistic' characteristics and does not allow for a plurality of communities (Bauman 2001: 48, 58). In accordance with Assmann, Bauman points to the importance of discourse and diversity and highlights the community's reliance on 'frequent and intense interaction' (Bauman 2001: 48, cf. 65, 136, 137, 142); however, his community is already formed. In the context of redefined theatre communities, I am interested in those communities, Bauman would call 'aesthetic' (2001: 65): temporary, voluntary, positively 'liquid' communities, formed and perpetuated through active participation.

In his seminal paper entitled 'Kollektives Gedächtnis und kulturelle Identität', translated by John Czaplicka as 'Collective memory and cultural identity' (1995), Jan Assmann links cultural memory to collective identity and marks it off from communicative memory. While communicative memory is tantamount to '*Alltagsgedächtnis*' (Assmann 1988: 9), 'everyday memory' (Czaplicka 1995: 126), cultural memory encompasses the idiosyncratic inventory of texts, pictures and rites that are geared towards re-utilization and through which a society upholds and underpins its unity, uniqueness and sense of self. Assmann argues that a society is visible through its cultural heritage, not only for others but also for itself, and relies on this cultural knowledge to performatively replicate its own identity (see Assmann 1988: 12, 15–16). The following three examples lend themselves well to illustrate this reciprocity of cultural heritage and communal identity.

In ancient Greek theatre, cultural heritage was not only formed, but acted out. The architectural structure of the amphitheatre allowed for the chorus to act as the audience's mirror, thereby connecting them to the action on stage. Actors and spectators were united in the performance event and created cultural memory together, which at the same time strengthened and promoted a collective cultural identity. Ancient Greek theatre is a perfect example for how cultural heritage and communities are interlinked and reciprocally constitutive.

By implication, the obliteration of cultural history simultaneously obliterates existing cultural memory and consequently a community's identity. Filippo

Tommaso Marinetti's 'Manifesto of futurism' from 1909 is an example for the rejection of cultural memory. In it, Marinetti calls out for the destruction of museums, libraries and archives to cleanse the, to his mind, dull and ponderous culture and to pave the way for a new cultural identity (cf. Marinetti 2005). Marinetti's invocation of war and of the destruction of objectified and curated cultural memory are proof of his fear that the current cultural memory was standing in the way of the radical new identity he had envisaged.

A contemporary example for how a community can be severely disrupted by the destruction of cultural memory is the demolition of the UNESCO World Heritage Site Palmyra by the self-declared Islamic State. Besides ISIS's declared religious motivation, 'the group revels in the destruction as it highlights its ability to operate with impunity and it shows the powerlessness of the international community to put a halt to its actions' (Shaheen 2015). With its actions, ISIS engages in symbol politics and sets itself off from the values of the world community: it destroys sites of collective cultural value and stages its own value of religious homogeneity. These examples show that communities are created, held together and strengthened by the culture that they create. The destruction of culture is bound to break communities apart.[2]

When we examine the notion of community from a sense of place, like we do when speaking of Palmyra and ancient Greek theatre, we automatically link community to nearness, both emotionally and physically: we speak of attachment (a-*touch*-ment) and of *comm-unity*, of *together-oneness*. In contrast, Judith Butler calls upon her readers to understand and enable the creating of community as the *inversion* of farness and nearness. She criticizes 'communitarianism' in which only those communities are valued and acknowledged that are based on physical, emotional and ethical proximity (see Butler 2012: 134–35). Communities, Butler argues, must also be formed in disregard of nearness, because we are solicited by *all* Others: 'those we do not know, and even those we did not choose, could never have chosen' (Butler 2012: 140). Accordingly, we can argue that verbatim theatre responds ethically to both suffering at a distance and within 'relations of proximity', thus honouring global connectedness (Butler 2012: 134, also see 138, 147, 149). Theatre generally emphasizes nearness, because it brings a diverse group of people together in one space, the dark auditorium, 'where strangers sit next to one another to look in the same direction at other humans living in the same space and time as them' (Stephens 2016: 30). Verbatim theatre is particularly well suited to incorporate farness into this nearness by bringing voices of people together on stage who are at least as diverse as the audience watching them.

Robin Soans' *Talking to Terrorists* (2005b), for instance, deals with the global issue of terrorism. For this play, Soans and a number of actors interviewed people from the United Kingdom, the Republic of Ireland, Israel, Palestine, Uganda and

Denmark. However, most interviewees never actually met and are only connected topically, through the writing on the page. Because it lacks the communal interaction and instead focuses on enlightening its spectators about the issues of terrorism, Soans' play is an example for political verbatim, albeit with a communal verbatim element – a part of the cast was, after all, involved in the interview process. Political verbatim practitioners' firm belief is that '[b]y watching how people give evidence [...] I think an audience feels that they are empowered and able to arrive quite dispassionately at the truth in their own minds' (Kent 2013: 139). If at all, the only community created is between the actors and the audience, but not with the interviewees.

In the context of his performance project *Formative Theatre* (2006–present), Vahid Evazzadeh argues that communities in art are built upon a collective of people caring and willing to participate. Besides participating in the performance as performers or interviewees in a verbatim play, people participate as audiences by feeling addressed by the theatre-making (cf. Evazzadeh 2015). This understanding of reception as participation can again be tied back to Butler and the Levinasian Other whose face calls upon us precontractually, without our prior consent, in the form of ethical solicitation (see Butler 2012: 135). I argue that this notion is compatible with Jacques Rancière's notion of the emancipated spectator. Rancière's prime tenant is that 'viewing is also an action' (2011: 13). He stresses how much the construction of meaning is built upon an active interaction: 'The spectator [...] acts, [...] observes, selects, compares, interprets[,] [...] links[,] [...] composes[,] [...] participates in the performance by refashioning it in her own way' (Rancière 2011: 13). Structurally, the very same strategies are at play in the creating and maintaining of community, which is an interactive process and, *au fond*, a hermeneutic spiral.

Not only in the context of *Formative Theatre*, therefore, is community to be understood as participation and to manifest itself as transnational and transcultural. Communal connection is generated through the collaborative interaction between individuals. In communal verbatim theatre, communities are primarily built through this form of collaboration, both among interviewer and actor, as well as between the interviewees themselves, who, as a group of individuals, participate in the same project independent from each other, while their stories are later edited together. The connection is created on a meta-level through the participation in the same project, which creates coherence and connection. This community-building process is strengthened through verbatim theatre's traditional, circular devising and staging process: a theatre company travels to a place, talks to residents, edits the collected words in rehearsal and goes back for more interviews and rehearsals until the play reaches its final form; the play is then performed all over the country to finally return to the community where it originated (cf. Paget 1987: 317;

Kaufman and Tectonic Theatre Project members 2001: vi). By returning the play to its origin, the company creates the opportunity of a dialogue between former interviewees. Seeing not only themselves but also fellow participants represented on stage gives former interviewees an opportunity to get into conversation with each other beyond the theatre venue. The main difference between *Talking to Terrorists* and *The Laramie Project* is that in Soans' play, the stories are collected to instruct the spectators rather than to work with a community.

So far, we can constitute that redefined theatre communities do not rely on physical or ideological proximity, but on the voluntary, reciprocal exchange between individuals that comes from the wish to work together. Instead of basing community on sentiments – on liking those on the 'inside' and disliking those on the 'outside', something that Butler would rightfully condemn as communitarian (cf. Butler 2012: 134–35) – the connection between the selves is created through participation. As this chapter tries to work towards new definitions, my understanding of community is radically positive and idealistic. I am aware of the fact that understanding community as teleological participation towards a goal would also allow for a community of terrorists. While, to speak with Butler again, being called upon by the Other is precontractual (see Butler 2012: 135), the building of a community is a voluntary act and relies on continued participation. When we accept Assmann's theory about a cultural memory, then we must accept that cultural memory is constitutive for the subsistence of communities and that all cultural performativity is involved in forming the glue between the selves who form the community. This understanding of community allows for involuntary communities, such as a community of war victims, a label that would be attributed to individuals by the 'greater community' or by society. When communities are broken through grave acts of violence, a healing process needs to incorporate these acts into the cultural memory, because they are inevitably a part of the community's identity – whether they are used productively or repressed is up to the community. An effective and rewarding way to work through such traumas is through communal action as it can, for instance, be achieved by means of communal verbatim theatre.

Community and Communal Agency in Moisés Kaufman's The Laramie Project

A powerful example for the use of communal verbatim theatre as a tool to attempt a healing of a broken community is Kaufman's *The Laramie Project*. The play is not only built around the tragedy of Matthew's murder, but also around the town of Laramie, the type of place it is and the way of life it stands for within the United States:

> [Laramie is] a good place to live. Good people – lots of space. [...] There's so much space between people and towns here, so much time for reflection. [...] I moved here after living in a couple of big cities. [...] I loved it there. But you'd have to be out of your mind to let your kids out after dark. And here, in the summertime, my kids play out at night till eleven and I don't think twice about it.
>
> (Kaufman and Tectonic Theatre Project members 2001: 6–7)

The utterance is edited from various characters' voices. They unanimously describe Laramie as a small, provincial, exceptionally friendly and safe town where everybody knows everybody else, a 'town with a strong sense of community' (Kaufman and Tectonic Theatre Project members 2001: 9). The reality of a murder committed by two of its residents violently clashes with Laramie's self-image. In his interview, Jedidiah Schultz describes the breakdown of the Laramie community after the murder:

> Now, after Matthew, I would say that Laramie is a town defined by an accident, a crime. We've become Waco, we've become Jasper. We're a noun, a definition, a sign. We may be able to get rid of that ... but it will sure take a while.
>
> (Kaufman and Tectonic Theatre Project members 2001: 9)

Schultz puts Matthew's murder in the context of two other racially motivated hate crimes: the 1916 lynching of Jesse Washington in Waco, Texas, commonly referred to as the 'Waco Horror', and the 1998 lynching of James Byrd Jr. in Jasper, Texas. Schultz's description of the town is an example of how an act of violence tears through a community, because it confronts it with its unconscious ideologies, moral judgements and repressed cognitive models.

The aftermath of the murder had 'brought to the surface how we think and talk about homosexuality, sexual politics, education, class, violence, privileges and rights, and the difference between tolerance and acceptance'. The project arose out of Kaufman's 'desire to learn more about why Matthew Shepard was murdered, about what happened that night, about the town of Laramie' (Kaufman and Tectonic Theatre Project members 2001: vi). It was never the company's goal to 'pry [...] into a town's unraveling' (Kaufman and Tectonic Theatre Project members 2001: 10). The aim of the project had been to restart a dialogue that had been stifled by the extensive media coverage following the incident. Rebecca Hilliker, head of the theatre department at the University of Wyoming, stresses her students' need to talk: 'When this happened they started talking about it, and then the media descended and all the dialogue stopped' (Kaufman and Tectonic Theatre Project members 2001: 11). Tectonic Theatre Project and Hilliker share the belief that communication and a collective engagement is what can restore community. People have the opportunity to vent emotions and through exchange gain closure. With diverse opinions comes a dynamic that supports the process: 'you may not like what [my students] have to say, and you may not like their opinions, [...] [but] I'd rather have opinions that I don't like – and have that dynamic in education' (Kaufman and Tectonic Theatre Project members 2001: 11). In harmony with Hilliker's call for a dynamic interaction, the voices of Laramie are authentically curated: devastated voices from Matthew's family meet homophobic voices of hate as well as pragmatic or indifferent voices. Presenting these diverse opinions without value judgements is what can help the community learn about the reasons for the crime and prevent such crimes in the future.

Some of the play's characters repeatedly point to a collective responsibility for the incident. 'We're a product of our society' (Kaufman and Tectonic Theatre Project members 2001: 62), explains Shannon, a friend of Aaron McKinney's, who had killed Matthew together with Russell Henderson. Father Roger Schmit even argues that 'right now our most important teachers must be Russell Henderson and Aaron McKinney. They have to be our teachers. How did you learn? What did we as a society do to teach you that?' (Kaufman and Tectonic Theatre Project members 2001: 89). Schmit wishes for Henderson and McKinney to tell their story to the public, so that this broken community has the opportunity to understand and address the structural conditions that had promoted the hate crime, accept what had happened, and thereby begin to (re-)construct a new collective community that is aware of its history. A strong example is Romaine Patterson's *Angel Action* (1999). Patterson had come up with the project as a means of showing the nation that 'there is a better way of dealing with that kind of hatred. [...] [W]e are a group of people bringing forth a message of peace and love and compassion' (Kaufman and Tectonic Theatre Project members 2001: 79–80). To counter Reverend Fred Phelps' anti-gay hate sermon, Patterson's group had dressed up as angels with giant wings and silently and peacefully surrounded the Reverend to drown out his sound and block his view. This action is on the one hand problematic, because it infringes the Reverend's freedom of speech. At the same time, it presents a form of peaceful protest and is an attempt at de-escalation.

Patterson's *Angel Action* shows how working towards overcoming a crisis can create new communities. The play provides examples for how a few people taking action can create communal action on a larger scale: from the small band of angels to hundreds of people marching behind a banner for Matthew Shepard (cf. Kaufman and Tectonic Theatre Project members 2001: 63). New communities are also formed on accounts of people's wish to express solidarity. Laramie is portrayed as a town that gradually faces up to its responsibility for its tragedy and then works to re-position itself and to reclaim a new identity that is aware of its violent potential. The play is as much about Laramie and Matthew's murder as it is about what such incidents can do to a community and how a shattered community can restore itself through communal agency.

Verbatim Theatre's Limits

In the face of such ambitious objectives, what are the limits of verbatim theatre? For one, there is no unmediated human contact between the story-givers and their audience. One exception is that of the aforementioned 'fed back' performances, which do, however, not exist in political verbatim. In the case of a 'fed back' performance, a direct interaction would be possible but is not necessarily given, because the interviewees who might come to watch the play will not necessarily be willing to speak to fellow interviewees or other audience members. Second, even in the case of performances that make use of the 'feeding back' process, there is no guaranteed long-lasting, tangible effect. I have no knowledge of the people of Laramie still collaborating in art projects with each other that have arisen out of *The Laramie Project*. This issue is proactively interrogated in the play: 'What's come out of this that's concrete or lasting? [...] [N]obody anywhere, has passed any kind of laws, antidiscrimination laws or hate crime legislation' (Kaufman and Tectonic Theatre Project members 2001: 99) – the Matthew Shepard and James Byrd Jr. Hate Crimes Prevention Act was not passed until October 2009. Within the theatrical context I am only aware of Kaufman, who did a follow-up project entitled *The Laramie Project: 10 Years Later* (2009) to 'see how the people of the town had changed' as a way of paying tribute to the 'ongoing story of an American town' (Kaufman and Tectonic Theatre Project members 2014: 103–04). It is not verbatim theatre's goal to create a perpetual series of meetings and re-meetings and to engage with these 'ongoing stories' in order to generate new creative work in the way performance projects can.[3] Beyond the original devising process and performances, verbatim theatre trades continued exchange for the permanence of a published, re-performable playtext.

Second, only about 10 per cent of the original material ends up being used in the finished play. Alecky Blythe explains that in the edit she tries 'to distill the characters and the key moments for dramatic effect' (Blythe quoted in Soans 2005: 102). From a constructivist point of view, this reinforces verbatim plays' candidness, because it pays tribute to our known selective perception. Kaufman and his company had edited *The Laramie Project*, a 100-page play, out of 'more than two hundred interviews' (Kaufman and Tectonic Theatre Project members 2001: vii).

What is more, this idiosyncratic devising and editing process gives rise to questions concerning the limits of veracious representation. Did the theatre company do their (albeit subjective) best to preserve the interviewees as true to their 'real' selves as possible? I am using parentheses because the actors are, of course, dependent on the image the interviewees present of themselves. As it is unlikely for any of the interviewees to present an unpolished version of themselves, both the actors and the interviewees fall into the trap of conformism by following the 'rules of the game' of such an interview setup. To tie this idea to Butler's argument, is the danger of conformism more imminent when we act, live, think out of oneness? I believe that Butler would tie (the idea of a need for) conformism to communitarianism, because the forming of a community on grounds of conformist thinking is again a community based on proximity. Since a community, in Butler's view, cannot be formed on the grounds of nearness, a redefined theatre community must be built on a diversity that is retained – to give dynamics (cf. Hilliker quoted in Kaufman and Tectonic Theatre Project members 2001: 11) – and at the same time transcended, in the sense that bridges are built between unconnected selves through dialogue. That is, the emancipated self can be called upon by the face of the Other and respond from its own point of view – without the need to enter into opposition.

Conclusion: Verbatim Theatre and/as Communal Practice

In the introduction to *The Laramie Project*, Kaufman explains why he chose to create a verbatim play. He emphasizes that by 'paying careful attention [...] to people's words, one is able to hear the way these prevailing ideas affect not only individual lives but also the culture at large' (Kaufman and Tectonic Theatre Project members 2001: v). By thinking about the limits of documentary art and the impossibility of an objective representation, spectators are forced to question their own role as address-ees and interpreters, that is creators of a text's meaning, and thus become 'active participants' (cf. Brecht quoted in Rancière 2011: 4). Through their participation, spectators open themselves up to an ethical encounter with the Other, which results in the building of a community between various groups: the interviewees participate with the actors to give their stories. The actors interact with the individual stories to devise a play. The spectators come to the performances and open themselves up to be called upon by the presented personal stories and thus essentially the interviewees. It is the editing that forms the glue between the individual stories. It is the actors, who form the glue between the interviewees and the spectators, who consequently become witnesses. Though not free from limitations, (communal) verbatim theatre works towards creating a 'true community' between artists and 'ordinary' people in order to meet Brecht's demand that is here revisited by Rancière: 'Theatre is a place where an action is taken to its conclusion by bodies in motion in front of living bodies that are to be mobilized' (2011: 3). Any communal verbatim play begins with a theatre company asking a community to give their stories to the verbatim project and thereby be mobilized into participation. In performance, communal verbatim extends this offer to spectators. Redefined theatre communities with verbatim thea-tre are characterized by a willingness of participants (interviewees and spectators alike) to be addressed by the theatre-making and to participate in the cultural event, thereby engaging in the creating of their community's cultural memory.

REFERENCES

Assmann, Jan (1988), 'Kollektives Gedächtnis und kulturelle Identität', in J. Assmann and T. Hölscher (eds), *Kultur und Gedächtnis*, Frankfurt am Main: Suhrkamp, pp. 9–19.

—— (1995), 'Collective memory and cultural identity' (trans. John Czaplicka), *New German Critique*, 65, pp. 125–33.

Auerswald, Bettina (2017), 'Promises of the real? The precariousness of verbatim theatre and Robin Soans's *Talking to Terrorists*', in M. Aragay and M. Middeke (eds), *Of Precariousness: Vulnerabilities, Responsibilities, Communities in 21st-Century British Drama and Theatre*, Berlin: De Gruyter, pp. 109–24.

Bauman, Zygmunt (2001), *Community: Seeking Safety in an Insecure World*, Cambridge, MA: Polity.

Bottoms, Stephen (2006), 'Putting the document into documentary: An unwelcome corrective?', *TDR*, 50:3, pp. 56–68.

Bottoms, Steve, Freedman, Ben and Poskitt, Mimi (dirs) (2010), *Counted? A Documentary-Play about British Democracy*, Look Left Look Right and Roundhouse, London, 15 April.

Brittain, Victoria and Slovo, Gillian (2004), *Guantanamo: 'Honor Bound to Defend Freedom': Taken from Spoken Evidence*, London: Oberon.

Butler, Judith (2012), 'Precarious life, vulnerability, and the ethics of cohabitation', *Journal of Speculative Philosophy*, 26:2, pp. 134–51.

Evazzadeh, Vahid (2015), 'Formative theatre: A new approach by the Counter Institute', *Redefining Theatre Communities: Community Perspectives in Contemporary Theatre-Making*, University of Malta, 14 September.

Hare, David (2009), *The Power of Yes: A Dramatist Seeks to Understand the Financial Crisis*, London: Faber & Faber.

Kaufman, Moisés and Tectonic Theatre Project members (2001), *The Laramie Project*, New York: Vintage.

—— (2014), *The Laramie Project* and *The Laramie Project: Ten Years Later*, New York: Vintage.

Kent, Nicholas (2013), 'Nicholas Kent', interview with Will Hammond and Dan Steward, in W. Hammond and D. Steward (eds), *Verbatim Verbatim: Contemporary Documentary Theatre*, London: Oberon, pp. 133–68.

Kopeinig, Rosalia (2015), 'Show.Rooms (schau.Raeume): An interdisciplinary performance project', *Redefining Theatre Communities: Community Perspectives in Contemporary Theatre-Making*, University of Malta, 16 September.

Marinetti, Filippo Tommaso (2005), 'Gründung und Manifest des Futurismus', in W. Asholt and W. Fähnders (eds), *Manifeste und Proklamationen der europäischen Avantgarde (1909–1938)*, Stuttgart: Metzler, pp. 3–7.

Paget, Derek (1987), '"Verbatim theatre": Oral history and documentary techniques', *New Theatre Quarterly*, 3:12, pp. 317–36.

Rancière, Jacques (2011), *The Emancipated Spectator* (trans. Gregory Elliott), London: Verso.

Shaheen, Kareem (2015), 'ISIS blows up Arch of Triumph in 2,000-year-old City of Palmyra', *The Guardian*, 5 October, http://www.theguardian.com/world/2015/oct/05/isis-blows-up-another-monument-in-2000-year-old-city-of-palmyra. Accessed 25 May 2016.

Soans, Robin (2005a), 'Should terrorists be given a voice?', interview with Dominic Cavendish, *The Telegraph*, 23 April, http://www.telegraph.co.uk/culture/theatre/drama/3640875/Should-terrorists-be-given-a-voice.html. Accessed 29 April 2013.

—— (2005b), *Talking to Terrorists*, London: Oberon.

Stephens, Simon (2016), *Simon Stephens: A Working Diary*, London: Bloomsbury Methuen Drama.

Editors' Note

For an extensive critical account on historical and contemporary verbatim and documentary theatre initiatives, see Forsyth and Megson (2009). For topical discussions on the techniques and methodologies of verbatim theatre, please see Belfield (2018) and Hammond and Steward (2008).

Further reading

Belfield, Robin (2018), *Telling the Truth: How to Make Verbatim Theatre*, London: Nick Hern Books.

Forsyth, Alison and Megson, Chris (eds) (2009), *Get Real: Documentary Theatre Past and Present*, Basingstoke: Palgrave Macmillan.

Hammond, Will and Steward, Dan (eds) (2008), *Verbatim Verbatim: Contemporary Documentary Theatre*, London: Oberon Books.

NOTES

1. I am grateful to Michael Sauter for pointing out the parallels between my notion of verbatim theatre's engagement with communities and Jan and Aleida Assmann's theory.

2. The concept of community is, of course, an ambiguous one. As I argue further below, understanding community as directional participation aiming towards a common goal also allows for communities of terrorists, which are subject to the very same threats and reinforcements described here.

3. A powerful example of such a project is Rosalia Kopeinig and Kartin Ackerl Konstantin's *schau.Raeume*, a global interdisciplinary performance project that specializes in the engagement with local communities, memoires and experiences of, particularly, tabooed topics (cf. Kopeinig 2015).

241

Conclusion

Marco Galea and Szabolcs Musca

For Jacques Rancière theatre is quintessentially a community endeavour, 'the community as a way of occupying a place and a time, as the body in action' (2011: 6). According to him, theatre has been struggling for centuries to go beyond the dichotomy of actor/spectator by reinventing the role of the spectator. He attacks the modernist narrative whereby art (including theatre) acquires legitimization by some intrinsic aesthetic quality and exists 'isolated in a world of [its] own' (Rancière 2009: 33). What we have tried to achieve in this book is to trace, through the examination of different practices, the engagement of theatre with the concept of community, grounded in time and space. Like Rancière, we have no confidence that theatre is a democratic art, where the boundaries between makers and consumers, or the hierarchies amongst theatre-makers, can be eradicated. It is in this light that ideas like turning spectators into 'experts', the allocation of resources to practitioners or the institutional control over amateur performers are discussed in this book. Although contemporary theatre practices are committed to go beyond the boundaries between actors and spectators, for aesthetic and political reasons, the notion itself reasserts these boundaries.

The essence of community is that it includes members according to explicit or implicit criteria. There are criteria (not always transparent or justified) about who forms part of the nation community, who is accepted within a local one, or even in a special interest community. Drawing on Aristotle, Rancière speaks of 'the distribution of the sensible' (or as his translator suggests, 'what is common to the community'), the rules that enable different levels of participation in the activities of the community (Rancière 2013: 7–8, 109). This is a problem that several writers in this book discuss, with regard to national communities, smaller geographical communities and also artistic communities. However, the other side of the coin is just as important. Who is excluded from the community and how are they represented? Some of the chapters in this book deal with theatre projects about, or with groups or even individuals who are at, the margins of established communities: (post-)migrants, drug users, sexual minorities or communities being disrupted by gentrification. A common element in all the discussed projects is that they only came about through the intervention of professionals who are themselves accepted and respected members of society, practitioners who have access to institutional resources and funding that is not available to the subjects/performers at the centre of these projects at the margins. It is troubling that, at least in all the examples in this book, the marginalized groups only come to the attention of the theatre when these professionals mediate for them. Otherwise, the unmediated perception (or the one mediated by the media) is a completely different and more negative one. Taking a cue from Spivak, can we say that the subaltern has no voice or is it that the dominant culture is not equipped to understand that voice and needs to have it translated (see Spivak 1988: 271–313)?

It is a characteristic of communities that they do not exist in isolation. Whilst the members of given communities develop strategies to communicate amongst themselves, they need different strategies to communicate with members of other communities. Within theatrical contexts, festivals are important tools for creating lines of communication across different national or linguistic borders. Some form of linguistic translation is often resorted to in order to facilitate the transmission of meaning. Translation is in itself a negotiation of meanings, but also of power relations, even when the objective is collaboration and mutual understanding. As a rule, also within the context of theatre festivals, translation happens between major languages, or from major languages to less used ones and hardly ever the other way round (see Aston and O'Thomas 2015: 15–19). Commissioning agencies and the forces of globalization need to be countered by what Spivak refers to as 'focus[ing] on transgressions and impossibilities – rather than acknowledg[ing] the normative' (2010: 40). This is especially important in an age when metropolitan centres that were seen as beacons of exchange of cultures and cosmopolitanism seem to be paralysed by isolationist politics.

Embracing new technology in performance might be a way of overcoming the isolation some communities experience if they do not fit into the logic of performance that is perceived primarily as an economic enterprise. 'Virtually linked artistic communit[ies]' might be a tool for levelling 'artistic, geographical, and economic hierarchies' (Felton-Dansky 2018: 154) but technology-heavy formats that travel well are as attractive in the theatre as they are in other spheres of entertainment. Indeed, as discussed in this book, this kind of theatre adopts some of the tools and the terminology of franchised game shows and video games. The tension between the needs of local communities and the attractions of a globalized society is present in the theatre as much as it is elsewhere and needs to be problematized.

It is our hope that this volume has highlighted some of the major issues in the intersection between theatre and community and that the contribution the book makes towards redefining theatre communities will encourage others to engage in this debate.

REFERENCES

Aston, Elaine and O'Thomas, Mark (2015), *Royal Court: International*, Basingstoke: Palgrave Macmillan.

Felton-Dansky, Miriam (2018), *Viral Performance*, Evanston, IL: Northwestern University Press.

Rancière, Jacques (2009), 'Contemporary art and the politics of aesthetics', in B. Hinderliter, W. Kaizen, V. Maimon, J. Mansoor and S. McCormick (eds), *Communities of Sense: Rethinking Aesthetics and Politics*, Durham, NC: Duke University Press, pp. 31–50.

—— (2011), *The Emancipated Spectator*, London: Verso.

—— (2013), *The Politics of Aesthetics*, London: Bloomsbury.

Spivak, Gayatri Chakravorty (1988), 'Can the subaltern speak', in C. Nelson and L. Grossberg (eds), *Marxism and the Interpretation of Culture*, Urbana, IL: University of Illinois Press, pp. 271–313.

—— (2010), 'Translating in a world of languages', *Profession*, pp. 35–43.

Notes on Contributors

Stefan Aquilina is director of research and internationalisation of the School of Performing Arts and Theatre Studies Lecturer at the University of Malta. His main area of research is modern theatre in Russia, especially Stanislavsky and Meyerhold, but he has wider interest in the cultural transmission of embodied practice, amateur theatre, devised performance and reflective teaching. Aquilina's publications include *Stanislavsky in the World* (co-edited with Jonathan Pitches, Bloomsbury, 2017), *Interdisciplinarity in the Performing Arts: Contemporary Perspectives* (co-edited with Malaika Sarco-Thomas, University Malta Press, 2018) and numerous essays in journals like *Studies in Theatre and Performance; Theatre, Dance and Performance Training; Journal of Dramatic Theory and Criticism; Theatre History Studies; Stanislavski Studies* and *Theatre Studies International.*

Bettina Auerswald is an early career researcher who has studied English, German and film and theatre at the University of Augsburg and at the University of Reading, UK. She holds an MA in English literature, English linguistics and new German literatures and the first state exam for grammar school teaching. She is currently working on her Ph.D. thesis on the poetology and ethical aspects of verbatim theatre. She has presented papers at conferences across Europe and published a book chapter entitled 'Promises of the real? The precariousness of verbatim theatre and Robin Soans's *Talking to Terrorists*' in *Of Precariousness: Vulnerabilities, Responsibilities, Communities in 21st-Century British Drama and Theatre* (eds Mireia Aragay and Martin Middeke, De Gruyter, 2017). Her research interests are in contemporary British theatre, early film, documentary art and the ethical concepts of responsibility and community. She also has a background in acting, directing, dramaturgy and sound design.

Ágnes Bakk is a Ph.D. research fellow at Moholy-Nagy Art and Design University in Budapest (Hungary) and a junior research fellow at Sapientia University in Cluj (Romania). Her work focuses on immersive performances and VR. She holds a BA in theatre studies as well as Hungarian and Finnish literature and language from the Babes-Bolyai University Cluj and an MA in theatre studies from the Károli Gáspár University, Budapest. Currently she is working at the Hungarian

REDEFINING THEATRE COMMUNITIES

National Digital Archive as an editor, focusing on digitization, new technologies and online platforms in theatres and museums. She worked as project manager at several performing arts companies and institutions including Jurányi Art Incubator House, Góbi Dance Company, the Natural Art Disasters Company, Verzio Human Rights Documentary Film Festival and Moholy-Nagy University of Art and Design, Budapest. Since 2014 she has been the co-organizer of Tű Fokán Fesztivál (The Eye of the Needle Festival) in Hungary and is also the co-founder of the organizing foundation. In 2015 she served as member of the organizing committee of IETM Budapest meeting, being responsible for the new technology sessions. She is the founder of the performing arts and new technologies blog: www.zip-scene.com.

Ruben Paul Borg is senior lecturer at the Faculty for the Built Environment, University of Malta. He graduated from the University of Malta in architecture and civil engineering, specialized in structural engineering at the Technical University of Milan, Italy and completed a doctorate in civil engineering materials at the University of Sheffield, UK. He was elected chairman of the European Council of Civil Engineers for Knowledge and Technology, member of the Board of Directors of the International Initiative for a Sustainable Built Environment, expert member of the European Committee for Standardization CEN TC350: Sustainable Construction and member of the International Federation for Structural Concrete, Commission 7: Sustainable Concrete. He is representative for Malta of the Institution of Civil Engineers UK, member of the Executive Board of the Building Industry Consultative Council, Government of Malta and member of the Scientific Committee for the Megalithic Structures of Malta. He is a visiting academic in various international institutions including the Technical University of Milan and the Brno University of Technology and is reviewer for leading international scientific journals. He has led various research projects and published widely in materials engineering and concrete durability, sustainable construction and structural vulnerability of cultural heritage. In 2013 he was awarded the International Energy Globe Award for the Sustainable Development Centre Project.

Maria Elena Capitani holds a BA and an MA in English and French from the University of Parma (Italy), by which she was awarded the title of 'Doctor Europaeus' in April 2016 for her dissertation 'The politics of re-(en)visioning: Contemporary British rewritings of Greek and Roman tragedies'. In 2014 and 2015 she was a visiting scholar at the Universities of Barcelona (Spain) and Reading (UK). Her research interests lie in twentieth- and twenty-first-century British literature and culture, with special focus on drama, fiction, intertextuality, identity and translation for the stage. She has presented papers at international conferences across Europe and published various articles/chapters on contemporary British dramatists such as Martin Crimp,

Sarah Kane, Tony Harrison, David Greig and Liz Lochhead. She teaches English literature and language at the University of Parma and is currently working on the proposal for a monograph based on her Ph.D. thesis.

Vicki Ann Cremona is chair of the School of Performing Arts at the University of Malta. She graduated from the Université de Provence, France and was a visiting scholar at Lucy Cavendish College, University of Cambridge. She was appointed ambassador of Malta to France between 2005 and 2009, and to Tunisia between 2009 and 2013. She is an executive member of the International Federation of Theatre Research (IFTR) and has contributed towards founding Icarus Publishing Enterprise, a joint initiative between TARF, Odin Teatret (Denmark) and The Grotowski Institute (Poland). She has various international publications, mainly about theatrical events and public celebration, particularly carnival, commedia dell'arte, theatre anthropology, Maltese theatre and costume. Her most recent publication is entitled: *Carnival and Power: Play and Politics in a Crown Colony* (Palgrave Macmillan, 2018).

Vicky Featherstone became the artistic director of the Royal Court Theatre in London in 2013, a post she took up after guiding the National Theatre of Scotland through its formative years. She had previously been artistic director of Paines Plough when Sarah Kane was writer-in-residence. Throughout her career she has directed the first productions of numerous plays by important contemporary British playwrights, some of which she commissioned as artistic director. Her work at the Royal Court has included working extensively with young people and children who live in London, but she has also given renewed importance to the theatre's International Playwrights' Programme. In January 2018 she was declared the most influential person in British theatre by *The Stage*, mainly for her work to highlight and eradicate sexual harassment and abuse in the performing arts industry.

Marco Galea is senior lecturer in theatre studies at the University of Malta. His main area of specialization is theatre in Malta in the nineteenth and twentieth centuries and he is particularly interested in issues of language, identity and representation. He has published articles and book chapters in this area and has edited a number of books, including a two-volume anthology of nineteenth-century play-texts in the Maltese language, a book on the representation of the other in Maltese culture and more recently, a book of theatre reviews from the second half of the twentieth century. In recent years he has been coordinating, on behalf of the School of Performing Arts at the University of Malta, the efforts to create a digital archive for the performing arts in Malta.

Pujya Ghosh is a Ph.D. candidate in theatre and performance studies at the School of Arts and Aesthetics, Jawaharlal Nehru University. She has also taught sociology and theatre at the Shri Ram School for the last two years. Her research interest lies in the relation between politics and performance. She is especially interested in the period of the 1960s and 1970s and the way it marked the cultural, intellectual and political shift that has been the consequence of that period. Currently she is working on the contemporary Maoist movements and its representation through performance. She has been working towards a critical methodological approach to political and theatrical event featuring oral history, cultural memory and Badiou's philosophy and trying to create an apt theory-history interface. Her work deals with spaces of political, performance interventions, civil society, spectatorship, community engagement and citizenship.

Hasibe Kalkan is associate professor at the Department of Dramaturgy and Theatre Criticism at the University of Istanbul in Turkey. She specializes in intercultural theatre, performance analysis, Turkish theatre in Germany and theatre semiotics. She holds a Ph.D. from the University of Istanbul with a thesis on documentary theatre, a BA in German language and literature from the Hacettepe University (Turkey) and an MA from the University of Marmara where her research focused on 'Otherness in Turkish female writers living in Germany'. Besides her scholarly work, she also worked as translator and dramaturg for the Istanbul State Theatre and as theatre critic for several journals and newspapers. Hasibe has been the recipient of various research grants in Germany and she was a fellow of the International Research Centre Interweaving Performance Cultures at the Freie Universitat in Berlin. She is a member of International Association of Theatre Critics (IATC), International Federation for Theatre Research (IFTR) and Gesellschaft für Interkulturelle Germanistik (GIG).

Szabolcs Musca is research fellow at the Centre for Theatre Research (CET) at the University of Lisbon (Portugal) and founding director of New Tides Platform (UK), currently leading an international research project on theatre and migration in Europe. He is project lead of Migrant Dramaturgies Network, an international research network composed of academics, theatre-makers and organizations. Szabolcs holds a Ph.D. from the University of Bristol and he worked as a researcher, lecturer and theatre critic for over ten years, both in the United Kingdom and continental Europe. Szabolcs is regional managing editor at *The Theatre Times* and an active member of the Translation, Adaptation and Dramaturgy Working Group within the International Federation for Theatre Research (IFTR). He is also member of the Theatre and Performance Research Association (TaPRA), the International Network of Italian Theatre and the European Association for the Study of Theatre and Performance (EASTAP).

Mark O'Thomas is pro vice chancellor at the University of Greenwich. He was formerly dean of academic affairs at Newcastle University, head of the School of Fine & Performing Arts at the University of Lincoln and the founding director of the Institute for Performing Arts at the University of East London. Mark also spent ten years at the BBC as a subtitler and channel director. He has worked as a playwright, translator and dramaturg for a number of theatres including Soho Theatre, The Royal Court Theatre and the Royal National Theatre, and has adapted a number of novels for the stage where his credits include Jorge Amado's *Dona Flor and her Two Husbands* (2006) and Fernando Pessoa's *Book of Disquiet* (2012). His publications include *Royal Court: International*, written with Elaine Aston and published by Palgrave Macmillan in 2015.

George Sachinis is a graduate of the Royal Central School of Speech and Drama (MA in advanced theatre practice), and the Institute of the Arts at Duke University (performance art and literature strand). He received his B.Sc. in civil engineering from Duke University and he also holds an M.Sc. from Berkeley University. He is the founder of Ohi Pezoume performing arts company and coordinator of the UrbanDig Project. In the mornings, he works as a civil engineer at Athens Water Company (EYDAP) where he has created its operations centre and represents the company at the steering committee of GWOPA/UN Habitat. He has been a board member of the Network for the Rights of Children and of the steering committee of Reactivate Athens. He has facilitated workshops and classes in theatre direction and devising. In 2006 he was a nominee for the 'Promising young artist' award by the Greek Theatre and Music Critics Association.

Naďa Satková holds a Ph.D. from Masaryk University, Brno (Czech Republic), and she is currently working at the Institute for Theatre Research at the Janáček Academy of Music and Performing Arts in Brno. Naďa's research interest lies in theatre history, especially the second half of the twentieth century. Her research focuses on artistic, operational and production issues of Czechoslovak theatre in this period and explores issues and processes of repertoire building and censorship, the consequences of 1968 and the specifics of the state reviewing system in regional theatres. Her research also deals with contemporary British drama and theatre historiography and she published articles on Joe Penhall's plays (*Revue Theatralia*, 2013) as well as on Tennessee Williams' *Orpheus Descending* in Jiří Svoboda's 1960's direction (*Czech Theatre Review*, 2015). Naďa also worked as a research fellow at the Department of Theatre at the Jagiellonian University of Krakow (Poland) and she was co-organizer of the Brno Theatralia Conference 2016: *Czech and Slovak Scenography for Shakespeare*.

David Schwartz is a theatre practitioner and scholar. He holds a Ph.D. from the Babes-Bolyai University Cluj (Romania) where his research focused on the political and ethical aspects of the interactions between artists and marginalized groups including migrants, elderly people, working-class families and people evicted from their homes or threatened with eviction. He is interested in counter-hegemonic perspectives towards local and global history and the social and human impact of post-socialist transition. He is the co-founder of *GAP – Gazeta de Artă Politică* (*Journal of Political Arts*) and of the Political Theatre Platform. David is also a member of the self-organized artists' and workers' collective MACAZ – Bar Theatre Cooperative based in Romania. Since 2009, David has been involved in several community theatre performances as part of the *4th Age* project, a community arts programme developed together with the residents of the Moses Rosen Retirement Home in Bucharest, Romania.

Ionuț Sociu is a cultural journalist and theatre critic based in Bucharest, Romania. His articles, translations and short stories were published in several Romanian journals and anthologies since 2004. Between 2010 and 2012 he studied at Bard College Berlin. He is the co-founder of the Political Theatre Platform and the *GAP – Gazeta de Artă Politică* (*Journal of Political Arts*), an independent publication of both critical reflection and activism focusing on literature, film and performing arts.

Evi Stamatiou is an actor, director and writer who works across stage and screen with fourteen years of international experience. She is a Ph.D. candidate in actor training and direction at the Royal Central School of Speech and Drama at the University of London, and she won the Governors Bursary Award for her contribution to the school and the field. She trains actors in conservatoires and universities and she is currently head of acting at the University of Chichester. Her academic work has featured in publications by Intellect Books, Routledge, Bloomsbury Methuen Drama and McFarland & Co. She specializes in comedy and in using a variety of text-based and devising practices that tackle representation issues in the acting industry, having workshopped new writing for various platforms, including Lincoln Centre Theatre Directors Lab. She is also an associate artist at New Theatre Royal in Portsmouth, UK.

Marius Bogdan Tudor holds an MA in contemporary history from Central European University in Budapest (Hungary) and a BA in English and Dutch from the University of Bucharest. His research focuses on the interplay between the socialist state and factory workers in Romania in the late 1940s and early 1950s. Since 2013, he has been an editor of *GAP – Gazeta de Arta Politica* (*Journal of*

Political Arts) and has been involved in research specifically for documentary theatre projects and performances in Romania.

Zoe Zontou is a senior lecturer in drama and theatre studies at Liverpool Hope University. Her principal research interests lie in the field of applied theatre with people in recovery from alcohol and drug dependencies. Her research covers a wide range of topics, including autobiography in performance, addiction studies and cultural theory, which are examined through their relationship with applied theatre. She has worked as a practitioner and researcher in a number of organizations, and has published in the area of applied theatre research and practice. Publications include the edited volume *Addiction and Performance* (Cambridge Scholars, 2014) that she co-authored with James Reynolds, 'Upon awakening: Addiction performance and aesthetics of authenticity', in O'Grady, ed., *Risk, Participation, and Performance Practice: Critical Vulnerabilities in a Precarious World* (2017) and 'Under the influence of... affective performance' in *Performance Research*, 22:7 (2017). She has also published articles in *RiDE: The Journal of Applied Theatre and Performance* and *The Journal of Applied Arts and Health*.

Index

Milton Keynes UK
Ingram Content Group UK Ltd.
UKHW052142040324
438897UK00032B/605